Economics as a process

Economics as a process

Essays in the New
Institutional Economics

Edited by RICHARD N. LANGLOIS
The University of Connecticut

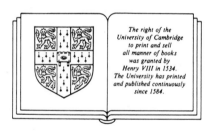

The right of the
University of Cambridge
to print and sell
all manner of books
was granted by
Henry VIII in 1534.
The University has printed
and published continuously
since 1584.

CAMBRIDGE UNIVERSITY PRESS

Cambridge
New York   Port Chester   Melbourne   Sydney

33 0
E 1998

Published by the Press Syndicate of the University of Cambridge
The Pitt Building, Trumpington Street, Cambridge CB2 1RP
40 West 20th Street, New York, NY 10011, USA
10 Stamford Road, Oakleigh, Melbourne 3166, Australia

First published 1986
Reprinted 1987
First paperback edition 1989
Reprinted 1990

Printed in the United States of America

Library of Congress Cataloging in Publication Data
Main entry under title:
Economics as a process.
Consists of original and rev. versions of papers
presented at a conference at Airlie House in Virginia.
Mar. 1983.
Includes bibliographics
Institutional economics – Addresses, essays,
lectures.   I. Langlois, Richard N.
HB99.5.E24   1985   330   85-12780

British Library Cataloguing in Publication Data
Economics as a process: essays in the new
institutional economics.
1. Institutional economics.
2. Langlois, Richard N.
330.15′5   HB99.5

ISBN 0-521-30174-2 hardback
ISBN 0-521-37859-1 paperback

Contents

v

Preface

In a certain sense, this volume owes its existence to youthful exuberance. Its genesis really traces to the years 1978–80, when I was researching my Ph.D. dissertation at Stanford University. Originally motivated by an interest in the problems of technology and technological change, I had begun to discover certain more-or-less unconventional approaches to economic theory. Indeed, it seemed to me that I had stumbled upon an oddly coherent body of ideas – oddly coherent in that, although the ideas themselves seemed to fit together remarkably well, the writers whose ideas they were appeared almost entirely unaware of one another or of the commonalities I perceived. The notion of bringing some of these authors together naturally suggested itself, even if such a suggestion was, at the time, a wholly fanciful one.

When I accepted a postdoctoral position at New York University in 1980, I had met none of the authors in this volume (with the exception of Stephen Littlechild, who had visited Stanford in the winter quarter of 1980). But during the next years I had occasion to meet several of them and even to work closely with one or two. I slowly became persuaded that the idea of a conference might not be so fanciful after all. With the assistance of my colleagues (Richard Nelson, Gerald O'Driscoll, and Mario Rizzo were particularly helpful and encouraging), I managed to secure funding and to fill out a roster of participants.

Indeed, under the administrative aegis of the C. V. Starr Center for Applied Economics at New York University and with the support of the Liberty Fund, Inc., of Indianapolis, the plan for a conference blossomed into a plan for *two* conferences. The first took place in October 1982 in Greenwich, Connecticut. Eight authors each presented for discussion the outline of a proposed paper. As an aid to that discussion, I prepared and circulated an introductory synthetic essay, a revised and shortened version of which appears as Chapter 1 of this volume. The second conference, in March 1983 at Airlie House in Virginia, saw the presentation of the eight completed papers.

In addition to the paper-givers, a number of discussants attended one or both sessions. They were James Buchanan, George Mason University; Marie-Thérèse Flaherty, Harvard Business School; Almarin Phillips, University of Pennsylvania; Mario Rizzo, New York University; David Teece, University of California at Berkeley; Karen Vaughn, George Mason University; and Sidney Winter, School of Organization and Management, Yale University. Dr. Louis M. Spadaro, retired dean of the Fordham Business School, served as moderator for both meetings.

This volume contains all eight papers presented at the Airlie House conference, along with my introductory chapter and a new Chapter 10. Several of the authors have revised their papers since that conference and have added some new material.

Many of these authors, I should also note, are precisely the ones I was reading in the period 1978–80. Although youthful exuberance has somewhat given way – as it ought – to an increased recognition of the subtleties and complexities of what I have chosen to label "the New Institutional Economics," I nonetheless remain strongly convinced of the coherence and fruitfulness of the ideas you will find in this volume. Quite apart from any programmatic unities the papers may (or may not) display, they all clearly share a suggestiveness and a sense of new possibilities; this is, as I hope you'll agree, a book of overtures rather than codas.

I would like to thank the administrators and staff of the C. V. Starr Center for Applied Economics for their good efforts and the Liberty Fund for its most generous support. I would especially like to thank Kenneth S. Templeton, Jr., now no longer with the fund, for his help in making the conferences a reality. On behalf of the authors, I would like to thank an anonymous reader for Cambridge University Press for helpful suggestions and Colin L. Day, the press's editorial director, for his assistance and patience in seeing this project to publication.

Richard N. Langlois

West Willington, Connecticut

Contributors

RICHARD N. LANGLOIS, the editor, was educated at Williams College, Yale University, and Stanford University. He taught for three years at New York University, where he was affiliated with both the C. V. Starr Center for Applied Economics and the Center for Science and Technology Policy. He is now an assistant professor of economics at the University of Connecticut, Storrs.

RONALD A. HEINER is professor of economics at Brigham Young University.

AXEL LEIJONHUFVUD is professor of economics at the University of California, Los Angeles.

STEPHEN C. LITTLECHILD is professor of commerce and head of the Department of Industrial Economics and Business Studies at the University of Birmingham.

BRIAN J. LOASBY is professor of management economics at the University of Stirling.

RICHARD R. NELSON is Elizabeth and A. Varick Stout Professor of Social Science and Economics and director of the Institution for Social and Policy Studies at Yale University.

GERALD P. O'DRISCOLL, JR., is a senior economist with the Federal Reserve Bank of Dallas.

ANDREW SCHOTTER is associate professor of economics and co-director of the C. V. Starr Center for Applied Economics, New York University.

OLIVER E. WILLIAMSON is Gordon B. Tweedy Professor of the Economics of Law and Organization at Yale University.

CHAPTER 1

The New Institutional Economics: an introductory essay

RICHARD N. LANGLOIS

If there is to be no sudden establishment of a new intellectual order among economists, can there at least be a new direction that will gradually draw economists away from their tired repetition of stale and sterile arguments? Some economists believe this new direction could come from the creation of a new "institutional economics," which would take as its main focus the study of human action, in both its individual and group manifestations.

      —Leonard Silk
New York Times
September 24, 1980

1.1   Introduction

The essays in the volume are, to say the least, a rather diverse lot. It may thus seem somewhat odd to maintain that these chapters are reflections of certain identifiable common themes and that these themes represent new directions in economic theory. Anyone who would bundle such essays into a single book, and who would further describe them all as essays on "the New Institutional Economics," surely owes the reader an explanation.

That is what this chapter tries to do – to identify a set of common themes that (I assert) run through the chapters of this book. More ambitiously yet, I will try to connect the currents in this book with a larger stream of thought that has lately begun flowing through economic thought.

The skein of ideas I will be concerned with comprises (if I may switch metaphors abruptly) a number of identifiable strands. Principal among these, in my view, would be the evolutionary theory of Nelson and Winter (1982) and other work influenced by Joseph Schumpeter (1934, 1942); the modern Austrian school (Kirzner 1981), especially as influenced by the work of F. A. Hayek (1948, 1967); the transaction-cost

I would like to thank Stephan Boehm, James Buchanan, Bruce Caldwell, Roger Koppl, Ludwig Lachmann, Gerald O'Driscoll, Mario Rizzo, and Viktor Vanberg for helpful comments on an earlier draft of this paper.

economics of Oliver Williamson (1975, 1979); and certain aspects of the property rights literature inspired by Ronald Coase (1937, 1960). There are other affinities and sources of influence, notably Herbert Simon (1955) and the behavioralist school.

To paraphrase Mark Blaug (1980), I am concerned with how this particular group of economists explains economic phenomena. My intention is not to define the boundaries of any school or research program, except perhaps incidentally. Even less do I plan to attack orthodoxy or anything else. It is the themes themselves that interest me. This is in part a detective story, an attempt to ferret out the inexplicit bases of a common pattern of reasoning; and it is also in part an exercise in intellectual engineering, a rational reconstruction (in the broad sense) of an underlying framework. As a result, what I have to say will be partly descriptive and partly critical. The danger of a synthesis of this sort is that the unity of thought it portrays can be more the product of intellectual gift wrapping than a manifestation of the ideas themselves; how much this is so in the present chapter the reader will have to judge. (In Chapter 10, where I explore some of the relevant methodological issues in greater depth, I will renounce even these slight pretensions to be speaking for others.)

1.2   Institutionalism old and new

The first problem is to find a name for this bundle of ideas. None of the options is wholly satisfactory, but for present purposes "the New Institutional Economics" is probably the best choice. The name was popularized by Williamson (1975) and is now fairly widely known. I will spare the reader most of the taxonomic pros and cons. The principal advantage of this name is its currency, along with the fact that it captures one of the main themes that sets the ideas in question apart from the mainstream view. Among the disadvantages is that I may be using the term here in a sense slightly different from, or at any rate broader than, the one it has taken on in association with Williamson's work.

Another disadvantage of this name is that it encourages one to associate this new brand of institutional economics with the original Institutionalism of the early century. And this is not an empty concern. For it is perhaps fair to say that this modern institutionalism reflects less the ideas of the early Institutionalists than it does those of their *opponents*.

The American Institutionalist school was a diverse and eclectic group that included the likes of Thorstein Veblen, John R. Commons, Wesley Mitchell, and Clarence Ayres. In fact, it was so loosely structured a school that the major commonality among its members was perhaps their opposition to the developing neoclassical viewpoint. It is true that many of the concerns for which these writers are remembered are similar to the ones I am dealing with in this essay. That economics is too narrow a field and should include more ideas from philosophy and from the other social sciences; that economic phenomena should not be analyzed solely in terms of static equilibria but as processes with a history and a future; that economics should be a more "evolutionary" science – all of these are themes as congenial to the old institutionalists as to the new.

Writing in 1898, Veblen assailed the economics of his time for not being a truly evolutionary science, "a genetic account of the economic life process" (Veblen [1898] 1919, p. 72). He considered the classical economics of Adam Smith and his followers to be merely taxonomic, mired in a prescientific state from which evolutionary biology had, since Darwin, suc essfully extricated itself. By contrast, the marginalist or early neoclassical economists – whom he identifies, interestingly enough, with Carl Menger and the Austrian branch of the marginalist revolution – did succeed in creating a theory of value that *is* suitably genetic, as far as it goes. But, to Veblen, the marginalists continue to labor under a faulty conception of human nature drawn from an outmoded hedonistic psychology, which accounts for their misguided preoccupation with a creature called *homo economicus*. Veblen's justly famous caricature of this creature is a microcosm of his critique of the marginalists.

The hedonistic conception of man is that of a lightning calculator of pleasures and pains, who oscillates like a homogeneous globule of desire of happiness under the impulse of stimuli that shift him about the area, but leave him intact. He has neither antecedent nor consequent. He is an isolated, definitive human datum, in stable equilibrium except for the buffets of the impinging forces that displace him in one direction or another. Self-imposed in elemental space, he spins symmetrically about his own spiritual axis until the parallelogram of forces bears down upon him, whereupon he follows the line of the resultant. When the force of the impact is spent, he comes to rest, a self-contained globule of desire as before. Spiritually, the hedonistic man is not a prime mover. (Veblen [1898] 1919, p. 73)

Marginalism, he is saying, is a Newtonian approach to economics. Its models are cast in terms of forces obeying determinate laws, and explanations for economic phenomena are sought not in a causal and sequential process taking place in time, but in the necessary and sufficient conditions for an atemporal equilibrium. The economic agent thus becomes a passive reactor rather than a true actor. The agent's behavior conforms to, and is rational in the light of, the specified forces to which he or she is subject; it is never influenced by habit, convention, institutions, or other factors not given in the choice-problem he or she faces.

Putting aside the several complex issues the passage raises – issues to which I return in Chapter 10 – this remains, I think, a critique with which one can be sympathetic on a number of grounds. The problem is that the methods of analysis used by Veblen and the Institutionalists were not themselves particularly congruent with the spirit of this critique.

To complain about the mechanistic Newtonian character of neoclassical models, and to object to an unrealistic hedonistic psychology that makes *homo economicus* passive and inhuman, is certainly to strike a very humanistic note. One would thus expect that Veblen would insist on substituting a more humanistic, a more "realistic," psychological assumption. In fact, quite the opposite is the case. Caught up in the materialism of his day, Veblen actually argued for a kind of proto-Skinnerian behaviorism,[1] and wished to rid economics of any sort of human intelligence and purpose (Kirzner 1976, p. 36; Seckler 1975, passim). The conflict between his humanistic rhetoric and his behaviorist psychology is a tension that Veblen was never able to resolve, and it largely vitiated the promise of his evolutionary alternative to marginalism.[2]

But the significant point is not that Veblen and the Institutionalists largely failed to live up to their own rhetoric; the true irony is that it was precisely the *target* of Veblen's attacks – Carl Menger – who was laying the groundwork for a very fruitful approach to the evolutionary and the institutional.[3] As William Jaffé (1976) has pointed out in his dehomogenization of the marginalist revolutionaries, Menger, far from concentrating on Newtonian equilibrium and ignoring institutions, was actually interested in disequilibrium economics and institutional economics: "Thorstein Veblen's strictures upon what he considered the Austrian

---

[1] Note that behaviorism (the psychological doctrine) is to be distinguished from behavioralism in the sense of Herbert Simon.

[2] "Forced from humanism, unable to accept either historicism or behaviorism, Veblen fled into obscurantism; that is one of his secrets" (Seckler 1975, p. 85). See also Coats (1954, 1976) for the view that "Veblen's attempt to formulate an alternative 'evolutionary' research programme in economics failed completely" (Coats 1976, p. 47). One can tell a similar, if not exactly identical, story about most of the other early institutionalists. The desultory and idiosyncratic Commons, for example, whom Williamson (1975, pp. 3, 254) lauds for seeing the individual transaction as the "ultimate unit of analysis," simultaneously adhered to an incompatible methodological holism in which "individual wills are congealed into a form of collective volitiency or will-to-action" (Gruchy 1972, p. 41).

[3] Indeed, to Seckler, "Veblen's choice of Menger and the Austrian School for attack becomes perhaps one of his greatest, although completely unintended, jokes" (Seckler 1975, p. 145).

preconception of human nature fit Jevons's or Walras's theory much better than they do Menger's" (Jaffé 1976, p. 521).

Menger spent a good part of his career embroiled in an intellectual battle over methodology – the *Methodenstreit* – with the German Historical School. The latter attacked theoretical economics for ignoring the diversity and effects of social institutions; more than that, they contended that this diversity invalidated all theoretical inquiry, since it implied a multiplicity and idiosyncrasy in human behavior refractory to analytical generalization. Menger's response was not to deny the importance of institutions, but rather to argue that institutions are *themselves* social phenomena in need of theoretical explanation (Lachmann 1971, pp. 55 – 6). Thus Menger has perhaps more claim to be the patron saint of the new institutional economics than has any of the original institutionalists. For it is in Menger's sense – and not in the antitheoretical sense – that these more recent writers are institutionalists.[4]

Thus, unlike earlier debates – and contrary to many perceptions about more recent debates – the current dialectic between neoclassical economics and institutionalism does not involve a disagreement about the possibility or value of pure theory. The problem with the Historical School and many of the early Institutionalists is that they wanted an economics with institutions but without theory; the problem with many neoclassicists is that they want economic theory without institutions; what we should really want is both institutions and theory[5] – not only pure economic theory informed by the existence of specific institutions, but also an economic theory *of* institutions.

1.3   Emerging themes

There are always a number of dimensions along which one could scrutinize an intellectual structure. The following interrelated themes are thus not the only ones possible, but they do seem to me to distill much of the essence.

1. Although definitely rational in a true sense, the agent of economic theory is not best conceived as rational in the narrow sense of maximizing within a framework of known alternatives.
2. Economic phenomena are in large measure the result of learning over time by economic agents; economic explanation

[4] See Vanberg (1982) for a similar treatment of old versus new institutionalism. Indeed, Vanberg uses the term "der neue theoretische institutionalismus" – the new theoretical institutionalism.
[5] I am indebted to Roger Garrison for this concise way of summarizing the matter.

should thus be a dynamic exercise – dynamic not merely in the sense of dynamic neoclassical models, but in a sense best rendered as evolutionary.

3. The coordination of economic activity is not merely a matter of price-mediated transactions in markets, but is supported by a wide range of economic and social institutions that are themselves an important topic of theoretical economic inquiry.

These themes do not emerge with equal emphasis in all the works I will cite; some writers who explore one of the themes may even do so in a manner antagonistic to the other themes. But I maintain that all three are necessary for a complete account.

1.4   Rationality

Complaints about the conception of rationality in neoclassical economics have a long history. Such complaints are usually interpreted – not always incorrectly – as denials that economic agents do behave, or should be represented as behaving, rationally. In the present case, such an interpretation would be unwarranted. The real issue is not whether agents should be seen as rational, but whether their rationality should be portrayed exclusively as the conscious maximization of an explicit objective (such as utility) within the constraints of well-defined alternatives.

Since I spend a good deal of time on the question of rationality in Chapter 10, let me not dwell on it here. I should note in passing that this theme is perhaps most evident in the three chapters following this one. In Chapter 2, Stephen Littlechild ties together the themes of rationality and of process: His three of types of market process are driven by three different conceptions of the nature and appropriate scope of rationality in modeling. In Chapter 3, Brian Loasby is also concerned with both process and rationality, and he finds his lens in the growth-of-knowledge literature that lies in the foreground of present-day philosophy of science. And, in Chapter 4, Ronald Heiner uses results from signal-detection experiments to explore the nature of rational behavior and extends his attempts to model that behavior using the reliability-condition framework he has recently introduced (Heiner 1983). In Chapter 8, Oliver Williamson also raises the issue of rationality in economics, aligning himself with the semistrong conception found in the work of Herbert Simon. This he distinguished both from the strong form of rationality in neoclassical economics and from a weaker form – what he calls "organic" rationality – that he associates with evolutionary modeling.

1.5   The dual role of institutions

1.5.1   Competition as a process

As I've already suggested, the connection between institutions and economic theory is a bidirectional one. On the one hand, institutions influence economic phenomena, and this implies a need for economic theories in which institutional influences and constraints play a role. Perhaps the best illustration of this sort of institutionalism lies in the area of competition theory, where process views of competition are coming together with property rights approaches to create an alternative to the traditional neoclassical microeconomics of competition (and to its policy handmaiden, the so-called structure-conduct-performance paradigm). In the other direction, institutions and economic theory meet to the extent that theory can be brought to bear to explain the various economic and social institutions themselves. This section examines the first of these topics, and Section 1.5.2 takes a look at the second.

There are a number of ways to describe the difference between a process view of economics (and hence of competition) and what I believe it is fair to call the mainstream standard. One of these ways may be to distinguish the former as "dynamic" and the latter as "static," at least as long as we are careful about what we mean by those terms.[6]

The heart of the distinction is that, in a process analysis, events are represented as taking place sequentially in real time.[7] By contrast, in a neoclassical analysis (as I am using the term), one is normally concerned with an equilibrium situation – an equilibrium defined not as the end-result or rest-state of a process, but as the condition of logical consistency among a group of mathematical relations. Thus a process analysis can be static in the sense that the process may have an eventual equilibrium state. And a neoclassical analysis can be dynamic to the extent that a variable labeled "time" may enter into relations whose consistency constitutes the equilibrium. But the meanings of dynamic and static are very different in the two cases.

Mathematical general-equilibrium theory in the tradition of Walras is the best-developed area of economics in which the static conception of equilibrium reigns, although the basic approach has filtered down to almost all other areas, including competition policy. General-equilibrium theory is built entirely around this idea of equilibrium as the logical consistency of relations. One searches for a fixed point, a particu-

---

[6] On the slipperiness of these terms see Machlup (1963).
[7] Time can also enter as a variable in a nonprocess model, but it necessarily plays a very different role. On this see O'Driscoll and Rizzo (1985, chap. 4), who distinguish between the Bergsonian time of process models and the Newtonian time of neoclassical equilibrium analysis. See also Fusfeld (1984).

lar vector of prices and quantities for which all the system's equations are simultaneously satisfied.

In a series of articles in the 1930s and 1940s, Hayek (1948, chaps. 2, 4, 8) argued that, although this model is valuable for illustrating the complex interconnectedness of the economy, to take it literally is to misconstrue much of the economic problem facing society. That problem, he argued, lies less in allocating a given set of resources according to consistent logical principles than in adapting successfully to changed conditions and in using effectively the knowledge dispersed throughout society. As an alternative to the Walrasian logical-consistency notion of general equilibrium, he offered a process approach in which economic agents are portrayed as having plans or strategies and in which equilibrium occurs when those plans come into mutual consistency after a process of learning (Hayek 1948, chap. 2).

Many of the theorists who helped to raise the general-equilibrium edifice to its current state of elegance have lately expressed rather similar misgivings. Frank Hahn (1973) has even reinvented Hayek's proposal and offered it as a new research program for general-equilibrium theorists – an offer that, unhappily, has so far attracted few takers (Littlechild 1982).

The static (logical-consistency) equilibrium approach is also prominent in applied competition theory. Here, as in general-equilibrium theory, the problem to be solved by competition is the allocation of a given set of resources to given ends. Aside from imperfect information (the failure of one or more buyers or sellers to know all the relevant facts of the hypothesized allocation problem), the principal impediment to a socially efficient allocation is the possession of "market power" by an agent, that is, the ability of the agent to affect the market price by manipulating the amount he or she sells. Not surprisingly, the normatively preferred market structure is atomistic or perfect competition, a situation in which no seller (or buyer for that matter) is able to affect the market price of the commodity in question.[8]

In this theory, the discipline of the market consists entirely in limiting the discretion producers have in setting the prices they will charge. One competes not by taking action but, in a real sense, by being unable to take action.

Perfect competition limits discretion completely. No action a firm takes can affect the price it can obtain for its product. There are also a number of "imperfect competition" variants in which the firm has

---

[8] I am, of course, ignoring a number of other assumptions of this model: perfect homogeneity of product, exogenous cost-curves deriving from fully understood production functions, etc.

discretion to adjust within a range its price asked and quantity offered. The most famous version of this, of course, is monopoly, in which there exists, for reasons unexplained, only one firm selling a given product in a given market. Unlike the perfectly competitive firm, which would lose fully all its customers if it charged more than the going rate, the monopoly would lose only *some* of its customers if it increased the price of its product. In view of this, the monopoly can maximize its profits by setting a price higher than its marginal costs, a maneuver that not only transfers income from consumers to the monopoly (relative to the equivalent perfect-competition case) but also results in a level of output less than the "social optimum."

Another version of imperfect competition is that noted variant of monopoly, oligopoly. The number of firms involved here ranges between two (duopoly) and perhaps a half-dozen, a circumstance that leaves oligopoly theory in a position somewhat analogous to that of the three-body problem in physics: Whereas the analysis of one body is analytically tractable, the analysis of an intermediate handful is not.

In an oligopolistic situation, price and quantity decisions among firms are very much interdependent. This is not a problem in the competitive case because no one's actions can affect the ruling price; and in the monopoly case, there *is* no one else. But life is not so simple in oligopoly. Since the optimum price depends not only upon variables subject to the oligopolist's own control but also on variables subject to the control of competitors, the oligopolist's choice at any time is governed by his expectations about the behavior of those competitors.

As a consequence, the theoretical hope – dating from Cournot (1838) – that social optimality could be deduced solely from the number of firms in a market had to be abandoned in favor of the structure-conduct-performance (SCP) paradigm. According to this schema, one evaluates performance (proximity to social optimality) by examining not only the market structure but also the conduct or behavior of the firms in the market. This is not in theory a move toward a process view (although it sometimes has that effect in practice): One looks at behavior only to fill in the blank of indeterminacy created in oligopoly theory by the problem of expectations; one looks exclusively for evidence of collusion or of "anticompetitive practices" in order to determine whether the oligopoly in question should be viewed as closer to the competitive or to the monopoly pole.

One might well complain that I have painted a misleading caricature of the literature of industrial organization. There have indeed been many subtle and interesting kinds of industry analysis carried out ostensibly under the SCP banner. But this work typically refuses to take the *formal* theory seriously, relying instead on a sort of economic intuition and common sense that, if formalized, would look much more like a process view of competition than like the SCP paradigm.[9] Taking the formal theory seriously can indeed lead to absurd conclusions; and it has led many economists, representing a fairly wide range of the political spectrum, to advocate, for example, the forcible chopping up of all "concentrated" industries irrespective of the history, growth rate, competitive environment, technology, institutional constraints, or any other factor specific to the case.

It is a persistent theme among the writers I'm concerned with in this essay that the heterodoxy they advocate is not merely a break with recent tradition but actually a return to an earlier, perhaps sounder, tradition (Nelson and Winter 1982, p. 45; Loasby 1976, p. 47; Klein 1977, p. 68; Kirzner 1981, p. 112). And, in the theory of competition, the earlier tradition is that of Adam Smith and the classical economists:[10] "Smith's concept of competition was decidedly not one in which the firm was passive with respect to price but was, rather, one in which the market moved toward equilibrium through the active price responses of its various participants" (McNulty 1967, p. 397; see also McNulty 1968). Moreover, Smith never viewed competition as involving perfection; he talked exclusively of "free" competition, "a phrase designed to capture the meaning of *free entry into* competition, against a background of medieval restrictions and regulations" (Dennis 1977, p. 99, emphasis in original).

The Walras-Cournot vision lay somewhat dormant during the early part of the century, a time dominated by the thought of economists such as Alfred Marshall, J. B. Clark, and Frank Knight. But Walras was rediscovered in the 1930s, and by the fifties and sixties had come to dominate economic thought almost completely. But there always remained a few voices of protest. In addition to Hayek (1948, chap. 5), there was J. M. Clark (1940, 1961), who long advocated a processlike view that he called "workable" competition. Most influential of all was probably Joseph Schumpeter, who offered a provocative account of competition as "creative destruction."

Schumpeter admitted the validity of the perfect-competition model (or, more correctly, of a commonsense empirical counterpart of some-

[9] This is essentially the same argument that Richard Nelson makes in Chapter 6 in the context of the productivity-growth slowdown of the 1970s.
[10] Alfred Marshall, who, a bit like Menger, always kept one foot firmly in the classical tradition, also receives generally good marks from these authors (Nelson and Winter 1982, p. 44; Loasby 1976, p. 47). Although his well-known partial-equilibrium analyses did not usually reflect it, Marshall was quite interested in biological analogies and evolutionary ideas (see Loasby in this volume).

thing like the perfect-competition model); but he argued that there was also a quite different, and far more important, kind of competition – a dynamic kind of competition arising from innovation and change: "This kind of competition is as much more effective than the other as a bombardment is in comparison with forcing a door, and so much more important that it becomes a matter of comparative indifference whether competition in the ordinary sense functions more or less promptly" (Schumpeter 1942, pp. 84–5). Moreover, these two forms of competition, he argued, are in many respects incompatible, and success in bringing about perfect competition must necessarily come at the expense of the more dynamic variety. In particular, this dynamic sort of competition very likely requires a more oligopolistic-looking market structure as well as countless active business practices that, when viewed through the lens of perfect competition, appear "monopolistic."

This conception of two kinds of competition has had a significant heuristic value. It has led some economists to talk fairly sensibly about the Schumpeterian tradeoff (Nelson and Winter 1982, chap. 14) and to associate that tradeoff with the necessary tension between "static efficiency" and "dynamic efficiency" (Klein 1977). At the same time, the idea of two kinds of competition has led other economists to reduce Schumpeter's dynamic competition to the terms of an optimizing allocation. In these models, innovation (of a fairly diluted sort) becomes just another allocative variable under the firm's control; and, by examining the appropriate marginal conditions, one can pronounce on the optimal market structure (Arrow 1962a; Loury 1979; Dasgupta and Stiglitz 1980a, 1980b). Other economists have attempted to regress market structure against variables such as research and development (R&D) spending or number of patents in order to determine econometrically which market structure is optimal. (For a review, see Kamien and Schwartz 1975.)

There are a number of subtle issues involved here. But let me suggest that, whatever heuristic advantages the idea of two kinds of competition may have, it is to a large degree misleading. A far better way to put it, it seems to me, is that there are two ways of looking at competition, not two different forms of competition. These two ways are mutually exclusive: Either competition is a state of affairs or competition is a process. It seems clear from Schumpeter's examples that when he talked about "ordinary" competition, what he had in mind were situations in which an industry had come into temporary equilibrium – in the sense that change had more or less stopped and process competition slowed. But, as I've already suggested, this sort of equilibrium is very different in form from the sort of equilibrium on which the Cournot-Walras models – and their conclusions – are based (Hayek 1948, p. 94; Kirzner 1973, pp. 91 – 2). More to the point, there is a good case that, when examined carefully, even situations that Schumpeter would have classed as noninnovative temporary equilibria are actually animated by something far more like process competition than by the sort of competition envisaged in the SCP paradigm. Adam Smith's version of process competition may not have involved the bold qualitative changes with which Schumpeter was concerned; but, as Axel Leijonhufvud stresses in Chapter 9, Smith's whole system was animated by the increasing division of labor and thus by innovation.[11] And as Kirzner has argued, all forms of competition should be seen as part of a process (Kirzner 1973, esp. pp. 129 – 30). What is at stake is not an empirical question about which kind of competition is more important; rather, what is at issue is the lens through which we view competition. This is not without implications. For if we see competition consistently in process terms, we are less likely to find ourselves jamming a set of complex phenomena into a narrow theoretical box.[12] More important, we are also less inclined to see market structure as a significant policy variable and more inclined to take our normative concerns in more sophisticated – more institutional – directions.

In the first place, market structure in a process view loses a good deal of the exogeneity the SCP paradigm tends to lend it. In Schumpeter's discussion of the incompatibility of perfect competition and innovation, many economists read what has come to be called the Schumpeterian hypothesis: that large firms innovate more than small firms.[13] More recently, economists have begun to realize that to ask how market structure affects innovation may be to ask the wrong question. This has led to the reverse Schumpeterian hypothesis, usually traced to Almarin Phillips (1971): It's not so much that large firms lead to innovation as that innovation leads to large firms. In the shake-out that invariably occurs in an innovative regime, the successful innovators will become larger and the unsuccessful will contract or disappear, leaving an in-

---

[11] As Nathan Rosenberg suggests in a related context, "Schumpeter accustomed economists to thinking of technical change as involving major breaks, giant discontinuities or disruptions with the past. This rather melodramatic conception fitted in well with his charismatic approach to entrepreneurship. But technological change is also (and perhaps more importantly) a continuous stream of innumerable minor adjustments, modifications, and adaptations" (Rosenberg 1976, p. 166).

[12] The most egregious example of this is the literature that attempts to calculate the "social costs of monopoly power" in the economy. For a recent critique, see Littlechild (1981).

[13] For an analytical treatment, see Fisher and Temin (1973); for a general survey, see Kamien and Schwartz (1975).

dustry in which the larger firms will necessarily appear to the econome-
trician as innovative.[14] In other words, industry structure is an endogenous result of a competitive learning process (Hayek 1978).

Once again, it is important to see that this learning process is not
limited to the kind of dramatic discovery associated with technological
innovation brought about by formal R&D. Another natural outgrowth
of a process view of competition is an attention to the extent to which
day-to-day learning by experience plays a role in shaping industry structure. Of particular significance in this context is the phenomenon of
endogenous costs – costs that can decrease over real time in a manner
not captured in the traditional concept of economies of scale.[15] This is
part of Leijonhufvud's point in Chapter 9 of this volume, where he
elaborates on Adam Smith's notion of the division of labor and on the
role that learning and innovation play in that process. Also relevant are
the recent life-cycle theories of innovation, which tell a stylized story
about the evolution of technology and the pattern of innovation in an
industry as it matures (Abernathy and Townsend 1975; Abernathy and
Utterback 1978; Abernathy 1978; Utterback 1979).

In all of these cases, what is at work is a particular kind of economic
process. And, as in most such processes, the development through competition of industry structure presupposes a framework that sets the
boundary conditions and provides filtering and selection mechanisms
(Hayek 1967, 1973; Nelson and Winter 1982). It is this framework that
we should be concerned with when we talk of the role and importance of
social institutions in competition. One implication is that we should be
concerned, for both analytic and normative purposes, with the implications of alternative frameworks – of alternative institutional arrangements – rather than with particular states of affairs (e.g., concentration)
independent of the circumstances under which those states are brought
about.

This comparative-institutional approach is in sharp contrast with the
approach of neoclassical economics (as it is often practiced), which seeks
to derive its normative conclusions from the welfare theorems of gen-

[14] Nelson and Winter (1982, chaps. 12, 13) have investigated precisely this phenomenon
with their evolutionary model. For other related models of Schumpeterian competition, see Futia (1980).
[15] The best discussions of the effect of real time on costs are probably those by Alchian
(1959) and Hirshleifer (1962). Especially relevant is Hirshleifer's interpretation of the
long run versus the short run as involving a progressive reduction in uncertainty over
time. The most oft-cited work on learning-by-doing is Arrow (1962b). For recent
discussions of the so-called learning curve or experience curve, see Spence (1981).
(Both the Arrow and Spence analyses are, of course, in a maximization context.) For a
recent treatment of the importance of the empirical in the evolution of technology, see
Rosenberg (1982).

eral-equilibrium analysis.[16] Those conclusions consist in comparing real world states of affairs with the hypothetical states of affairs that, in the general-equilibrium model, can be shown to be Pareto optimal. It is this practice – and it is a widespread one – that Demsetz (1969) branded the "nirvana" approach, the comparison of actual situations with an impossible ideal. And, to the extent that the failure of competition to live up to this hypothetical standard is taken as justification for government intervention, the welfare comparison necessarily implies a hidden value judgment that such government intervention is the more efficient institutional arrangement (Dahlman 1979).

In competition theory, the comparative-institutional approach comes most visibly into collision with the welfare-economic approach (as embodied in the neoclassical microeconomics of competition and the SCP paradigm) over the question of barriers to entry. The issue can be described simply. The excess of revenues over costs that (by definition) a monopoly or oligopoly is able to maintain is at the same time a potential profit opportunity for someone who would enter the market. To put it another way, there are potential gains from trade in a situation of imperfect competition that are not being exploited. In the literature of externalities since Coase (1960), the analogous question would be cast in a language of property rights and transaction costs; that is, a property-rights theorist would try to isolate those transaction costs that prevent an exploitation of the apparent profit opportunity[17] and he would ask whether a redefinition of the appropriate property rights could increase the gains from trade. By contrast, the standard industrial organization literature persists in asking the same question in noninstitutional terms, a fact that arguably qualifies this literature as a relatively backward area of theory.[18] To the extent that it is answered at all, the question of why an apparent profit opportunity is not being exploited is treated in this literature in terms of barriers to entry arising naturally within the logic of allocation. Most often, the plausibility of such barriers is closely bound up with the static nature of the hypothetical allocation problem or with particular ad hoc – one might even say contrived – assumptions about the knowledge and behavioral responses of the barrier-creating firms.[19] Few if any economists would argue that

[16] For an interesting comparison of these approaches, see Nelson (1981).
[17] More correctly, he would try to isolate the transaction costs that, when taken into account, explain why the apparent profit opportunity is not a profit opportunity at all.
[18] I am indebted to Gerald O'Driscoll for this observation. His Chapter 7 in this volume pursues many of the themes I'm developing here.
[19] The best known of these assumptions is probably the Sylos postulate. For a canonical exposition, see Scherer (1980, p. 244). For a recent critique of the barriers-to-entry literature, see Demsetz (1982) and, from a different angle, Latsis (1976, pp. 33–9).

there are never barriers of this sort; competition is surely full of imperfections relative to any ideal of perfection. But many economists would certainly argue that such ad hoc barriers, to the extent that they exist, are far less important for economic analysis and policy than the legal barriers that come from investing competitors with the legal right to prevent entry – as, for example, through patents, franchises, medallions, regulatory boards, and the like (Demsetz 1974; O'Driscoll 1982).

The property-rights approach is one way to look at competition in institutional terms. One shortcoming of this approach, in my view, is that, as it is usually practiced, the analysis proceeds with much the same static-allocation objectives in mind as its more conventional counterpart. This is often an extremely useful way to approach things; but, if we take seriously the themes of bounded rationality and economic process, we might well be more concerned with the adaptability properties of an institutional structure (Hayek 1948; Nelson 1981) than with its optimality properties in some narrower sense. The economic problem in such a world may be less to generate Pareto optimality than to increase, as the biologist might put it, the ecological diversity and complexity of the economy (Hayek 1973; Klein 1977). There is no reason to think that a property-rights approach cannot handle these concerns, even if the conclusions we draw from the analysis turn out in some cases to be different.[20]

1.5.2   The evolution of social institutions

I have argued that to study competition with an eye toward the institutions – such as property rights – that guide and mold it is a far more interesting and sophisticated approach than to analyze particular states of affairs – such as concentration. Market structure is something that develops as part of the competitive process; and the meaning of an observed structure will depend crucially on the path by which it was reached and on the pattern of property rights that supports it.

If we step back a bit further, however, we see that the institutional structure is not itself entirely exogenous. Property rights and other institutional support systems have themselves emerged as part of a process of social interaction, and this process is also fair game for theory. In fact, the appropriate theory may very well be closely related to theories of process competition. As Ludwig Lachmann (1971, p. 68) puts it, "the theory of institutions is the sociological counterpart of the theory of competition in economics."

[20] See Rizzo (1980) for an economic analysis of the common law from a dynamic perspective.

In what is clearly the seminal article in the literature of property rights, Coase (1960) called attention to the fact that property rights are, in a certain sense, arbitrary; in the absence of transaction costs, it is irrelevant[21] which of two conflicting parties is assigned the right to carry out his or her activities – since, through bargaining and exchange, the right will ultimately come to rest in the hands of the party who values it most highly. When there *are* costs of bargaining and exchange, the initial distribution of rights does matter. And it is a topic of controversy whether and to what extent the legal system (the common law as possibly modified by legislation) operates so as continually to alter rights assignments in favor of those whose possession of the right would increase aggregate wealth.[22] Broadly speaking, though, it does seem that we can explain the historical development of property rights and the common law itself as the emergent result of interaction among individuals; and we may even safely agree with Demsetz (1967, p. 350) that "the emergence of new property rights takes place in response to the desires of the interacting persons for adjustments to new benefit-cost possibilities" – as long as we are careful about the process by which such emergence takes place.

There seems to me to be a conflict or tension within the economic literature of social institutions, particularly that influenced by the important work of Coase (1937) on the theory of the internal organization of firms. Although the issue may in the end be merely one of emphasis, there is a sense in which writers on this topic can be distinguished into two groups: those who try to explain institutions as *instances* of market-like contracting among individuals and those who see institutions precisely as *alternatives* to such contracting.

The former approach is probably best epitomized by an oft-quoted remark by Alchian and Demsetz: "To speak of managing, directing, or assigning workers to various tasks is a deceptive way of noting that the employer continually is involved in renegotiation of contracts on terms that must be acceptable to both parties. Telling an employee to type this letter rather than to file that document is like my telling a grocer to sell me this brand of tuna rather than that brand of bread" (Alchian and Demsetz 1972, p. 778). But surely Alchian and Demsetz don't mean this literally. Continually renegotiating contracts is precisely what the employer is *not* doing; the efficiency value of the employer-employee rela-

---

[21] That is, it is irrelevant from the point of view of which party ultimately comes to possess the right; the initial distribution is certainly relevant to the participants, since it determines the eventual distribution of wealth.

[22] For an excellent discussion, see the symposium on the efficiency of the common law published as the March, 1980, issue of the *Journal of Legal Studies*.

tion lies if anywhere in making unnecessary the continual renegotiation of contracts. The social institution here consists in the shared understanding that there are people called employers and people called workers; that employers pay workers and direct them within a particular (perhaps tacitly recognized) sphere of activities; and that workers can quit whenever they choose. It is certainly true that the employee relation and the market-contract are both voluntary contracts; but they are very different *kinds* of contracts – and therein lie all the interesting analytic issues.

What Alchian and Demsetz presumably mean – and this is why I say the matter may boil down to one of emphasis – is that this institution operates as if the employer and employee were continually renegotiating marketlike contracts. The "as if" here might mean that the employer-employee relation is morally equivalent to the market-contracting structure; or, more significantly for present purposes, it might mean that the former fulfills in a world of high renegotiation costs the function that the latter would fulfill in the absence of transaction costs. Similarly, the practice of driving on the right-hand side of the road – to give an example of a simpler institution – fulfills the function that, in a very different world, could be performed by individual negotiations between oncoming motorists.

In order to put transaction costs in their proper context, we have, it seems to me, to return to one of the themes with which I began this essay: the conception of economic process. A necessary preliminary, though, is to define what it is one means by an institution – a term I have so far used rather loosely.

Andrew Schotter offers the following useful definition: "A social institution is a regularity in social behavior that is agreed to by all members of society, specifies behavior in specific recurrent situations, and is either self-policed or policed by some external authority"[23] (Schotter 1981, p. 11). His economic theory of social institutions is based on game theory, especially the concept of a supergame in which a particular game is played again and again. In such recurrent games, players may find it to their advantage to settle upon strategies that, although perhaps inferior from the point of view of any single game, are superior in the long run. The strategy is a norm of behavior, a rule that

---

[23] The emphasis here should be on the idea of an institution as a regularity of behavior that specifies action in particular recurrent situations. That the institution is "agreed upon by all members of society" is less important in our context, and is certainly questionable or perhaps meaningless outside the confines of the game-theory formalism Schotter uses.

says "always react in manner X to event Y." Social institutions are made up of rules of this sort.

For example, if two players find themselves repeatedly engaged in a game of the well-known prisoners' dilemma form, they may eventually agree tacitly on the rule "always cooperate," an outcome that would be unlikely – that is, that would not be a Nash equilibrium – in a one-shot game. Indeed, Schotter suggests that one can think of players as passing such rules along to the heirs that replace them in the game; over time, these descendants may follow the rule without understanding the reason for its adoption – and may be better off if they follow this rule than if they consciously attempted to solve anew the game they face.[24]

In addition to prisoners' dilemma games, Schotter also considers what he calls "coordination" games. The recurrent game of deciding which side of the road to head for when another car approaches head on is an example; these games differ from prisoners' dilemmas in that they are self-policing – it is in no one's interest to deviate from the norm once it is established. In both cases, the resulting institutions have a clear informational function,[25] which Schotter (1981, pp. 139–42) connects with the notion of entropy within the formalism of information theory.[26]

It might seem a rather larger jump from simple norms and social conventions to institutions such as the employer-employee relation or the corporate firm. In fact, Viktor Vanberg (1982) has argued that the two are fundamentally different, and that the evolutionary approach

---

[24] In some interesting recent work, Robert Axelrod has shown that the emergence of such norms in prisoners' dilemma situations is not at all an unlikely occurrence. He staged a computerized tournament for which game-theorists from around the world submitted strategies. One interesting conclusion was that the most successful strategy in the tournament turned out to be one of the simplest – the tit-for-tat strategy, in which the player echoes in the present period whatever his opponent did in the previous period. That such a simple strategy won repeatedly over more complex strategies illustrates some of the arguments Heiner has advanced about the value of simplicity in complex environments (Heiner 1983 and in this volume). More interestingly for our purposes, the tit-for-tat strategy and most of the other successful strategies have the following characteristic in common: they show a willingness to cooperate, a propensity for swift and sure punishment of any noncooperation by the opponent, and a willingness to forgive the opponent quickly for his noncooperation. This suggests that norms of cooperation with these properties would have strong survival value over the alternatives, and that we thus might expect to see many such norms in society. See Axelrod (1980a, 1980b, 1981, 1984).

[25] For an excellent verbal treatment of the informational role of social institutions, see Sowell (1980).

[26] As Dahlman (1979, p. 148) suggests, the intellectual content of the concept of a transaction cost reduces to a single idea: resource losses caused by a lack of information. Looking at the information content of norms in the manner Schotter suggests may thus be a way finally to get an analytic handle on this slippery concept.

favored by writers such as Adam Smith and Carl Menger for explaining law, money, and other basic institutions should be supplemented with a contractarian approach, involving greater reference to conscious design, when corporate structures are at issue. This is similar to Menger's distinction between "organic" institutions and "pragmatic" institutions (Menger 1963). Now, it is certainly true that a social norm is in some sense a different kind of social institution from a corporation. In Hayek's terms (1973, pp. 30, 50), the rules of behavior embodied in the former are "abstract," applying to a wide class of persons and activities, whereas the body of rules that govern a business firm are aimed toward specific goals. But both qualify as institutions. As Lachmann (1971, p. 81) writes,

It might be said that the undesigned institutions which evolve gradually as the unintended and unforeseeable result of the pursuit of individual interests accumulate in the *interstices* of the legal order. The interstices have been planned, though the sediments accumulating in them have not and could not have been. In a society of this type we might distinguish between the *external* institutions which constitute, as it were, the outer framework of society, the legal order, and the *internal* institutions which gradually evolve as a result of market processes and other forms of spontaneous individual action. (Emphasis in original)

What unifies both types of institution, and what makes the same methods of analysis more or less applicable to both, is that both are in large measure regularities of behavior understandable in terms of rules, norms, and routines (Nelson and Winter 1982, chaps. 4, 5). In one case the rules will be general, abstract, and widely applicable; in the other the rules will be specific and narrowly focused; but the basic logic is the same.

Furthermore, in considering an organization such as the firm, we have to distinguish between particular firms and the general organization concepts they reflect. Any individual firm may be of pragmatic origin; it is consciously designed in the sense that someone consciously filed incorporation papers, acquired financing, hired secretaries, and did all the things one associates with creating a firm. At the same time, however, that firm does not spring full-blown from anyone's head. Its ultimate size, its economic success, its particular characteristics become known only as the result of an economic process. Moreover, the general organizational concepts that one uses in designing a firm – such as the idea of the M-form studied by Chandler (1962) – certainly develop in an organic way from earlier forms.

We should thus not be surprised to find that Williamson's framework for analyzing what he describes generically as "governance structures" is quite congruent with Schotter's way of looking at the more general problem of analyzing social institutions. As we've already seen, his method is a comparative-institutional one. And his algorithm is this: to identify which governance-structure is most efficient – that is, which is most effective in economizing on transaction costs. The range of governance-structures with which he's concerned typically includes the spectrum from markets to hierarchies. In his original 1975 formulation, Williamson tackles the problem with a four-part organizational failures framework. More recently (Williamson 1979, 1981, and in this volume), this framework seems to have been distilled down to two factors: bounded rationality and opportunism. The first I will discuss in some detail in Chapter 10; the second refers to the tendency of transacting agents to exploit informational advantages, a tendency Williamson describes as "self-interest with guile." One interesting aspect of these two factors is the extent to which they correspond to the two types of game situations Schotter analyzes: bounded rationality is precisely the problem faced in a typical coordination game, and opportunism is at the heart of the prisoners' dilemma.

In broadest outline, the type of analysis Williamson advocates is this. Isolate two or more discrete institutional alternatives – various forms of corporate organization, for example. Analyze each alternative for its ability to operate effectively in the face of bounded rationality and opportunism, given the kinds of transactions that take place within it. This approach clearly marries the themes of bounded rationality and institutional analysis. But where does the process theme fit in? Both Williamson and Schotter address this question in their chapters in this volume. I myself have treated the issue in detail elsewhere (Langlois 1984), and I devote much of Chapter 10 to a detailed methodological analysis of institutional explanation. At the risk of oversimplification, however, we might summarize the issues in the following way.

Understood as an explanation for the existence of an institution, the transaction-cost approach must face two problems. One of these is what we might call the disequilibrium problem; the other is the path-dependency problem.

The disequilibrium problem is related to the idea of a flexibility-efficiency tradeoff of the sort I mentioned above under the rubric of Schumpeterian competition. One implication of this tradeoff is, in effect, that efficiency is not an absolute concept: it can't be defined independently of the organization's environment. A firm in a very rapidly changing environment may have very bad transaction-cost properties but be far more efficient – far better able to survive – than a relatively less flexible organizational structure with good transaction-cost properties in equilibrium. It's not clear how important this problem is in practice, although I conjecture that it may be quite significant in situations of rapid technical change. In any event, it's far from clear that one can't do comparative-institutional analysis in a way that accounts for these dynamic considerations. Most current analyses do seem to assume that the criterion for the organization's survival is efficiency in the allocation of resources rather than flexibility or something like it.

The path-dependency problem is closely related. Here the question is whether, once having scrutinized an organizational form and found it more efficient than existing alternatives, we can immediately say that we have explained why this organizational form exists and the alternatives do not. And the answer is probably that we cannot. The process by which more efficient forms supplant less efficient ones need not work smoothly and unfailingly. For example, those organizations well designed to economize on transaction costs in the long run may find themselves selected out by a very inhospitable selection environment in the short run, leaving behind an observed population of relatively ill-adapted forms. A complete explanation may have to suggest not only why a structure is efficient now but why it was efficient throughout its evolutionary history, which means specifying the process by which structures are selected.

Again, the significance of this problem in practice is not entirely clear. It does seem that it would be more important in explanations of organizational form – which are relatively specific and short-lived sets of behavior patterns – than in explanations of simpler and more abstract social norms.

In any case, these problems are troubling if we interpret comparative-institutional transaction-cost analysis as providing an explanation of the *origin* of an institution or organization. If, however, we reinterpret such analysis in a more limited way as instead explaining, as it were, the raison d'être or rationale of the structure in question, then an efficiency analysis of this sort is not only justifiable but perhaps logically necessary. In an evolutionary system, for example, one must ultimately appeal to efficiency arguments to explain why observed structures are able to survive; to do otherwise would be to risk the sort of tautology Darwinian biology was long, and wrongly, accused of embodying – that survival is its own explanation (Gould 1977, pp. 42–3). In this sense, the comparative-institutional analysis of Williamson and the organic explanation of institutions in the manner of Menger should be seen as slightly different, but nonetheless complementary, research programs.

22   Richard N. Langlois

References

Abernathy, William J. 1978. *The Productivity Dilemma*. Baltimore: Johns Hopkins University Press.
Abernathy, William J., and Phillip Townsend. 1975. "Technology, Productivity, and Process Change." *Technological Forecasting and Social Change* 7(4):397.
Abernathy, William J., and James Utterback. 1978. "Patterns of Industrial Innovation." *Technology Review* (June/July):41.
Alchian, Armen. 1959. "Costs and Output." In *The Allocation of Economic Resources*, ed. Moses Abramovitz et al. Stanford: Stanford University Press.
Alchian, Armen, and Harold Demsetz. 1972. "Production, Information Costs, and Economic Organization." *American Economic Review* 62(5), December.
Arrow, Kenneth J. 1962a. "Economic Welfare and the Allocation of Resources to Invention." In *The Rate and Direction of Inventive Activity: Economic and Social Factors*, ed. R. R. Nelson. Princeton: Princeton University Press.
1962b. "The Economic Implications of Learning by Doing." *Review of Economic Studies* 29:155.
Axelrod, Robert. 1980a. "Effective Choice in the Prisoner's Dilemma." *Journal of Conflict Resolution* 24:3–25.
1980b. "More Effective Choice in the Prisoner's Dilemma." *Journal of Conflict Resolution* 24:379–403.
1981. "The Emergence of Cooperation Among Egoists." *American Political Science Review* 75:306–18.
1984. *The Evolution of Cooperation*. New York: Basic Books.
Blaug, Mark. 1980. *The Methodology of Economics*. Cambridge: Cambridge University Press.
Chandler, Alfred D., Jr. 1962. *Strategy and Structure*. Cambridge: MIT Press.
Clark, John M. 1940. "Toward a Concept of Workable Competition." *American Economics Review* (June): 241–56.
1961. *Competition as a Dynamic Process*. Washington, D.C.: Brookings Institution.
Coase, Ronald H. 1937. "The Nature of the Firm." *Economica*, 4 (November).
1960. "The Problem of Social Cost." *Journal of Law and Economics* 3 (October):1–44.
Coats, A. W. 1954. "The Influence of Veblen's Methodology." *Journal of Political Economy* 62:529–37.
1976. "Economics and Psychology: The Death and Resurrection of a Research Programme." In *Method and Appraisal in Economics*, ed. S. J. Latsis. Cambridge: Cambridge University Press.
Cournot, Antoine Augustin. 1838. *Recherches sur les principes mathématiques de la théorie des richesses*. Paris: Hachette.
Dahlman, Carl. 1979. "The Problem of Externality." *Journal of Law and Economics* 22:141–62.
Dasgupta, Partha and Joseph Stiglitz. 1980a. "Industrial Structure and the Nature of Innovative Activity." *Economic Journal* 90:1266.
1980b. "Uncertainty, Industrial Structure, and the Speed of R&D." *Bell Journal of Economics* 11(1):1–23.
Demsetz, Harold. 1967. "Toward a Theory of Property Rights." *American Economic Review*, papers and proceedings, p. 347.
1969. "Information and Efficiency: Another Viewpoint." *Journal of Law and Economics* 12:1.

1974. "Two Systems of Belief about Monopoly." In *Industrial Concentration: The New Learning*, ed. Harvey J. Goldschmid, et al. Boston: Little, Brown.

1982. "Barriers to Entry." *American Economic Review* 72(1):47–57.

Dennis, Kenneth. 1977. *Competition in the History of Economic Thought*. New York: Arno Press.

Fisher, Franklin, and Peter Temin. 1973. "Returns to Scale in Research and Development: What Does the Schumpeterian Hypothesis Imply?" *Journal of Political Economy* 81:56–70.

Fusfeld, Daniel R. 1984. "Analytic Time and Historical Time in Economic Theory." Working paper presented at the annual meeting of the Eastern Economic Association, New York City.

Futia, Carl. 1980. "Schumpeterian Competition." *Quarterly Journal of Economics* 94:675–96.

Gould, Stephen Jay. 1977. *Ever Since Darwin*. New York: Norton.

Gruchy, Allan G. 1972. *Contemporary Economic Thought: The Contributions of Neo-Institutionalist Economics*. Clifton, N.J.: Augustus M. Kelley.

Hahn, Frank. 1973. *On the Notion of Equilibrium in Economics*. Cambridge: Cambridge University Press.

Hayek, F. A. 1948. *Individualism and Economic Order*. Chicago: University of Chicago Press; Gateway, 1972.

1967. *Studies in Philosophy, Politics, and Economics.* Chicago: University of Chicago Press.

1973. *Law, Legislation, and Liberty.* Vol. 1, *Rules and Order*. Chicago: University of Chicago Press.

1978. "Competition as a Discovery Procedure." In *New Studies in Philosophy, Politics, Economics, and the History of Ideas*. Chicago: University of Chicago Press.

Heiner, Ronald A. 1983. "The Origin of Predictable Behavior." *American Economic Review* 83(4):560–95.

Hirshleifer, Jack. 1962. "The Firm's Cost Function: A Successful Reconstruction?" *The Journal of Business* 35(3):249.

Jaffé, William. 1976. "Menger, Jevons, and Walras De-homogenized." *Economic Inquiry* 14:511–24.

Kamien, Morton I., and Nancy Schwartz. 1975. "Market Structure and Innovation: A Survey." *Journal of Economic Literature* 13:1–37.

Kirzner, Israel M. 1973. *Competition and Entrepreneurship*. Chicago: University of Chicago Press.

1976. *The Economic Point of View*. Kansas City: Sheed and Ward.

1981. "An 'Austrian' Perspective on the Crisis." In *The Crisis in Economic Theory*, ed. D. Bell and I. Kristol. New York: Basic Books.

Klein, Burton H. 1977. *Dynamic Economics*. Cambridge: Harvard University Press.

Lachmann, Ludwig. 1971. *The Legacy of Max Weber*. Berkeley: Glendessary Press.

Langlois, Richard N. 1984. "Internal Organization in a Dynamic Context: Some Theoretical Considerations." In *Information and Communications Economics: New Perspectives*, ed. M. Jussawalla and H. Ebenfield. Amsterdam: North-Holland.

Latsis, Spiro J. 1976. "A Research Programme in Economics." In *Method and Appraisal in Economics*, ed. Spiro J. Latsis. Cambridge: Cambridge University Press.

Littlechild, Stephen C. 1981. "Misleading Calculations of the Social Costs of Monopoly Power." *Economic Journal* 91:348–63.

1982. "Equilibrium and the Market Process." In *Method, Process, and Austrian Economics: Essays in Honor of Ludwig von Mises*, ed. Israel M. Kirzner. Lexington, Mass.: D. C. Heath.

Loasby, Brian J. 1976. *Choice, Complexity, and Ignorance.* Cambridge: Cambridge University Press.

Loury, Glenn C. 1979. "Market Structure and Innovation." *Quarterly Journal of Economics* 93:395–410.

Machlup, Fritz. 1963. *Essays on Economic Semantics.* Englewood Cliffs, N.J.: Prentice-Hall.

McNulty, Paul J. 1967. "A Note on the History of Perfect Competition." *Journal of Political Economy* 75:397.

1968. "Economic Theory and the Meaning of Competition." *Quarterly Journal of Economics* 82:639–56.

Menger, Carl. 1963. *Problems of Economics and Sociology.* Trans. F. J. Nock. Urbana: University of Illinois Press.

Nelson, Richard R. 1981. "Assessing Private Enterprise: An Exegesis of Tangled Doctrine." *Bell Journal of Economics* 12:93–111.

Nelson, Richard R., and Sidney G. Winter. 1982. *An Evolutionary Theory of Economic Change.* Cambridge: Harvard University Press.

O'Driscoll, Gerald P. 1982. "Monopoly in Theory and Practice." In *Method, Process, and Austrian Economics: Essays in Honor of Ludwig von Mises,* ed. Israel Kirzner. Lexington, Mass.: D. C. Heath.

O'Driscoll, Gerald P., and Mario J. Rizzo. 1985. *The Economics of Time and Ignorance.* Oxford: Basil Blackwell.

Phillips, Almarin. 1971. *Technology and Market Structure: A Study of the Aircraft Industry.* Lexington, Mass.: D. C. Heath.

Rizzo, Mario J. 1980. "Law Amid Flux: The Economics of Negligence and Strict Liability in Tort." *Journal of Legal Studies* 9(2):291–318.

Rosenberg, Nathan. 1976. *Perspectives on Technology.* New York: Cambridge University Press.

1982. *Inside the Black Box.* New York: Cambridge University Press.

Scherer, Frederick M. 1980. *Industrial Market Structure and Economic Performance.* 2d ed. Chicago: Rand McNally.

Schotter, Andrew. 1981. *The Economic Theory of Social Institutions.* New York: Cambridge University Press.

Schumpeter, Joseph A. 1934. *The Theory of Economic Development.* Cambridge: Harvard University Press; New York: Oxford University Press, 1961.

1942. *Capitalism, Socialism, and Democracy.* New York: Harper and Brothers; Harper Colophon, 1976.

Seckler, David. 1975. *Thorstein Veblen and the Institutionalists.* Boulder: Colorado Associated University Press.

Simon, Herbert. 1955. "A Behavioral Model of Rational Choice." *Quarterly Journal of Economics* 69:99–118.

Sowell, Thomas. 1980. *Knowledge and Decisions.* New York: Basic Books.

Spence, A. Michael. 1981. "The Learning Curve and Competition." *Bell Journal of Economics* 12(1):49–70.

Utterback, James M. 1979. "The Dynamics of Product and Process Innovation." In *Technological Innovation for a Dynamic Economy,* ed. C. T. Hill and J. M. Utterback. New York: Pergamon Press.

Vanberg, Viktor. 1982. *Markt und Organisation: Individualische Sozialtheorie und das Problem Korporativen Handelns.* Tubingen: J. C. B. Mohr.

Veblen, Thorstein. 1898. "Why Is Economics Not an Evolutionary Science?" *Quarterly Journal of Economics* 12:373–97. Reprinted in *The Place of Science in Modern Civilisation.* New York: W. B. Huebsch, 1919.

Williamson, Oliver E. 1975. *Markets and Hierarchies: Analysis and Antitrust Implications.*
New York: The Free Press.
——— 1979. "Transaction Cost Economics: The Governance of Contractual Relations."
Journal of Law and Economics 22(2):233–61.
——— 1981. "The Modern Corporation: Origin, Evolution, Attributes." *Journal of Economic Literature* 19:1537.

CHAPTER 2

Three types of market process

STEPHEN C. LITTLECHILD

2.1   Introduction

During the last half-century or so, economic theory has focused upon the individual decision and the state of equilibrium in which individual decisions are perfectly coordinated. There is increasing acknowledgement, however, that markets are typically *not* in equilibrium. Individual decisions and market outcomes at any particular moment in time must be seen in the context of a series of such decisions and outcomes. Decisions today are made in the light of the observed outcome of previous decisions and the conditions expected to obtain in the future. Decision making is increasingly seen as a process extending over time, and attention is shifting to the associated market process that reflects the sequence of decisions.

In this chapter I shall attempt to compare three main types of market process that have been discussed in the literature. For simplicity, these will be termed the neoclassical (*NC*), the Austrian (*A*), and the radical-subjective (*RS*). There are, of course, many variants of these types, notably the proposal by Hahn (1973), which embodies elements of all three.

The first part of this chapter examines the differences between the three types of process from a theoretical or modeling perspective, particularly the different assumptions about how the decision makers perceive the world, how these perceptions change over time, how additional information may be sought, and how the decision maker can limit his exposure to uncertainty. There is also some discussion about the problems of mathematical modeling and the role that equilibrium plays in each process.

The second part of the chapter is concerned with some implications for the explanation of, and public policy towards, various business practices and institutions, including advertising, industrial organization, and regulation or nationalisation.

27

2.2   The neoclassical approach

We shall term neoclassical (*NC*) the kind of model used by such writers as Stigum (1969), Rothschild (1973), and Frydman (1982), in which each agent characterises future prices by means of a probability distribution and continually updates this distribution in the light of observed values of the relevant variables. The distinguishing feature of the *NC* approach is not, however, the concept of the probability distribution, since a continually revised point estimate could be consistent with this approach. Nor does it depend upon Bayesian techniques being used to update the distribution, since in principle any forecasting technique (e.g., distributed lag or exponential smoothing) could be used. (In both these respects, the work of Grandmont [1977] on temporary equilibrium is a special case of the general *NC* approach.)

The crucial feature of the *NC* approach is that *the form that the future can take is known in advance.* "Tomorrow" can be characterised as a vector of random variables, where the range the values can take is known today and, more important, so is the set of variables itself. The *NC* agent lives in a world of Knightian risk. He is unsure what the price of honey will be tomorrow, but he knows that honey will be traded. Conversely, he never finds honey in the shops if he had not previously expected it to be there (see Stigum 1969, p. 549; Littlechild 1977, secs. VII-IX).

2.3   The Austrian approach

We shall identify the Austrian (*A*) approach with the work of Kirzner (1973, 1979), which in turn reflects the ideas of Mises and Hayek (and, to a lesser extent, Schumpeter). Here the agent may be characterised as knowing some things and not knowing others. The problem is not uncertainty (or risk) but ignorance. Over time, however, the agent discovers things of which he or she was previously unaware. The Austrian model differs from the *NC* model with point estimates in two respects. First, the revision of forecasts is not merely an updating in the light of experience – it may take place autonomously, as when, for example, the agent discovers a hitherto unsuspected source of supply. Second, this new opportunity is not necessarily a better value for a known variable – it may be a completely new variable: For example, a consumer may discover honey for the first time.

Risk (and uncertainty) are not the essence of the *A* approach (à la

Kirzner). "Tomorrow" is a vector of which the agent knows some components but not others; he or she knows there will be other components, but not what they will be; consequently, the agent cannot form a probability judgement as to the likelihood of their occurring.

2.4 The radical subjectivist approach

Both the NC and the A models just discussed are subjectivist in the sense that the agents act upon their perceptions of the world, which are in general different from what the world is really like. We therefore use the term "radical subjectivist" to describe the distinctive approach taken by Shackle (1969, 1979), Lachmann (1976, 1977), and Wiseman (1983). They emphasize the imagination needed to create the alternatives between which decisions are made, and hence the inevitable uncertainty associated with the outcomes of decisions. In this view, the future is not so much unknown as it is non-existent or indeterminate at the time of the decision. The agent's task is not to estimate or discover, but to create. He must therefore exercise imagination. The agent is aware of the flimsiness of his conjectures about the future and the vulnerability of his plans to the independent imagination of other agents. The agent's environment thus exhibits a qualitative as well as quantitative uncertainty – what Langlois (1984) has referred to as "structural" rather than "parametric" uncertainty.

One further significant difference may be noted here. In the NC and A approaches, the objects of choice are specified independently of the agent. Furthermore, an agent's knowledge and beliefs are quite independent of his or her preferences, except insofar as an agent is more likely to search for and discover opportunities of interest (e.g., someone who likes honey will, over time, come to know of a wider range of varieties of honey and will be able to make better estimates of future honey prices). In the RS approach, by contrast, the dividing line between preferences and beliefs is unclear. Agents will tend to devise schemes of action that appeal to them. Their predictions of consequences will be influenced by what they wish to happen – and also by what they fear. They may choose to ignore those things they find unattractive. As Shackle remarks, "I decide by choosing that imaginative vision which I prefer. To give me 'more information' might spoil it" (Shackle 1965, p. 308). There is evidence from both psychology and economics to suggest that such "cognitive dissonance" is widespread (Arrow 1982).

2.5   Reducing uncertainty

In all three types of process, the agent is uncertain about the environment in which he or she operates; and in all cases his or her perceptions change over time in such a way that further or revised decisions continually become appropriate. Yet the nature of this learning process is quite different. The *NC* approach is characterised by *risk and revision* (of probability estimates), the *A* approach by *ignorance and alertness* (to hitherto unperceived opportunities), and the *RS* approach by *indeterminacy and imagination.*

The three types of process focus attention on quite different devices that might be used by agents as a means of increasing their information about their environment or reducing their exposure to uncertainty.

Neoclassical models have greatly developed the concept of *search,* in which the benefits of lower prices are set against the costs of acquiring the information and the precise location of such prices. Effort has been devoted to calculating optimal stopping rules, and a variety of observed phenomena (notably unemployment and price dispersion) have been explained in terms of the cost of search (Stigler 1961; Alchian 1969). From the Austrian perspective, the concept of search, although by no means rejected, is inadequate to deal with the problem of ignorance. Search presumes that the agent already knows what to search for and how to search: in an Austrian world, however, these things are not obvious. The task is to discover what is worth searching for, and a cost-benefit analysis is inapplicable.

Two other devices for coping with ignorance seem appropriate. First, Kirzner (1978) has argued that the likelihood of discovering an opportunity will depend upon the value of that opportunity. According to this argument, higher taxes on income or capital gains will reduce the likelihood of profitable opportunities being discovered; government ownership or regulation will have a similar effect.

Second, though this is not an argument made by Kirzner, it would seem possible for an agent deliberately to seek out a position where profitable opportunities may be expected. A financier may observe the poor performance of a particular company and suspect that it could be run better – but not know precisely how. The financier may buy control of the company in order to gain access to the flow of information that seems likely to reveal more precise opportunities. In effect, the agent perceives an opportunity to perceive an opportunity.

From the radical-subjectivist perspective, a different course of action is indicated. Search can reveal information about the past but not (directly) about the future. Discovery of opportunities presumes those opportunities already exist (e.g., arbitrage). But if uncertainty derives from the as-yet-undetermined actions of other agents, then it is necessary either to become privy to the decisions of those other agents (e.g., by agreement or collusion), or to reduce one's dependence on them (e.g., by securing supplies or outlets).

We shall return to these topics later in the chapter. The point to establish here is simply that, insofar as the three types of process reflect different sources of uncertainty, so the agents may be expected to take different courses of action to reduce the uncertainty.

2.6   Mathematical modeling

I have suggested that the *NC* approach is characterised by risk and estimation, the *A* approach by ignorance and alertness, the *RS* approach by indeterminacy and creativity. To what extent can these approaches be modeled mathematically?

Various *NC* models have already been developed, notably by the authors mentioned. The essential ingredient is the forecasting function, which specifies future variables (typically prices) as a function of previous observations. Bayesian methods are often preferred as being more general than arbitrary forecasting functions and also as embodying a notion of "optimal" response to new information.

A models have not been represented mathematically, with one (quasi-Austrian) exception (Littlechild and Owen, 1980). There would seem to be no great difficulty in doing so, however. Alertness can be represented as a probability of discovery. Furthermore, agents can be equipped to deal with whatever turns up in the future, even though they might not know this at the time. For example, even if they have never tasted honey before, their utility functions can include honey; but they will not discover whether they like it until they discover honey itself.

Insofar as agents in *RS* models base their expectations upon their imagination rather than upon (mere) observation of the past, their forecasting functions are unlikely to be of a convenient form (e.g., continuous) – if, indeed, they can be said to have a forecasting function. *RS* models pose the fundamental difficulty of how to model creativity. If the analyst embodies in the model from the beginning the things to be created, this effectively transforms the *RS* model into the *A* model. It could be argued that creativity may be thought of as the discovery of a pre-existing opportunity. (For example, a new slogan on a T-shirt could have been discovered by anyone, though this can be realized only after the event.) But does this capture the essential open-endedness of creativity?

Both *NC* and *A* models may be set in motion by specifying initial environments and then left to run. *RS* models, if they are to remain truly *RS*, cannot. On the other hand, the complexity of *NC* models, reflecting the burden of calculation put upon the *NC* agent, makes those models relatively intractable. Models embodying bounded rationality have been constructed (Nelson and Winter 1982), and quite different approaches offer prospects of modeling extreme uncertainty (Heiner 1983), but these lie beyond the scope of the present discussion.

2.7   Equilibrium

Both *NC* models and *A* models stress the concept of equilibrium. For *NC* models, the key questions are what constitutes an equilibrium in a market process (for example, the concept of stochastic equilibrium has been introduced); whether an equilibrium exists and is unique; whether the market process converges to an equilibrium; what conditions are required to ensure convergence; and so on. In fact, all the traditional questions are applied in this new context. The purpose of studying processes seems to be the better understanding of equilibrium. Attention is therefore focused on processes in which equilibrium exists, or upon the properties of the process in the state of equilibrium (Hahn 1973; Littlechild 1982b).

A models emphasise the importance of equilibrium not as a description of the actual state of the process but as determining its likely future direction. "Opportunities have a tendency to be discovered," says Kirzner; hence the process is pulled towards the equilibrium point, even though the latter is continually moving as underlying exogenous factors change. Boulding's well-known "dog chasing the cat" illustration exemplifies this *A* model.

Kirzner's analysis of the equilibrium tendency has been the subject of some discussion in Austrian circles (Kirzner 1982 and references therein). How far is it possible to assert, on purely theoretical grounds, that the market process tends to coordinate rather than discoordinate? Kirzner's view is that entrepreneurship consists in the discovery of opportunities thrown up by exogenous change but not yet noticed by other market participants. In this sense, the entrepreneurial market process is one of continual discovery and increased coordination. Critics point out that this analysis downplays (or even ignores) the possibility of mistakes. If a market participant acts on the basis of a perceived opportunity that turns out not to exist, he may further discoordinate the market (as, for example, when a speculator makes a loss and accentuates price fluctuations by mistakenly buying at the peak rather than the trough). On this view, the tendency to coordination is an empirical matter. It is true that market participants are *trying* to foresee the future correctly, and that market forces will *tend* to eliminate the unsuccessful participants; but they cannot guarantee that every entrepreneurial action (or even most such actions) will increase coordination in the market.

This line of criticism is in sympathy with the *RS* approach, which stresses the importance of uncertainty, and hence the likelihood of mistakes. Shackle (1972) has also suggested another difficulty. There may be situations in which the very concept of equilibrium is ill-defined. Consider a market in which durable assets (e.g., undated government securities) are bought and sold with a view to a subsequent rise or fall in price. The price at any time will reflect the relative numbers of bulls and bears. But the subsequent movement of prices will convert some bears to bulls (or conversely) and this will cause further movements in prices. Even a temporarily constant price will eventually disappoint the expectations of some participants, and hence cannot last. Such markets are inherently restless.

Shackle's (1972, p. 433) own suggestion is a "Keynesian kaleido-static process":

The method implicit in the *General Theory* is to regard the economy as subject to sudden landslides of re-adjustment to a new, precarious and ephemeral, pseudo-equilibrium, in which variables based on expectation, speculative hope and conjecture are delicately stacked in a card-house of momentary immobility, waiting for 'the news' to upset everything again and start a new disequilibrium phase.

A kaleidic process is not entirely inconceivable in the *NC* and *A* approaches, but they are not well designed to handle such phenomena.

In the remainder of the chapter we consider some implications of the three different approaches for various business practices and institutions.

2.8   Advertising

What is the function of advertising in these models? In *NC* models, it *conveys information,* presumably more cheaply than do other means. It can also be *misleading,* in the sense that buyers can be told something that is not true but that would be too costly for them to verify (before purchase). But there is no mechanism in the *NC* model for *changing tastes.* (However, if the agent himself views tastes as uncertain but costly to explore, then advertising can presumably *change beliefs about tastes* by encouraging exploration. See Rothschild [1974] on two-armed bandits.)

For *A* models, advertising can, in addition to providing information, *alert consumers to the existence of unsuspected opportunities* (hence its frequently brash nature to attract attention: Kirzner 1974, chap. 4). Here again, advertising does not change tastes, but may appear to do so insofar as it *reveals tastes* to the hitherto unsuspecting consumer. ("Try this, you'll like it.") The agent's real tastes are assumed to be given, though he or she may not properly appreciate them. Once again, Kirzner does not address the issue of whether agents may make mistakes as a result of advertising; if they do, advertising cannot be said to be coordinating on purely theoretical grounds.

For *RS* models, a new possibility arises. Tastes are not previously given; they have to be created. Advertising can help to *form tastes*, by stimulating (replacing?) the agent's own imagination (Littlechild, 1982a). It cannot be said that such advertising is coordinating or even true or false. For the *RS* model, the possibility of changing preferences by advertising does exist, in the sense of influencing the formation of future preferences. Whereas *NC* and *A* models regard the changing of tastes as outside the scope of economics, *RS* models consider it a fundamental part of economics.

This raises different issues of public policy. For *NC* models, the issues are whether advertising is an economical means of conveying information, how far it may be deceptive and what costs it imposes, whether the level of advertising provided is socially optimal, and whether truth-in-advertising policies are cost-effective. For *A* models, there is little to criticize in advertising if attention is not focused on mistakes. For *RS* models, the issues for public policy concern the kinds of influences that should be brought to bear on the consumer as he or she exercises imagination. Issues of efficiency blend very quickly into issues of morality.

2.9   Property rights and industrial organization

The "new institutional economics" places great emphasis on property rights. It is therefore of interest to examine a few examples to see how each of the different types of process approaches the analysis of property rights.

Consider the familiar question of whether the workman or his employer will own the workman's tools. An important consideration is how far the tools are liable to be damaged by careless actions on the part of the workman, and how costly it is to monitor the workman's behaviour.

Here there is no uncertainty as to the kinds of action that might (or might not) be taken; but the pattern of ownership will determine the total cost of owning and operating the tools, and it is predicted that ownership will be such as to minimise the total cost.

NC models are quite capable (in principle) of reflecting these costs. But suppose that a further factor is taken into account: the possibility that unexpected developments will render the tools more or less valuable (e.g., the discovery of a new use for them or the discovery of cheaper substitutes). It is now relevant to consider which party is best able to "predict" and respond to such unexpected change – or, perhaps, which party is most optimistic or apprehensive about the possibility of such a development. *NC* models do not seem adequate to encompass this factor, whereas *A* and *RS* models do.

To take a second example, if I am quite sure what kinds of actions my neighbour contemplates, I might be indifferent between his owning the field at the bottom of my garden and my owning it but renting it out for him to graze his horse in. But once I take into account that he may discover some new use for the field that I haven't yet thought of, but would find objectionable, it will be in my interest to own the field so as to put the use of it under my own control. More generally, ownership of a resource reduces exposure to unexpected events. Property rights are a means of reducing uncertainty without needing to know precisely what the source or nature of the future concern will be.

Money is a third example. *NC* analysis incorporates the transaction-cost element but does not give adequate weight to the role of money as a generalized store of value. That is, wealth may be held in the form of money in order to buy something in the future that cannot yet be specified.

Finally, consider the size and scope of the firm. There has recently been a growing appreciation of the firm as a device for reducing the costs of market transactions. Horizontal, vertical, and conglomerate mergers may all be seen, albeit in slightly different ways, as alternatives to contracts between constituent firms. An important element here is the cost (even the possibility) of drawing up contracts to take care of every eventuality. Mergers are, inter alia, a means of reducing exposure to uncertainty. Insofar as this uncertainty can be represented in the form of a (reasonably stable) probability distribution, it is within the scope of *NC* models. But insofar as the firms wish to guard against quite unexpected events, the very nature of which cannot be adequately predicted, then *NC* models do not appear adequate.

Is there any distinction between *A* and *RS* models with respect to property rights? Probably not, if the unexpected developments are assumed to be purely exogenous to the parties concerned. But insofar as the parties themselves may, under some circumstances, have an incentive to design and bring about outcomes that had not previously been anticipated, and insofar as there is an element of conflict in which surprises play a significant role – in short, insofar as competition rather than cooperation is the relevant alternative – then *RS* models embodying imagination would seem more appropriate than *A* models embodying discovery.

One final point might be made here. There has been some criticism in Britain of the fact that many mergers appear to be unplanned and poorly thought out, often leading to no increase in profit over what the component firms might separately have earned (Meeks 1977). From an *NC* perspective, a more rigorous appraisal seems justified, couched in terms of probability distributions of future prices and outputs, and so on. But how far can such appraisals be relied upon? Is business strategy merely a calculation of probabilities? Is there no distinction between regular decisions as to the size of output and irregular decisions as to the kind of business one ought to be in? Businessmen seem to make such latter decisions partly on the basis of a hunch: a feeling that, although current demand is high, it cannot last, or that in another industry opportunities are bound to arise, though they cannot be specified in any detail at present. Such strategic decisions reflect entrepreneurial vision, but they are often so unclear and tentative that they can scarcely be described as discovering and exploiting an opportunity that others have not yet noticed. They seem more consistent with the *RS* approach: Within that framework, what basis is there *other than* hunch for taking long-term decisions?

2.10   Regulation and nationalisation

What will be the effects of regulation or nationalisation upon an industry's performance? *NC* models direct our attention to the effects of ownership on the choice among available alternatives: the Averch-Johnson overcapitalisation hypothesis; the reduced incentive to adopt peak-load pricing; the tendency to favour large subscribers; the looser controls on costs and wages; the increased preference for a quieter and simpler life; and so on.

Kirzner (1978) has drawn attention to the effects of regulation (and government ownership) on the discovery of new opportunities. Restrictions on entry and limitation on profit reduce the likelihood that opportunities will be noticed. As a result, changes in the pattern of demand are likely to be noticed later and technical innovations adopted more slowly.

RS models suggest attention to the process by which alternatives are drawn up for decision and to the techniques that might be adopted to ensure the successful implementation of the chosen plan. Any proposed course of action involves an imagined future. All decision makers have to convince those who monitor their performance of the plausibility of their plans. Compared to private ownership, regulation and nationalisation impose a different kind of filter on the imaginative vision, as well as on the choice of project. Different objectives will be paramount in designing projects; different weights will be attached to predictions of the future; different time-horizons will be relevant. In particular, there will be pressure to put forward and choose those projects that are demonstrably acceptable, those for which there is a "proven need." Projects that rely on imaginative vision or hunch will find it more difficult to gain acceptance, despite the importance (from the *RS* perspective) of this element in long-term decision making.

Insofar as decisions as to the scope of government control are made (or justified) on "economic" grounds, such factors as economies of scale are frequently involved. We have noted that this is only one factor influencing the size and scope of firms. Mergers and diversification are structural methods for coping with radical uncertainty. Regulated and nationalised industries cannot have the same freedom to act in this respect. On the other hand, regulation and nationalisation very often involve restrictions on entry, which (inter alia) reduce the uncertainty from competition. Thus, there are techniques adopted to cope with structural uncertainty that are different from those the unregulated private sector would adopt. This is not to say that one or the other of these devices is preferable, but any evaluation for purposes of public policy will need to take into account uncertainty in a way that *NC* models do not easily allow.

2.11 Summary and conclusions

Three main types of market process have been discussed in the literature. The neoclassical type takes as given the set of products or actions that can exist and assumes that market participants continually revise their expectations concerning prices. The Austrian type (as developed by Kirzner) in effect assumes that data are known or unknown, with market participants discovering and reacting to new opportunities over the course of time. The radical-subjectivist approach points out that all action is taken in the light of imagined future conditions and hence emphasizes creativity and uncertainty. The neoclassical approach is relatively straightforward to formulate and has been much analysed; but its complexity does not make it easy to manipulate. Although the Austrian model has not been mathematically formulated, it would seem straightforward to do so. The radical-subjectivist model poses the problem of how creativity is to be represented in formal terms.

Many real-world institutions, such as advertising, property rights, firms, and government regulation are capable of analysis in terms of all three models of market process. However, the element of structural uncertainty, which seems an important ingredient of the real world, is missing from the neoclassical model and is downplayed somewhat in the Austrian model. The radical-subjectivist perspective seems necessary to obtain a full understanding. Issues of public policy are not so clear-cut, and not so narrowly "economic," as when neoclassical or Austrian models are applied; but it seems necessary to face these complexities rather than disregard them. It may also be necessary to abandon the ideal of a comprehensive mathematical model of the market process.

References

Alchian, Armen. 1969. "Information Costs, Pricing and Resource Unemployment." *Economic Inquiry* 7(2):109–28.

Arrow, Kenneth J. 1982. "Risk Perception in Psychology and Economics." *Economic Inquiry* 20(1):1–9.

Frydman, Roman. 1982. "Towards an Understanding of Market Processes: Individual Expectations, Learning, and Convergence to Rational Expectations Equilibrium." *American Economic Review* 72:652–68.

Grandmont, J. M. 1977. "Temporary General Equilibrium Theory." *Econometrica* 45(3):535–72.

Hahn, Frank. 1973. *On the Notion of Equilibrium in Economics.* Cambridge: Cambridge University Press.

Heiner, Ronald A. 1983. "The Origin of Predictable Behavior." *American Economic Review* 83(4):560–95.

Kirzner, Israel M. 1973. *Competition and Entrepreneurship.* Chicago: University of Chicago Press.

1978. *The Perils of Regulation: A Market-Process Approach.* Occasional Paper, The Law and Economics Center, University of Miami.

1979. *Perception, Opportunity, and Profit.* Chicago: University of Chicago Press.

1982. "Uncertainty, Discovery, and Human Action: A Study of the Entrepreneurial Profile in the Misesian System." In *Method, Process, and Austrian Economics: Essays in Honor of Ludwig von Mises,* ed. Israel M. Kirzner. Lexington, Mass.: D. C. Heath.

Lachmann, Ludwig. 1976. "From Mises to Shackle: An Essay on Austrian Economics and the Kaleidic Society." *Journal of Economic Literature* 14(1):54–62.

1977. *Capital, Expectations, and the Market Process.* Kansas City: Sheed, Andrews, and McMeel.

Langlois, Richard N. 1984. "Internal Organization in a Dynamic Context: Some Theoretical Considerations." In *Information and Communications Economics: New Perspectives,* ed. M. Jussawalla and H. Ebenfield. Amsterdam: North-Holland.

Littlechild, Stephen C. 1977. *Change Rules, O.K.?* Inaugural Lecture delivered at the University of Birmingham, May 28.

1982a. "Controls on Advertising: An Examination of Some Economic Arguments." *Journal of Advertising* 1:25–37.

1982b. "Equilibrium and the Market Process." In *Method, Process, and Austrian Economics: Essays in Honor of Ludwig von Mises,* ed. Israel M. Kirzner. Lexington, Mass.: D. C. Heath.

Littlechild, Stephen C., and Guillermo Owen. 1980. "An Austrian Model of the Entrepreneurial Market Process." *Journal of Economic Theory* 23(3):361–79.

Meeks, G. 1977. *Disappointing Marriage: A Study of the Gains from Merger.* Occasional Paper 51, Department of Applied Economics, University of Cambridge.

Nelson, Richard R., and Sidney G. Winter. 1982. *An Evolutionary Theory of Economic Change.* Cambridge: Harvard University Press.

Rothschild, Michael. 1973. "Models of Market Organization with Imperfect Information." *Journal of Political Economy* 81(6):1283–1308.

1974. "A Two-Armed Bandit Theory of Market Pricing." *Journal of Economic Theory* 9:185–202.

Shackle, G. L. S. 1965. "Comment" on V. Mukerji, "Two Papers on Time in Economics." *Artha Vijnana* 7(4):308.

1969. *Decision, Order, and Time in Human Affairs.* 2d ed. Cambridge: Cambridge University Press.

1972. *Epistemics and Economics.* Cambridge: Cambridge University Press.

1979. *Imagination and the Nature of Choice.* Edinburgh: Edinburgh University Press.

Stigler, George. 1961. "The Economics of Information." *Journal of Political Economy* 69(3):213–25.

Stigum, B. 1969. "Competitive Equilibrium under Uncertainty." *Quarterly Journal of Economics* 83(4):533–61.

Wiseman, Jack. 1983. "Beyond Positive Economics – Dream and Reality." In *Beyond Positive Economics?* ed. J. Wiseman. London: Macmillan.

CHAPTER 3

Organisation, competition, and the growth of knowledge

BRIAN J. LOASBY

It is now becoming widely recognised that many of the central unresolved problems in economics turn on questions of knowledge. Increasing attention is accordingly being paid to the formulation of explicit hypotheses about the relationship between expectations and facts (past or future), to the content of information sets and the costs of acquiring information (probabilistically defined), and to the information properties of market and organisational structures. What is striking about this work is its total neglect of the abundant literature on the growth of knowledge – even though this literature is now frequently called in aid to interpret the history of economic thought and to elucidate present controversies. Though many economists would nowadays agree that any one school of thought embodies a (necessarily) limited perspective, the agents whose situation is analyzed apparently suffer no paradigmatic constraints.

No doubt it is refreshing to find economists conferring greater analytical powers on their subjects than they claim for themselves; but it is not necessarily a good research strategy. In considering such standard themes as the response to (and sometimes the promotion of) change, and the possibilities of coordinating, by whatever means, a multitude of decisions, we should not be surprised to find only limited help from theories that ignore the problems of human knowledge. In this chapter, I propose to start from theories of the growth of knowledge and to see what suggestions might be made about the working of an economic system composed of organisations. Readers should perhaps be warned that they will not encounter any rigorous testing of carefully specified hypotheses; there will, however, be some shreds of evidence such as, in the hard sciences, may suffice to launch a new idea.

41

3.1   Popper, Kuhn, and Lakatos: conjectures and refutations, paradigms and research programmes

My starting point is the work of Sir Karl Popper. For present purposes, it is perhaps enough to say that Popper claims to show us how to escape from the search for verifiable knowledge – a search that Hume long ago showed to be a delusion, since no universal hypothesis may logically be derived from particular instances, no matter how numerous. We escape by embracing the logic of the proposition that a single counter-instance is enough to invalidate a universal hypothesis. Thus, instead of looking for evidence that is consistent with a proposition, we look for evidence that appears to contradict it; if we can find none, despite our best efforts, we then have some reasonable grounds for accepting the proposition under test, for the time being.

I do not propose to discuss the awkward question of why it should be reasonable to accept a proposition that has been corroborated by severe tests, or indeed how we might choose to define a severe test – not only because they are awkward, but because the arguments in this chapter do not seem to depend critically on the answers that we might give (though they are certainly not irrelevant to the problems of effective management). What is significant for this chapter is that these difficulties introduce an element of judgement into the definition of knowledge. There is no such thing as certain knowledge, in the sense of general empirical laws that can be shown to be universally true; what we may perhaps enjoy is what Ziman (1978) calls *Reliable Knowledge*, that is, knowledge that, in the opinion of those expert in the field, has stood up successfully to well-conducted tests of appropriate severity.

The growth of Popperian knowledge is necessarily a social activity: "The goal of science is to achieve the maximum degree of *consensuality*. Ideally the general body of scientific knowledge should consist of facts and principles that are firmly established and accepted without serious doubt, by an overwhelming majority of competent, well-informed scientists" (Ziman 1978, p. 6). This objective necessarily implies a particular way of doing science. If facts and principles are to become firmly established, they must be presented in a manner that is amenable to the judgement of peers. If there is, even in principle, no touchstone of objective truth available to use, we have to rely on intersubjective criteria.

That should not be a disturbing proposition to economists used to invoking intersubjective judgements of value in the market, resulting from the appraisals and decisions of competent, well-informed economic agents. The parallel goes further. Scientists seek to advance knowledge, but can do so only by exposing their own ideas to the testing of their fellows and to comparison with other new ideas from other scientists – just as entrepreneurs, seeking to better existing offerings, must expose themselves to the appraisal of customers and suppliers, and to the risk of being surpassed by competitors' offers. This exposure is fatal to most new ideas, both of scientists and of entrepreneurs. Competitive science, like competition in the marketplace, is at once a discovery procedure and a control mechanism.

In both, moreover, such competition requires a kind of collaboration: It has to be carried on within a more or less agreed framework. For the present, this theme will be developed only in the context of science. The concept of the controlled experiment, as popularly understood, is that by resting on a secure foundation of established knowledge, one can associate a deliberately contrived act with an observed effect. But if one accepts Popper's analysis, all knowledge is at best provisionally established; there is no ground at all on which one can be absolutely certain of standing firm. Controls and observation depend upon fallible theories. The Duhem-Quine thesis (Quine 1951), that it is logically impossible to test a single hypothesis, but possible only to test a set of hypotheses – a full listing of which may well be quite unmanageable – antedates Popper, but is likewise a corollary of the logical impossibility of inductive certainty. The Duhem-Quine thesis, and the simple logic of scientific discovery, leave wide open the question of what precisely should be deemed to be refuted by a refutation. Any acquaintance with current issues in any science or quasi-science will readily reveal that this is no mere point of logic; there seems no need to cite any examples from economics. If it were indeed to be left to each individual to make his or her own choice in these circumstances, not much would be left of the notion of consensible science, or of scientific progress.

Popper himself has always been aware of the need, not merely to create hypotheses for testing, but also to impose some methodological rules on the testing procedure. But though he recognises that any particular scientific activity necessarily takes place within a framework, he has not given much attention to the character of that framework, and seems to believe, moreover, that frameworks can readily be changed if they become inconvenient. Now it is precisely the framework, and the problems of changing it, that are the central concerns of both Kuhn and Lakatos. Kuhn's original theory of scientific revolutions (1962) was written in ignorance of Popper's work, whereas Lakatos (1970) was deliberately seeking to deal with the Popperian problem, and in what he believed was a more analytically useful way than Kuhn's. It is certainly more elaborate; for in place of a paradigm that defines the class of acceptable solutions to anomalies, and continues to do so until the accumulated weight of unresolved anomalies encourages a shift to a fresh paradigm, we are offered a research programme in which there is a clear distinction between hard-core propositions (both substantive and methodological) and a protective belt, within which hypotheses are openly subject to Popperian challenge and dismissal. Changes in the extent and density of this protective belt may be used to judge whether the research programme is progressive or degenerating, thus producing rational, though not decisive, criteria by which scientists may decide whether to join or leave it.

It is not appropriate in this discussion to enter upon a critique either of Kuhn or Lakatos; we shall simply observe that the apparently sharp distinctions become blurred as one approaches them: paradigms are fuzzy, and hard cores, in economics certainly, are soft at the edges – perhaps even in the centre. That, of course, is no more than can be said about the distinction between short and long periods in economics, which serves analogous purposes to the Lakatosian scheme. One should not seek more precision than the subject admits of; and the definition of scientific schools rarely admits of as much as we might like. It will be argued later that this lack of precision contributes to the growth of knowledge. Indeed, a scientific school embodies a kind of imperfectly specified contract rather like that of a firm (though in some respects more like that between a firm and regular, specialised suppliers) – a contract that may be reopened at any time in response to a change either in objectives or in perception.

However, the primary intention of this chapter is to develop this argument in reverse, and to consider firms as schools of thought. What I wish to propose is that the imperfectly specified contract that constitutes a firm should be deemed to comprise, not only understandings about pay and conditions on the one hand and duties on the other, but also understandings about the kinds of knowledge that will be employed and the criteria by which their adequacy will be judged. Nelson and Winter (1982) have prepared the way for this extension by their emphasis on the importance of skills and routines within the firm, and by their emphasis on economic change as change in routines. They have recognised (p. 111) that changes in routines might cause difficulties, because they might be thought to threaten the terms of the contract; and it must be remembered that it is the individual – subject to various social pressures – who decides whether a particular change is compatible with his or her interpretation of those terms. It is certainly not unknown for what appear to be minor changes to generate substantial strife.

3.2   George Kelly: man as scientist

We shall return to these issues shortly; but first I would like to consider knowledge from another, complementary, perspective. In his remarkable *History of Astronomy*, Adam Smith (1979) put forward a psychological theory of the growth of science in terms of the human desire for a scheme of ordering that would comfortably accommodate all the phenomena encountered thereafter, and thus allow the imagination to remain in its preferred state of indolence – until some recalcitrant observation generated fresh discomfort, leading to the search for a new ordering. For Adam Smith, as for Popper, science responds to problems; but unlike Popper, Smith tries to explain why. In *The Years of High Theory*, Shackle (1967) has unconsciously paraphrased Smith's argument (see Loasby 1983); but here I prefer to draw attention to a similar treatment by the American psychologist George Kelly (1963). A major reason for concentrating on Kelly is his "hard core" proposition that we should, for some purposes, consider people as scientists. To his fellow psychologists Kelly was suggesting that instead of regarding people as responding to stimuli, or drives, or whatever, we should regard them as people trying to make sense of the world and to do so by imposing some kind of interpretative framework upon it. Their actions therefore should be explained in terms of their perceptions.

Kelly emphasises the significance of bounded rationality (though not under that name) both for the professional scientist and for the amateur scientist whom he wishes to study. Because the universe is presumed to be an integrated whole, any perception of it is inevitably partial and inaccurate; we can interpret it only with the aid of models of our own creation. These models cannot be derived from the phenomena by some natural principle of selection and adaptation, since an integrated universe embodies no such principles: they are human inventions. In a very important sense, scientific knowledge is not discovered, but created – a view shared, for broadly similar reasons, by Kelly, Smith, Shackle, Popper, Kuhn, and Lakatos.

Furthermore, the creator has some measure of freedom, even if he or she subscribes to the most rigorous Popperian doctrines of falsification: Not only are alternative selections possible from the continuum under study, but the tests that are appropriate will differ. Thus it is not impossible that two theories that have some, but not all, phenomena in common could each gain corroboration by testing, but each be apparently refuted by tests that are strictly appropriate to the other. The first conclusion to be drawn, therefore, is that alternative, partly inconsistent, theories may survive, and indeed prove valuable as a basis for prediction and control. This is one of Kelly's basic theses, to which he gives the name of "constructive alternativism" (Kelly 1963, p. 15): He seeks to use it to liberate both psychologists and their disordered patients.

For the next conclusion, we must bring in Kelly's perception of the universe as a stream of events, many of them resulting from human actions that are based on human perceptions. As in Hahn's (1973) model, agents have policies as well as theories – but Kelly's interest is in evolution, not equilibrium. Thus the theories or frameworks that people use must continually demonstrate their serviceability by accommodating new events (or passing new tests, if one wishes to use sterner language). Since they are necessarily incomplete, it is not surprising that this process is likely to lead to some modification of the theories – that, after all, is what constitutes the growth of knowledge. But we should not assume a convergent process. Since different theories rarely deal with identical sets of phenomena, they are likely to be sensitive to somewhat different influences; moreover, insofar as theories are used as a guide to action, they will tend to generate different events. If two theoretical frameworks are to be adapted to data sets that are selected on different (even if overlapping) principles, then it is an open question how such adaptations will affect the relationship between these two frameworks. Arrow's (1974, p. 41) argument that an initial investment in selected information channels will be difficult to reverse provides an illuminating parallel, though his assumptions about knowledge are very different.

It is far from obvious that this question can be tackled by considering what is the equilibrium state of the system, since the unrefuted conjectures that would form an essential component of such a state are invented by people during the process that might lead up to it. None of the writers on the growth of knowledge considered here seems to think the concept of an equilibrium approach to knowledge worth considering, except insofar as it produces a concept of disequilibrium as a trigger to action. Their theories of knowledge are process theories; they are all, in a general sense, theories of learning by experience, in which the confrontation between an interpretative framework (or conjecture) and the phenomena it is intended to interpret leads to the strengthening, adaptation or, occasionally, overthrow of that framework. Experience, as Kelly (1963, p. 73) asserts, "is made up of the successive construing of events. It is not constituted merely by the events themselves." It cannot therefore be assumed that two people exposed to the same events (if we could agree on the definition of such a set) are therefore subject to the same experience. This is a critical point for the study of industries and of organisation.

3.3   Frameworks

Before we turn to these, however, we should pursue Kelly's argument a little further. As a clinical psychologist, Kelly was concerned with personality breakdown; and the interpretative framework he proposed was designed to help in the understanding and treatment of such breakdowns. People break down when they can no longer construe events in a way that others perceive as lying within a broad band of normal behaviour. In terms of this theoretical structure, this happens when events are changing at a rate beyond the individual's willingness to adjust, or in ways that seem impossible to fit into any acceptable pattern. The breakdown is a breakdown of coherent interactions between events and the framework that is to be used to interpret them; but as with interactions between supply and demand, it may be convenient to consider each component separately, and even, on occasion, to attribute the trouble primarily to disorientating events (most obviously when breakdown is deliberately created) or to the rigidity of personal frameworks. In this chapter, most attention is given to the latter.

It is with respect to the rigidity of frameworks that Popper's views are most sharply differentiated from those of Kuhn and Lakatos. The latter both argue that replacement hypotheses are almost always confined within the ambit of a particular research programme or paradigm; indeed, Kuhn maintains that many – perhaps most – scientists would find a change of paradigm impossible. Popper (1970, p. 56) agrees that change within an accepted framework is easier than the replacement of the framework, but sees no particularly formidable obstacles to replacement:

I do admit at any moment we are prisoners caught in the framework of our theories; our expectations; our past experiences; our language. But we are prisoners in a Pickwickian sense: if we try, we can break out of our framework at any time. Admittedly, we shall find ourselves again in a framework, but it will be a better and roomier one; and we can at any moment break out again.

The evidence seems to be against Popper on this issue, and perhaps the logic also. The social activity of conjecture and refutation through intersubjective competition depends on a very substantial measure of agreement on what is open to challenge: Of the many conceivable reactions to the falsification of a network of hypotheses, all but a few represent, for the relevant scientific community, not the advancement of science but its disintegration. For a particularly striking example, note the hostility of physicists to any suggestion of psychic effects, which is readily understandable as soon as one recognises that any general acceptance of such possibilities leaves very little established truth in physics.

As Ziman (1978, pp. 39–40) emphasises, compatibility with the accepted framework is a vital factor in assessing the claims of novel hypotheses:

> The text-book description of a physical science fails to do justice to the *network* of interrelated models, experiments, concepts, mathematical techniques, instruments, materials, properties, etc. that constitute the corpus of knowledge in that science. Our confidence in any particular element of this science cannot be rested solely upon one or two other elements, but is deeply embedded in our consciousness of a multitude of related facts and opinions. Not all the elements of the network are of equal weight or credibility, but they must all be taken into account in an assessment of the reliability of our knowledge in that field.

In particular instances, such as that of the missing neutrinos (Loasby 1976, p. 11; Ziman 1978, p. 35), this procedure seems to allow hypotheses to survive repeated Popperian refutations; yet, in general, the requirement that hypotheses should fit into the general received pattern of knowledge is a much more severe test. Of course it is not an infallible test, and at times is seriously perverse; but then, as Popper recognises as clearly as anyone, there is no infallible test, and no test at all without rules. All we need to add is that there are no rules without a framework.

Smith and Shackle offer similar psychological explanations for this attractive power of general frameworks: Quite simply, if we have a single general scheme into which we can fit all events, rather than a variety of specific schemes each of which has only a limited range, then we are spared the need to select the scheme appropriate for each occasion, and spared the disturbing thought that our explanations are somehow not quite right, and therefore not reliable. Kelly (1963, p. 9) also emphasises the importance that an individual normally places on the ordering of particular constructs within a hierarchical system, and indeed locates here a major cause of personal problems: "In seeking improvement he is repeatedly halted by the damage to the system that apparently will result from the alteration of a subordinate construct." Acceptance of a new hypothesis may entail the reopening of questions hitherto felt to be comfortably settled, and cause far more tiresome labour of thought than is required by some ad hoc solution, such as postulating the irrationality of some other person or group. Moreover, if once we embark on local reconstruction, we can have no guarantee that it will remain localised. If the network starts to unravel, who knows where the process may end? The physicists' hostility to the paranormal is characteristic both of man as scientist and of scientist as man.

People clearly differ in their readiness to undertake the risk of abandoning part of their own interpretative framework – partly, perhaps, according to their confidence in their ability to invent or to borrow some adequate replacement. But there may be dangers in judging this readiness from past experience. Though people differ widely in their stock of courage, it now seems to be accepted by medical psychologists that the stock, however large, can be exhausted: The bravest people, if repeatedly exposed to danger, may eventually behave like cowards. Similarly, although people may differ greatly in the elasticity of their minds, it seems plausible to believe that this elasticity can be exhausted; those who have already made great changes to their construction system may be least, rather than most, fitted to make the next change. Indeed, there is plenty of supporting evidence to be found among the creators of new scientific ideas or of political revolutions. Nor does it seem surprising from either a biological or human point of view that adaptability should be limited. As Nelson and Winter have emphasized, effective skills and routines are in large part unconscious, and not too easily changed; to design a human brain with emphasis on the ability to reconstruct routines over the widest possible range would not seem to be the optimal strategy for survival. At the level of human relationships, if a person were to be capable of instant rearrangement of his or her own interpretative framework, it is not clear that he or she could be recognised as an individual. Such a person would be very disconcerting to deal with, and would probably be shunned by people who wished to avoid disturbing challenges to their own less malleable construction systems.

The limited adaptability of any individual's framework, allied with its necessary inadequacy to cope with all the phenomena with which it might be confronted, point to the advantages of variability among individuals. One should not assume that any one scientist is capable of accepting (still less initiating) all the revisions that are compatible with the perpetuation of a single paradigm or research programme. Indeed, each individual may have his or her own perception of what that paradigm or research programme consists of. It is perhaps no accident that paradigms are fuzzy: They would be too constricting if they were not. The intersubjective collaborative competition that constitutes the discovery and control process that we call science does seem to require that its structures be imperfectly specified. As suggested earlier, imprecision in the right places can be extremely helpful.

These issues do not seem to be appreciated by Kuhn, who, even in his much attenuated revised version (1970), persists in his sharp distinction between work within a shared paradigm and revolutionary change. Lakatos certainly allows, indeed requires, the content of a research programme to change as a result of work in the protective belt, and, at least by implication, allows scientists to differ in the set of theories within this belt that they find useful at any one time; nevertheless, he writes as if the hard core were unambiguously defined and unquestioningly accepted by the adherents of a particular programme. Thus, although the supersession of one research programme by another is perhaps rather more like a constitutional change of government than the revolution on which Kuhn insists, nevertheless this is presented as quite a different kind of event – and a public event – from rearrangements within the protective belt. Ziman, however, although insisting on the need for scientists to agree on a great deal, does not expect them all to share in every detail a common core of explicable beliefs.

Even if a research programme may be regarded as an imperfectly specified contract, there does seem to be a need for alternative programmes that are substantially different. As Kelly argues, each construction system has a limited range of convenience; as he implies, each system has a limited scope for adaptation. The progress of human knowledge seems to require both Marshallian incremental change and Schumpeterian discontinuous change. That should not be surprising, since Marshall and Schumpeter were both quite explicitly writing about the growth of knowledge.

3.4   Organisational coherence

It is perhaps time to focus more explicitly on the analysis of change within firms and within industries. What therefore follows is an attempt to enlarge the range of convenience of a particular interpretative framework, by extending Kelly's proposition to include the manager and the entrepreneur as scientists. The emphasis is on organisations rather than entrepreneurs, not because they are necessarily more significant, but primarily because there seems, at this stage, more that can usefully be said about them. An organisation, then, is to be analysed as a "visible college" of scientists.

The visibility makes some difference, in imposing greater requirements of coherence than in a wider scientific community; but it is important to be clear what these are. Organisational efficiency requires specialisation of skills and routines, and this specialisation entails the learning of particular cues and responses – a particular framework for interpreting events. Organisational routines and the cues that evolve them are extensively analysed by Nelson and Winter (1982) and, more briefly, in the form of information structures by Arrow (1974). Now it is a central argument of this chapter that these frameworks are not simply subdivisions of a single elaborate structure that would encompass all the activities of the organisation. Such a system is not fully decomposable even in principle, and our limited human ability to handle analytical structures often leads us, as Kellian scientists, to tackle one kind of problem in ways that are quite incompatible with the methods used to tackle another, as physicists use for different purposes the liquid drop (densely packed) and shell (almost empty) models of the atomic nucleus. Each of these incompatible models has received the formal certification of a Nobel prize (Ziman, p. 37). The actions taken within an organisation need to be consistent; the frameworks within which they are embedded do not. This degree of freedom is also very helpful in maintaining an organisational coalition among members with very different personal objectives, and even very different ideas of where the organisation should be going. All that is required is that the frameworks should fit where they touch. The methods of preserving an organisational coalition discussed by Cyert and March (1963) ensure that they are not required to touch very often.

If we were concerned merely with a static equilibrium model of an organisation no more need be said. But organisations have to cope with a stream of events that will contain some surprises; and many of these surprises will flow from the organisation's own actions. If there is to be any response at all to these surprises, then someone's framework has to change, and it may then no longer fit adjacent frameworks where it touches them. The experiences of functionally organised companies seeking to diversify their product ranges pulled apart the frameworks used to handle these diverse products within the functional departments; the standard remedy of creating product divisions ensured that what no longer fitted was no longer required to touch. The obverse of this, as of any reorganisation, is that frameworks hitherto kept apart must be brought together; and such juxtapositions are liable to reveal unsuspected discords. The amalgamation of two divisions of ICI entailed the formal combination of two research departments whose members used radically opposed criteria for appraising projects. The operating consequences were mitigated by keeping the two groups in their own laboratories a few miles apart. Within the same company, the much greater explicitness entailed by the introduction of management by objectives disclosed a good deal of submerged conflict. Organisations are always vulnerable to surprise; well-ordered organisations are likely to be especially vulnerable.

Within a working group, the requirements of compatibility are normally much tighter; there must be close agreement on what constitutes a problem, and what kind of solution is to be looked for. But agreement need not be complete; indeed, given the difficulty of specifying contracts or research programmes, it would usually be very difficult to know if it were complete. It may sometimes be helpful if one member of the group perceives a problem or an opportunity in a situation that the others all consider to be fully consistent with their expectations; it will generally be an advantage if members have somewhat different – but not too different – ideas for responding to what they all recognise as a problem.

3.5   Alternative frameworks and the growth of knowledge

The growth of knowledge is a response to the failure of our existing theories to predict and control, a mismatch between expectations and perceived relevant events. What events are perceived to be relevant depends upon the intended scope of a theory; and insofar as an organisation's theories guide its actions, they determine what plans are tested in the market (or elsewhere): We thus have two reasons why different sets of expectations may give rise to different recognitions of failure and therefore different stimuli to search. Economists invariably assume a standard definition of failure, a standard trigger for search; even Nelson and Winter do so in their formal models, though not in their general discussion. Yet a very slight acquaintance with individuals or with organisations will disclose wide variations in the idea of a satisfactory performance. (Leibenstein alone has tried to build a theoretical structure on these variations.) If we are going to explain why some people, some firms, some countries seem to be much more effective in generating new knowledge, must we not seek part of the explanation in the differences in the way that they define their situations? This is not to deny that there are genuine differences in, for example, factor scarcity; but that can hardly be the whole story, and perhaps only a minor part of it.

However, recognition of the need for a better theory is only the first stage. The new theory has to be invented, and tested. It is not consistent with the argument of this chapter to maintain that only one new theory will stand up to tests, even in pure science. It may be difficult to devise a formal model of search that does not employ a set of "correct answers" as defined by the analyst; but such a model seems to owe more to its compatibility with a particular academic research programme than to its success in construing evidence. But even if it were true that the set of correct answers could be defined, the ability of any individual or group to find any one of them would be influenced by the particular framework employed.

Diversity of perceptions and diversity of conjectures provide two reasons for rejecting a model of discovery as a succession of draws by different people or firms from a single pool, in which the chances of success are strictly proportional to the number of draws that one pays for. This is a point of substantial importance; for if the model were correct, the chances of success would be just the same whether a given number of draws were to be made by a variety of firms or a single (private or state) monopolist: institutions would not matter. Any argument for competition would then need to be based on its effect on the number of draws, and it would need to be shown that such an effect would be desirable. The proper argument for competition, in science as in business, as a means to improving knowledge, is that it promotes alternative conjectures – and their critical examination.

The discovery of DNA is a striking example of the value of competition between groups of scientists who were using very different approaches to a recognised problem, each based on a framework that had been tested against their own very different patterns of experience (Watson 1968). The development of a commercially viable process for the manufacture of ICI's first systemic fungicide was the result of keen rivalry between two divisions of the company with contrasting scientific expertise and expectations. Peters and Waterman (1982) highlight the contribution of internal competition to corporate success. As a counterpoint to these examples, we may note Ziman's (1978, pp. 63–4) fears that the enormous costs of some kinds of scientific research will frustrate the competitive process that is essential to scientific progress. The construction of a single very big (and very expensive) accelerator to serve all high-energy physicists throughout the world "could, in the end, be damaging to the health of this branch of science. What system of competitive independence for research teams will be built into the bureaucracy that must eventually allocate research opportunities with this instrument? Could one feel quite sure that the results of incompetent research will be replicated, and errors eliminated, within such an organisation?"

3.6   Marshallian competition

Marshall's (1920) theory of the growth of knowledge is similarly based on competition among firms that have rather different ideas for changing their products or their methods of production: "[T]he alert business man strives so to modify his arrangements as to obtain better results with a given expenditure, or equal results with less expenditure . . . even in the same place and the same trade no two persons pursuing the same aims will adopt exactly the same routes. The tendency to variation is a chief cause of progress" (Marshall 1920, p. 355). A recent research study (Balestri 1982) shows the Marshallian process at work in the Prato woollen district of Italy. The former industrial structure, which was dominated by large integrated firms making heavy blankets and uniform cloth, using woollen rags as a principal material, collapsed after the war of 1939 – 45, and has been replaced by a fashion industry that is now much bigger, but deconcentrated and vertically disintegrated. There are now several thousand small firms, and none that could be called large – more than half the workers are in firms with no more than twenty employees. At every stage of production, experimentation is encouraged by the collaborative competition of many specialised enterprises. Several hundred firms have established market connections in the fashion trade, and create new designs for every season, thus completing a structure that is admirably fitted to cope with the unpredictability of fashion. Those firms whose designs are unsuccessful in one round join the non-designers as suppliers to the successful, and are thus preserved to re-enter the competition in the next round, in which their new design ideas may meet the new market test. Balestri (1982, p. 41) also seeks to explain the general level of success by the prewar experience of dealing with the great variety of rags used in blanket manufacture, which "shaped into local people's minds a mentality open to continuous screenings of new methods of production and new products."

The localisation of the industry facilitates a flexible structure, which is coordinated by a mixture of pure market relationships and the kind of cooperation between independent firms performing closely complementary functions (so necessary if a disintegrated industry is to serve a quickly changing market) to which Richardson (1972) has drawn atten-. tion. Non-price information is important, and is more effectively handled in a collaborative-competitive system that, like the invisible colleges of science, makes use of voice as well as exit. The industry has therefore avoided the tight cohesion that frustrates creativity, and achieved a success unparalleled in the European textile industry. It is now the largest woollen centre in the world.

Because the members of these firms have "assimilated the notion of precariousness" (Balestri 1982, p. 116), they are open to change originating from outside. Their interpretative frameworks, in Kelly's (1963, p. 80) phrase, are permeable to new constructs: "Permeability confers resilience, and thus promotes stability." As long as the changing requirements for success can be accommodated within these evolving frameworks, which outsiders do not use, these firms possess a capital stock of knowledge that provides an effective barrier to entry: It is not, however, a barrier that obviates continued learning.

3.7   Schumpeterian competition

Though research programmes, paradigms, or construction systems may be flexible, that flexibility is limited; and so is the flexibility of the organisation that relies on them to organise and extend its knowledge. Organisations have one potential advantage over individuals in promoting, or responding to, innovation: they can change the construction systems they employ by changing the set of members. But they have major disadvantages, too. As pointed out earlier, their visible college requires greater coherence than a scientific community; a paradigm shift imposes severe, and sometimes unmanageable, strains even on the latter, and is perhaps the greatest of all challenges to those at the top of an organisation, who have to encourage the development of a new group of frameworks, which intersect in new places, and therefore impose a doubly novel set of compatibility constraints. The more tightly structured, the more efficient in a conventional sense, the more severe is the problem of change, as Arrow (1974, p. 49) has pointed out.

These difficulties are compounded by the importance of the existing structures of routines and interpretative frameworks as an organisational truce (Nelson and Winter 1982, pp. 197–212); thus some changes, even if acceptable in themselves, may be opposed because they might seem to imply a willingness to allow the terms of the truce to be redefined to the disadvantage of those who object. Each organisation has its own implicit treaty, and its own tacit conception of what is acceptable. Not only is the organisational contract incompletely specified; it is unenforceable. Whether, in any particular organisation, this combination of incompleteness and unenforceability encourages rigidity or flexibility depends not so much upon the facts, as upon the constructions that are placed upon them. Thus there is no reason to believe that all firms in a particular industry will find the adoption of new techniques equally easy. Studies of the diffusion of innovation demonstrate clearly that they do not, and Rogers's (1962) analysis of the relevant factors may easily be expressed in terms of differences of construction system. The pioneer is "in step with a different drummer" (Rogers, p. 193).

It has been suggested earlier that the total capacity for change of each individual is likely to be limited; and it seems reasonable to extend this idea to organisations also. It is to avoid the commitment of existing organisations to established patterns of behaviour that Schumpeter's (1934, p. 80) entrepreneurs create new organisations, and it is their subversions of these well-corroborated frameworks that destroys them: "Where the boundaries of routine stop, many people can go no further, and the rest can only do so in a highly variable manner." Such people, and their organisations, suffer Kellian breakdowns. We should not forget that most organisations die; and the cause of death is often a failure to combine adaptation and coherence. Even simple failures such as unsuccessful products or excessive costs can be interpreted as failures of prediction and control, which imply failures of knowledge.

Yet it is not obvious that we should concentrate our efforts on improving the chances of organisational survival – especially if this is thought to imply restricting change to the rate and direction that organisations seem capable of adapting to. As Klein (1977) has argued, the stability of a system may be undermined by attempts to stabilise its elements. Thus the failure rate of organisations may not be an indication of system failure but of system success – just as an abundance of refutations may be a sign of rapid scientific progress. Since each organisation embodies a particular cluster of ideas, we might derive from Popper's advice to let our ideas die instead of ourselves the recommendation to let organisations die, as an aid to the growth of knowledge. (Complaints have been made that government organisations continue in existence long after their original rationale has disappeared, and that their persistence tends to frustrate progress.) But if we are to let organisations die, we do need to be sure that the result is not monopoly; we need to facilitate the dissolution of unsuccessful combinations, embodying degenerating research programmes, and the creation of new structures, which show promise of progressive programmes. Somehow or other, we need to maintain both the structured competition between organisations operating within imperfectly specified research programmes, and also the more fundamental competition between rival programmes. We need both Marshall and Schumpeter.

References

Arrow, Kenneth J. 1974. *The Limits of Organization*. New York: Norton.
Balestri, A. 1982. "Industrial Organisation in the Manufacture of Fashion Goods: The Textile District of Prato." M. Phil. thesis, University of Lancaster.
Cyert, Richard, and James March. 1963. *A Behavioral Theory of the Firm*. Englewood Cliffs, N.J.: Prentice-Hall.
Hahn, Frank. 1973. *On the Notion of Equilibrium in Economics*. Cambridge: Cambridge University Press.

Kelly, George A. 1963. *A Theory of Personality.* New York: Norton.

Klein, Burton H. 1977. *Dynamic Economics.* Cambridge: Harvard University Press.

Kuhn, Thomas S. 1962. *The Structure of Scientific Revolutions.* Chicago: University of Chicago Press.

Lakatos, Imre. 1970. "Falsification and the Methodology of Scientific Research Programmes." In *Criticism and the Growth of Knowledge,* ed. Imre Lakatos and A. Musgrave. Cambridge: Cambridge University Press.

Loasby, Brian J. 1976. *Choice, Complexity, and Ignorance.* Cambridge: Cambridge University Press.

1983. "G. L. S. Shackle as a Historian of Economic Thought." In *The Craft of the Historian of Economic Thought,* ed. W. J. Samuels. Greenwich, Conn.: JAI Press.

Marshall, Alfred. 1920. *Principles of Economics.* 8th ed. London: Macmillan.

Nelson, Richard R., and Sidney G. Winter. 1982. *An Evolutionary Theory of Economic Change.* Cambridge: Harvard University Press.

Peters, Thomas J., and Waterman, Robert H. 1982. *In Search of Excellence.* New York: Harper and Row.

Popper, Karl R. 1970. "Normal Science and Its Dangers." In *Criticism and the Growth of Knowledge,* ed. I. Lakatos and A. Musgrave. Cambridge: Cambridge University Press.

Quine, W. van O. 1951. "Two Dogmas of Empiricism." *Philosophical Review.* Reprinted in Quine, *From a Logical Point of View.* New York: Harper and Row, 1961.

Richardson, G. B. 1972. "The Organisation of Industry." *Economic Journal* 82:327.

Rogers, E. M. 1962. *Diffusion of Innovations.* New York: The Free Press.

Schumpeter, Joseph A. 1934. *The Theory of Economic Development.* Cambridge: Harvard University Press.

Shackle, G. L. S. 1967. *The Years of High Theory.* Cambridge: Cambridge University Press.

Smith, Adam. 1979. "History of Astronomy." In *Essays on Philosophical Subjects,* ed. W. P. D. Wightman. Oxford: Oxford University Press.

Watson, J. D. 1968. *The Double Helix.* London: Weidenfeld and Nicolson.

Ziman, J. 1978. *Reliable Knowledge.* Cambridge: Cambridge University Press.

CHAPTER 4

Uncertainty, signal-detection experiments, and modeling behavior

RONALD A. HEINER

[Knightian uncertainty] seems to lead only to the conclusion that no theory can be formulated for this case.

— Kenneth Arrow (1951, p. 417)

In situations of risk, the hypothesis of rational behavior on the part of agents will have useable content, so that behavior may be explainable in terms of economic theory. . . . In cases of uncertainty, economic reasoning will be of no value.

— Robert Lucas (1981, p. 224)

A problem has always existed in the conventional theory of behavior under uncertainty. What if agents are unable to organize their experience into subjective probabilities of potential events? Or what if the environment provides no objective frequency information for agents to observe? As the introductory quotations (spanning the last thirty years) indicate, the dominant tendency has been to view such questions as not amenable to theoretical analysis. Knightian uncertainty[1] is typically ignored or even viewed as a mistaken issue that hinders serious attempts to analyze behavior in risky situations.

Yet, even within accepted orthodoxy, misgivings are still expressed about the fruitfulness of standard formulations. For example, John Hey's (1979) recent survey of the literature of uncertainty in microeconomics concludes with the following assessment (p. 232):[2]

I thank the following persons for helpful comments and criticisms: Armen Alchian, James Buchanan, Dean Dutton, Daniel Friedman, Mark Isaac, Howard Kunreuther, Richard Langlois, Axel Leijonhufvud, Richard Nelson, Dennis Packard, Clayne Pope, Nicholas Rescher, Vernon Smith, Dean Truby, and Sidney Winter. Of course, I alone am responsible for the content of the chapter.
[1] See also the writings of G. L. S. Shackle (1969, 1972), which emphasize an even deeper, subjective uncertainty than does Knight (1933).
[2] See also Hey (1981, 1982).

Consider the original motivation for work in the economics of uncertainty . . . objections were voiced about the amount of information that an individual agent (in certainty theory) was assumed to have. For example, the theory of demand assumes that the agent knows the prices of all goods and his tastes (both now and . . . in the future). . . . . Economists threw up their hands at this . . . and set to work . . . producing the "new" microeconomics.

But what does the agent need to know in the new uncertainty theories?: the probability distribution of the prices of all relevant goods, the probability distribution of his income, and the probability distribution of his tastes. . . . Is this an improvement? . . . the optimization problems that . . . agents are supposed to be solving . . . are so complicated that the economic theorist . . . probably spent several months finding the solution. . . . The "as if" methodology is stretched to the breaking point. . . . Have we not gone wrong somewhere?

I wish to pursue these issues in the light of a series of experiments in psychology having to do with signal detection. These experiments suggest a different view of how to model behavior, one that is compatible with Knightian uncertainty and that also complements my recent analysis (Heiner 1983) about uncertainty as the source of predictable behavior. In particular, signal-detection experiments elicit systematic patterns of behavior that persist even when individuals cannot discern probability information.

I have three main objectives in mind: first, to describe the signal-detection experiments and discuss their implications for using probability and maximizing concepts to model behavior; second, to apply these implications to the *Reliability Condition* I previously suggested (Heiner 1983) as a way of modeling behavior under uncertainty; and third, to combine features suggested by the experiments and the reliability condition to build a simple analytical engine for analyzing behavior. I then briefly developed a few illustrations to suggest how the analysis might apply to economic theorizing. I also include a brief comparison with two recent topics in neoclassical theory – costly information and rational expectations. Finally, I conclude with a broader perspective about the conceptual issues raised in the discussion.

4.1   Signal-detection behavior and ROC curves

A variety of detection skills have been tested experimentally. These include various pattern-recognition and information-processing abilities, as well as other cognitive tasks.[3] To facilitate exposition, I will

[3] The principal reference on the signal-detection approach is Green and Swets (1974; for some of the major experimental designs, see pp. 30–52, 180–5, 209–23, 235–70, 276–345). See also Egan (1967, 1975); Coombs, Dawes, and Tversky (1970); Lindsay

confine attention to the earliest experiments, which are similar to hearing tests. However, the qualitative patterns to be discussed are robust over a wide range of different perceptual skills.

In the typical auditory experiment, a person must try to detect the presence of a signal amid background noise. Background noise is produced by a probability distribution of signal frequencies. The experimenter can calibrate the shape of the noise distribution, and determine how this distribution is shifted (including possibly a change in its shape) to incorporate the effect of adding a signal.

For example, suppose the noise distribution is normal with mean μ and variance δ^2. Adding a signal might shift μ from its initial value μ_n to a new value μ_s, where s and n denote, respectively, the presence or absence of the signal. In this special case, the noise distribution is shifted by $\Delta\mu = \mu_n - \mu_s$, thus retaining the same shape and variance, δ^2.[4]

Increasing the amplitude of the signal will concentrate the noise distribution (i.e., the variance δ^2 of the distribution will shrink at the same time its mean shifts by $\Delta\mu$). A loud signal compared to relatively weak background noise will be very easy to detect. Conversely, a weak signal masked by loud noise will be difficult to detect without making mistakes. Thus, the uncertainty in detecting the signal is positively related to the signal-to-noise ratio, denoted by d.[5]

A person is also informed about the size of gains, g, and losses, ℓ, that will accompany each correct or mistaken detection respectively.[6] In addition to d, g, ℓ, another parameter can be independently selected by the experimenter, namely, the probability of the signal's occurrence over a number of trials, denoted by $p(s) = 1 - p(n)$.

A person is asked to indicate whether he or she has heard the signal over a large number of successive trials in which the signal's actual presence is randomly distributed. Responding that a signal is present in a particular trial is denoted by S. Responding that only noise is present is denoted by N.

and Norman (1972); McNicol (1972); and Swets (1964). For a sample of literature references, see Adams (1963); Baldwin, Chambliss, and Wright (1962); Cannon (1970); Christ (1969); Colquhoun (1961); D'Amato (1970, pp. 157–189); Emmerich (1968); Heath (1977); Killeen (1982); MacDonald (1976); Moray and O'Brien (1967); Nevin (1969, 1982); Schulman and Greenberg (1970); Swets (1977); Tanner, Haller, and Atkinson (1967); and Tanner, Rauk, and Atkinson (1970).

[4] See Green and Swets (1974, pp. 53–85).
[5] In the special case mentioned above, $d = \Delta\mu/\delta^2$. For other possibilities see Green and Swets (1974, pp. 95–9). Besides the signal-to-noise ratio, a number of other factors influence a person's signal-detection performance, including differences in the hearing capabilities of particular individuals and a variety of environmental features that may either help or hinder proper recognition of the signals.
[6] See Green and Swets (1974, chaps. 2, 4).

	n	s	
N	#(N,n)	#(N,s)	#(N)
S	#(S,n)	#(S,s)	#(S)
	#(n)	#(s)	#(n) + #(s) or #(N) + #(S)

S = Agent responds that signal is present
N = Agent fails to detect the signal
#(E) = number of times event E occurs
n = only noise is actually present
s = signal is also present

Figure 4.1.

In contrast to the person being tested, the experimenter knows exactly when the signal is present or not, and can compare this knowledge with the person's observed responses in each trial. Figure 4.1 shows how these comparisons are computed. The number of times an event E occurs is denoted by #(E). Thus, the number of hits (detecting the signal when it is actually present) is denoted by #(S,s). Similarly, the number of misdetections, or false alarms (mistakenly detecting the signal when only noise is present), is denoted by #(S,n). The total number of times the signal occurs or fails to occur is given by #(s) = #(S,s) + #(N,s) and #(n) = #(S,n) + #(N,n), respectively. These in turn sum to the total number of trials, #(s) + #(n). From these data, the experimenter can estimate the conditional probability of hitting the signal when actually present, $p(S|s)$, or the chance of misdetections when only noise is present, $p(S|n)$. These probabilities are calculated using the appropriate frequencies from Figure 4.1.

$$p(S|s) = \frac{\#(S,s)}{\#(s)} \text{ and } p(S|n) = \frac{\#(S,n)}{\#(n)}. \tag{1a}$$

In addition to $p(S|s)$ and $p(S|n)$, their respective complements – failures to detect the signal (the miss rate) and correctly rejecting the

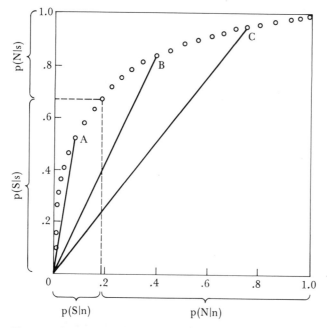

Figure 4.2. An empirically generated ROC curve. The above set of points represents an experimentally generated ROC curve for a given signal-to-noise ratio, d. The points move from the northeast corner monotonically down to the origin as either the signal probability is reduced or the ℓ/g ratio is raised. Note that the ratio $p(S|s)/p(S|n)$ systematically changes at different points along the curve. *Source:* Green and Swets 1974, p. 100.

signal when only noise is present (the correct rejection rate) – are calculated by

$$p(N|s) = \frac{\#(N,s)}{\#(s)} \text{ and } p(N|n) = \frac{\#(N,n)}{\#(n)}. \tag{1b}$$

The probability of the signal occurring, $p(s)$, and its complement, $p(n)$, are similarly given by

$$p(s) = \frac{\#(s)}{\#(s) + \#(n)} \text{ and } p(n) = \frac{\#(n)}{\#(s) + \#(n)}. \tag{2}$$

A person's detection behavior is usually represented by points in a unit-probability box, as shown in Figure 4.2. A particular signal-to-noise ratio, d, is selected and then a sequence of experiments is run for different combinations of loss and gain, ℓ and g, and different probabilities of the signal, $p(s)$.

Each combination of ℓ, g, $p(s)$ defines a single experiment in which a large number of detection trials are run to generate the frequency information shown in Figure 4.1. These frequencies are combined as discussed above to determine the chance of hits, $p(S|s)$, and misdetections, $p(S|n)$. A pair of these probabilities define a single point in Figure 4.2.

By selecting different combinations of $(\ell,g,p(s))$, we can run a series of experiments under the same set of listening conditions (i.e., for a constant signal-to-noise ratio, d). These experiments generate a sequence of points, $[p(S|n), p(S|s)]$, which form a curve commonly referred to as an ROC curve (for "receiver operating characteristic").[7] Such a curve is shown in Figure 4.2.

ROC curves are usually produced by either fixing the loss-gain ratio ℓ/g and varying $p(s)$, or by holding $p(s)$ fixed and varying the ratio ℓ/g. For example, let ℓ/g be held fixed, and start with high values of $p(s)$ (i.e., the signal is very likely to be present). The observed conditional probabilities will lie toward the northeast corner of the diagram (i.e., the person is likely to "detect" the signal whether it is actually present or not). As successively lower values of $p(s)$ are introduced, $p(S|n)$ and $p(S|s)$ will both monotonically converge toward zero (i.e., detections are less and less likely, whether the signal is present or not).

The same response pattern occurs if $p(s)$ is fixed and ℓ/g is successively increased. Three such points (A,B,C) are shown in Figure 4.2. This qualitative pattern holds for a variety of detection skills in addition to the simple auditory ones described here.[8] With an eye toward later developments, let me make four comments about ROC behavior patterns.

(1) Each point along an ROC curve indicates how accurately a person detects the signals. He or she is more "reliable" as either $p(S|s)$ increases or $p(S|n)$ decreases, or both. Accordingly, we can measure the reliability of a person's responses by the ratio $p(S|s)/P(S|n)$. This is shown graphically by the slope of a ray from the origin to a point on an ROC curve. Each ROC curve can thus be thought of as a *reliability curve* that shows the combinations of $p(S|s)$ and $P(S|n)$ achievable for a given set of detection conditions (parameterized by the signal-to-noise ratio d).[9]

(2) For a given ROC curve, the slopes of rays from the origin change for different points along the curve. Thus, *varying the frequency of detec-*

---

[7] See Green and Swets (1974, pp. 34–5).
[8] See n. 3.
[9] Detection conditions are also affected by other features of the shapes of both noise and signal distributions, as well as variables that affect a person's hearing capabilities.

tions systematically affects the reliability of those detections. Moreover, note a key feature of these curves: the slopes from the origin increase only for successive points closer to the origin (see Figure 4.2). Thus, greater reliability (a higher ratio $p(S|s)/p(S|n)$) can be achieved only by responding less frequently regardless of whether the signal is present or not. If the signal-to-noise ratio is low, this may require very infrequent detections in order to achieve even a moderate degree of reliability in detecting the signal.

(3) The preceding two remarks discussed changes in response reliability along a given ROC or reliability curve. Reliability can also be systematically affected by changing the listening conditions that define each curve. As one might intuitively expect, it is easier to detect a more powerful signal with a higher signal-to-noise ratio, d. Higher d will shift an ROC curve, causing it to bow more toward the northwest corner (where the signal is always correctly identified without any misdetections; so that $p(S|s) = 1$ and $p(S|n) = 0$).

Three such ROC curves for successively higher d are shown in Figure 4.3. Notice that, for each ROC curve, greater reliability always requires less frequent responding, as noted in remark 2. However, any given reliability (i.e., a given slope from the origin) is achievable with more frequent responding if the signal-to-noise ratio, d, is higher. The reason is that, when d is high, any increase in the chance of correctly hitting the signal increases the chance of misdetections more slowly than when d is low (so that the ratio $p(S|s)/p(S|n)$ drops more slowly with more frequent detections). When d is low, increased responding increases the rate of misdetections more rapidly for any given increase in correct detections (so that $p(S|s)/p(S|n)$ drops faster with more frequent detections).

(4) These characteristics of ROC curves are invariant to a wide range of listening conditions, irrespective of how easy or difficult it may be to identify the signals. In each case, higher ℓ/g or lower $p(s)$ produces a monotonic drop in the frequency of detections in a manner that increases the ratio $p(S|s)/p(S|n)$ (i.e., increases the reliability of detecting the signals). Different listening conditions still produce this same qualitative pattern, affecting only the rate at which the relative probabilities of correct or mistaken detections change as a person varies the frequency of detections.

4.2 Using probability and maximizing concepts to model behavior

The experiments were described in detail to suggest certain key features about the probabilities $p(S|s)$, $p(S|n)$, and $p(s)$ (and their respective complements, $p(N|s)$, $p(N|n)$, $p(n)$). These features have to do with

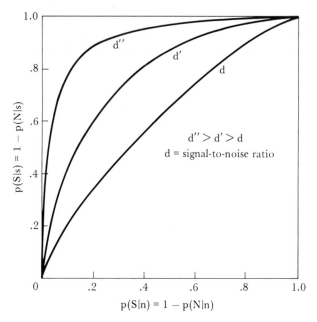

Figure 4.3. ROC curves for different signal-to-noise ratios. Above are three ROC curves produced for successively higher values of d. Note that the curves have the same qualitative shape. Only the degree of curvature is affected by changing d. As d increases, the curves will bow closer to the northwest corner, where $p(S|s) = 1$ and $p(S|n) = 0$ (i.e., where the signal is perfectly detected). *Source:* Green and Swets 1974, p. 60.

using probability and maximizing concepts to model behavior. First consider probability concepts.

In order to construct an ROC or reliability curve, the experimenter must calculate numerical estimates of $p(S|s)$, $p(S|n)$, $p(s)$ from a subject's signal-detection behavior. However, the subjects themselves may not be able to estimate these probabilities. To do so would require them to know accurately when the signal is actually present. Yet, this is just what the experiments are designed to prevent when low signal-to-noise ratios are used (i.e., inability to estimate $p(s)$, $p(S|s)$, $p(S|n)$ can be experimentally induced with sufficiently low signal-to-noise ratios). Nevertheless (as we have seen from the detailed description above), determinate values can always be calculated for $p(s)$, $p(S|s)$, $p(S|n)$ regardless of how uncertain the situation appears to the subjects being observed.

In a basic sense, these probabilities are conditional on the kind of uncertainty introduced into the experiment (in this case, by varying the signal-to-noise ratio) rather than reflecting any theoretical abstraction from uncertainty. Now think of uncertainty as indirectly resulting from agents' decision skills relative to the subtlety of the decision environment. We can then restate the preceding sentence as follows: The $p(s)$, $p(S|s)$, $p(S|n)$ probabilities are *conditional* on agents' ability to decipher their decision environment. Consequently, they do not depend on any special decision or perceptual skills, *including those that might be needed to assign probabilities to potential events.*

Now consider the above discussion in more general terms. The experiments suggest the probabilities $p(s)$, $p(S|s)$, $p(S|n)$ can be statistically well defined even though agents lack the competence to infer such probabilities from their own experience. The experiments cannot themselves justify extending this conclusion to other domains. Nevertheless, they do show that well-defined probabilities may exist in situations in which an inability to infer probability information can be experimentally induced and controlled. I believe this to be a point of great importance for theorizing about behavior.

In particular, suppose agents must act in a subtle, continually evolving environment. Suppose also that many future situations are historically unique to a degree that is beyond agents' ability to anticipate. This may also prevent agents from assigning meaningful probabilities to such events.

Next, imagine a sequence of situations produced by the environment. Even though many situations in this sequence may be historically unique, we may still be able to classify them as favorable or unfavorable for selecting a particular action. (In terms of the above experiments, favorable and unfavorable situations for detecting a signal would correspond to the signal being actually present or not.) Performance improves when the action is selected under favorable situations and, conversely, drops under unfavorable ones. These situations can be labeled *right* or *wrong* situations for selecting the action (denoted by the sets R and W, respectively). We can then calculate the probability of events R and W according to a frequency interpretation of the fraction of such events in a sequence of n situations; that is, $p(R) = \#R_n/n$, $p(W) = \#W_n/n$, where $\#S_n$ denotes the number of times situations in a set S occur in a sequence of n trials.

Note that it may be very difficult or even impossible for agents to determine $p(R)$, $p(W)$ from an ex ante perspective (because assigning historically unique situations into R and W may not be feasible before such situations actually occur). The same issue also applies to the conditional probabilities defined by $r = p(a|R)$ and $w = p(a|W)$, where a denotes a particular action and R and W denote favorable and unfavorable future situations for selecting it. (The probabilities r and w would correspond to $p(S|s)$ and $p(S|n)$, respectively, in a signal-detection experiment.)

Over a sequence of n future situations, we can determine the number of joint events $\#(a,W)_n$ and $\#(a,R)_n$, and then calculate r and w according to the proportions $\#(a,R)_n/\#R_n$ and $\#(a,W)_n/\#W_n$, respectively. Note that (analogous to $p(S|s)$, $p(S|n)$ in a signal-detection experiment) agents may be unable to infer such probabilities *even though they are in part generated by their own ongoing reaction to future situations*. Because the r and w probabilities result from agents' ongoing behavior (yet they are independent of whether agents can infer probability information), let us call them *behavioral probabilities*.

The signal-detection experiments also suggest (see points 1 – 4 in Section 4.2) that in addition to being statistically well defined, such behavioral probabilities can respond in quantitatively predictable directions to changes in the complexity of the environment or changes in agents' perceptual abilities. Consequently, they may be able to provide an analytical basis for modeling behavior without assuming that agents possess any special decision capabilities.

This conclusion is in marked contrast to conventional risk and utility theory, which typically assumes that agents act "as if" they are able to assign probabilities to all potential events. The latter probabilities (as distinct from the behavioral probabilities described above) are either postulated directly in the form of preference axioms over risky contingencies (subjective probabilities) or derived from "objective" frequency data assumed to be available to agents. Whatever the interpretation, conventional theorizing assumes agents choose according to a set of well-defined probabilities over all potential events. As such, even though many plausible situations exist in which agents may be unable to infer such information, it still has not seemed possible to analyze them fruitfully (as suggested by the statements of Arrow and Lucas quoted at the beginning of this chapter).

Now think of this in terms of using maximizing concepts to model behavior. Such concepts have often been used to justify why theorists should abstract from agents' perceptual abilities (i.e., agents act as if they have the necessary perceptual skills to maximize successfully). This is largely because maximization has been the primary motivating concept used to construct formal models of behavior. Suppose, however, we did *not* begin with optimizing concepts, but rather started from uncertainty factors that determine the achievable (r,w)-combinations for different actions as well as the likelihood (π) of favorable conditions for selecting them.

In particular, suppose we applied maximizing tools to the r, w, π probabilities (see Section 4.8.3 for a brief discussion of how to do so). Such tools would thereby become *conditional* on whatever uncertainty factors affect r, w, π, including factors that might severely restrict agents' ability to maximize in the traditional sense. Note how this represents a major shift in analytical perspective: Maximization ceases to be the primary unifying concept, but now becomes lexicographically subordinate to uncertainty features that characterize agents' competence relative to the difficulty of their decision problems. In this way, the r, w, and π probabilities enable one to use maximizing tools without tending to ignore agents' true decision capabilities.

Let us now summarize the above discussion. Two main points have been made: (1) Probabilities such as r, w, π can result from agents' behavior without assuming any ability to infer probability information or any other special perceptual capability. (2) Consequently, such probabilities provide a means of using maximizing concepts without having to abstract from agents' attainable decision skills. The analysis of behavioral probability concepts presented here may therefore have important implications for our ability to model behavior. With this possibility in mind, I now discuss how a previously suggested modeling structure (Heiner 1983) can use behavioral probabilities to analyze decision making under uncertainty.

4.3   A reliability condition for theorizing with behavioral probabilities

Let A, A' be different repertoires of *actions* available for choosing by an agent. In addition, let S^* represent the set of potentially realizable *situations* that might be encountered. Note that S^* may be open-ended in that its elements $s \in S^*$ are generated through an evolutionary or historical process. Consequently, many situations may be essentially unknown or unknowable until they actually occur.

The latter possibility may prevent agents from inferring the relative likelihood of potential future situations. This in turn may prevent agents from always choosing actions with the highest expected utility (even if they would otherwise do so if able to discern probability information). Consequently, it is *not* assumed that agents always pick the best action from a set A, either in the traditional sense of maximizing utility, or in the modern sense of maximizing expected utility. Rather, they must deal with uncertainty about whether particular actions are preferred to others that might otherwise be selected.

Various forms of uncertainty can be described by two classes of variables. The first describe the decision and perceptual capabilities of different agents, denoted by the vector **p**. The second describe the structure of the environment, including features that determine the complexity and instability of potential situations in S^*. These are called environmental variables, and are denoted by the vector **e**. The **p** and **e** variables together determine the structure of the uncertainty facing the agents, represented by the vector-valued function $\mathbf{U} = u(\mathbf{p},\mathbf{e})$. Uncertainty increases as either perceptual abilities become less effective, or the environment becomes less predictable, or both. (In terms of the above experiments, the signal-to-noise ratio represents a particular environmental variable that affects the uncertainty in detecting a signal amid background noise.)

Now suppose an agent must decide when to select a specific action, $a \in A'$, rather than other actions from $A = A' - \{a\}$. As already discussed, the agent may not always pick an action when it is preferred to other actions. However, regardless of the uncertainty involved in determining preferred actions, repeated selections from any given repertoire such as A will produce an average performance, denoted by $V_\mathbf{U}(A)$, which is conditional on $\mathbf{U} = u(\mathbf{p},\mathbf{e})$. If performance is also conditional on a particular subset of situations $S \subset S^*$, it is denoted by $V_\mathbf{U}(A|S)$.

As already suggested in Section 4.2, S^* can be divided into situations that are favorable (the "right situations") or unfavorable (the "wrong situations") for selecting an action. That is, $R \subset S^*$ contains those situations in which performance rises compared with that achievable when actions are selected only from A. Conversely, $W = S^* - R$ contains those situations in which selecting action a will reduce performance compared with selecting actions only from A.

Let ℓ represent the "loss" in average performance when action a is mistakenly selected under wrong situations, W (i.e., when doing so would be outperformed by selecting actions only from A); that is, $\ell(\mathbf{U}) = V_\mathbf{U}(A|W) - V_\mathbf{U}(a|W)$. Similarly, let g represent the average gain in performance when action a is correctly selected under the right situations, R; that is, $g(\mathbf{U}) = V_\mathbf{U}(a|R) - V_\mathbf{U}(A|R)$.

The formulas for ℓ and g mean that in general they depend on the uncertainty $\mathbf{U} = u(\mathbf{p},\mathbf{e})$ affecting both selections of action a and actions from A. Hence, the explicit dependence of ℓ and g on $\mathbf{U}$ is formally written as $\ell(\mathbf{U}), g(\mathbf{U})$. (Note that signal-detection experiments represent a special case in which ℓ and g are set exogenously by the experimenter and thus are not affected by changes in uncertainty determinants such as the signal-to-noise ratio.)

This also means that the probabilities of situations in R and W may depend on the uncertainty-conditioning performance achieved from repertoire A under different situations compared with selecting action a. Hence, these probabilities also depend on $U = u(\mathbf{p},\mathbf{e})$ and are written $\pi(U) = p_U(R)$ and $1 - \pi(U) = p_U(W)$.

Next, introduce the conditional response probabilities $r = p(a|R)$ and $w = p(a|W)$, which are generalizations of the $p(S|s)$ and $p(S|n)$ probabilities produced in signal-detection experiments. These also depend on the type of uncertainty affecting the decisions of agents and are thus written $r(U) = p_U(a|R)$ and $w(U) = p_U(a|W)$, respectively; $r(U)$ and $w(U)$ are the chances of correctly or mistakenly selecting action a under situations in R or W respectively (when doing so would raise or lower performance, respectively, compared with selecting actions only from A). We can thus use the ratio $r(U)/w(U)$ to measure the reliability of selecting action a rather than actions from A.

Recall that for each signal-to-noise ratio there are certain attainable combinations of the $p(S|s)$ and $p(S|n)$ probabilities (corresponding to a given ROC curve) as subjects vary their frequency of detections from never to always detecting the signal. The latter frequency can be measured by the unconditional probability, $p(S)$, that an agent will detect the signal. As this probability varies between zero and one, the conditional probabilities $p(S|s)$ and $p(S|n)$ trace out a particular ROC curve. In the general case, let the variable h denote the unconditional probability of selecting action a (i.e., $h = p(a) = 1 - p(A)$).

Analogous to an ROC curve, assume that varying the probability h (the likelihood of selecting a) will trace out the attainable combinations of $r(U)$ and $w(U)$ corresponding to a given structure of uncertainty $U = u(\mathbf{p},\mathbf{e})$. For given U, we can then write r and w as functions of h, denoted $r(h|U)$ and $w(h|U)$, respectively. The combinations of r and w produced as h varies between 0 and 1 can be thought of as a particular reliability curve conditioned by $U = u(\mathbf{p},\mathbf{e})$.

At the extremes of $h = 0$ and $h = 1$ (never or always selecting action a, respectively), the corresponding values for r and w must satisfy $r(0|U) = 0 = w(0|U)$ and $r(1|U) = 1 = w(1|U)$. However, for intermediate values of h, the attainable combinations of r, w depend on the uncertainty U affecting agents' behavior. As already suggested, the ratio $r(h|U)/w(h|U)$ measures the reliability of selecting action a instead of actions from A. Note, however, that r/w now depends on h (i.e., the reliability of selecting an action depends on how frequently agents decide to select that action).

Recall (as discussed in Section 4.3) that r and w are conditional on the achievable decision skills of the agents (described by the $\mathbf{p}$-variables) in comparison with the complexity of the decision environment (described by the $\mathbf{e}$-variables). Consequently, agents may be unable to determine r

and w even though these probabilities are in part generated by their own ongoing reaction to future situations. As such, it is *not* assumed that agents are able to estimate these probabilities (nor even that they have the cognitive equipment – say, in the case of a nonhuman agent such as an insect – to conceive of such probabilities in the first place). Rather, our purpose is to see how these probability concepts might be used to analyze behavior irrespective of whether agents are able to assess probability information.

In an earlier paper, I suggested an approach to this question; namely, develop a condition that determines whether agents can benefit from flexibility to select potential actions. The intuition behind this approach is that agents who are not fully competent to always select preferred actions (i.e., who are not able to maximize in the traditional sense) may consequently not be sufficiently reliable to benefit from selecting successively *more* actions. This will tend to restrict agents to smaller action-repertoires, with resulting behavioral patterns that are simpler than if all potentially optimal actions could be correctly chosen. In this way, regularities manifested in behavior are indirectly generated by uncertainty that limits the reliability of selecting potential actions.

With respect to the general setting described above, the question of behavioral flexibility for a particular action a amounts to determining whether $V_U(A \cup \{a\})$ exceeds $V_U(A)$. It can be shown (see Section 5.8.1) that this is equivalent to the following *Reliability Condition* intuitively motivated in an earlier paper (Heiner 1983):

$$\frac{r(h|\mathbf{U})}{w(h|\mathbf{U})} > T(\mathbf{U}) = \frac{\ell(\mathbf{U})}{g(\mathbf{U})} \cdot \frac{1-\pi(\mathbf{U})}{\pi(\mathbf{U})}.$$

We thus have a condition expressed directly in terms of the behavioral probability components r, w, π, along with the associated loss-gain variables ℓ and g. As already discussed, the ratio $r(h|\mathbf{U})/w(h|\mathbf{U})$ measures the reliability of selecting a particular action instead of other actions that might have been chosen. $T(\mathbf{U})$ can be interpreted as a *tolerance limit* or as a minimum lower bound on reliability that demarcates the point at which allowing flexibility to select an action will improve performance. The above condition thus intuitively means that actual reliability must exceed the minimum reliability required to improve rather than worsen performance. Only in this case will agents benefit from responding to potential information about when to select an action.

In simplest notational form, the Reliability Condition becomes $r/w > T$. The dependence on $\mathbf{U} = u(\mathbf{p},\mathbf{e})$ indicates potential interdependences among the major theoretical components r, w, π, ℓ, g. However, particular $\mathbf{p}$ or $\mathbf{e}$ variables may affect only (or mostly) the reliability

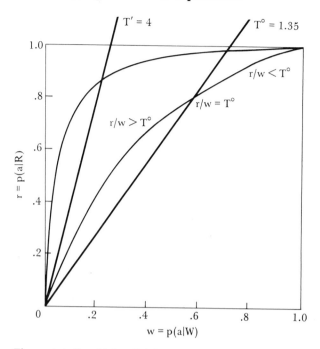

Figure 4.4. Combining ROC curves with the reliability condition. The less-bowed ROC curve corresponds to greater uncertainty in detecting when to select action a. The slopes of the above "T-lines" equal two different values of $T = \ell/g \cdot (1 - \pi)/\pi$. The Reliability Condition, $r/w > T$, is satisfied for those intervals along a particular ROC curve from the origin to where the curve intersects a given T-line.

(r/w) or tolerance limit (T) components of the condition.[10] For example, in the signal-detection experiments, the signal-to-noise ratio d affects only the attainable (r,w)-combinations along an ROC curve. The other (π,g,ℓ) components of T are independent of d.

Now incorporate the Reliability Condition into a diagram analogous to the unit-probability box in Section 4.2. Each type of uncertainty produces a particular reliability curve that shows the achievable (r,w)-combinations. Tolerance limits are represented by different rays from the origin (called "T-lines"), the slopes of which equal different values of $T = \ell/g \cdot (1 - \pi)/\pi$. An example is shown in Figure 4.4, which depicts two reliability curves and two T-lines. Less uncertainty shifts the reliability curve more toward the northwest corner where $r = 1$ and $w = 0$.

---

[10] If the $(\mathbf{p},\mathbf{e})$ variables are explicitly included, we have $\hat{h}[u(\mathbf{p},\mathbf{e}), T(u(\mathbf{p},\mathbf{e}))]$.

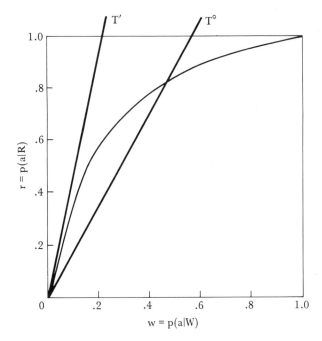

Figure 4.5. A bounded-reliability example. In this case, the reliability of selecting an action reaches a maximum, shown by the constant slope of the ROC curve as it extends out of the origin. Note that the reliability zone, $r/w > T$, suddenly drops to zero as the T-lines become steeper than this constant slope. (This type of situation is analyzed further in Section 4.8.2.)

Along any given curve, the segment from the origin to where the corresponding T-line intersects the curve shows the combinations of r and w that satisfy the Reliability Condition, $r/w > T$. As T increases, the slope of the T-line increases, thus shrinking the above segment (i.e., $r/w > T$ is violated more quickly as (r,w)-combinations move further from the origin). This means that an agent must select an action less frequently if required to be more reliable in order to benefit from selecting it. It is even possible for the Reliability Condition to be violated for any positive response frequency (as illustrated in Figure 4.5). When this happens, agents will benefit from complete inflexibility in selecting an action (even though favorable situations for selecting it may arise with positive probability $\pi > 0$).

This was the possibility emphasized in my earlier paper (Heiner 1983) – that uncertainty tends to produce behavioral rules that restrict the flexibility of behavior (so that uncertainty becomes the source of recurrent pattern manifested in behavior). We now have a richer structure with which to investigate this general theme.[11] Actions are not simply included or excluded from an agent's repertoire. Rather, there are certain zones of permissible frequencies for selecting different actions corresponding to (r,w)-combinations that satisfy $r/w > T$. Behavior can then be modeled by analyzing how these zones are affected by shifts in the reliability curves or tolerance limits of particular actions.

4.4   A simple analytical engine

Now consider how to combine the Reliability Condition $r/w > T$ with a few principles suggested by the signal-detection experiments. The objective is to construct a simple analytical engine (akin to basic supply-demand analysis) for investigating behavior – one that we can use without necessarily being aware of the methodological issues raised in previous discussion (about using probability and maximizing concepts to model behavior).

First, examine Figure 4.4. Note that the reliability curves retain the same qualitative features initially shown for ROC curves in Figures 4.2 and 4.3. The signal-detection experiments are thus used to suggest properties for the more general setting described in Section 4.3.

Three basic features emerge. The first was discussed in remarks (1) and (2) at the end of Section 4.2. Along a given reliability curve (defined for a given type of uncertainty U), the reliability ratio r/w falls as the probability of selecting an action increases. This implies the following property: (a) Along a given reliability curve, higher T requires a smaller probability of selecting an action in order to satisfy $r/w > T$. Two additional properties are implied from Figure 4.4: (b) For given T, less reliability (corresponding to a less-bowed reliability curve) requires a smaller probability of selecting an action in order to satisfy $r/w > T$; (c) less reliability requires the probability of selecting an action to drop faster as T increases in order to satisfy $r/w > T$.

[11] Some of the topics to be developed within economics include dynamics of expectation-formation and investment behavior; general uncertainty-behavioral-complexity characterizations; modeling connections with Shannon-Weaver information theory; reformulating the value-theory foundations of individual-decision and general-equilibrium models; evolution of market organization and evolutionary discovery of new industrial techniques; positive and normative theory of government institutions; etc. Thus, the uncertainty determinants can potentially affect both the reliability and tolerance-limit components of $r/w > T$. Clear implications follow from changes in particular **p** or **e** variables that (primarily) affect r/w or T, or which affect r/w and T in the same direction. A few illustrations are presented in Section 4.5.

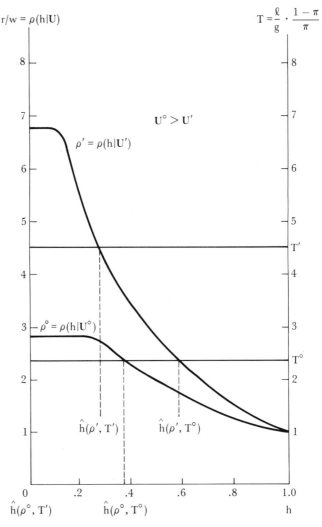

Figure 4.6a. The analytical engine in graphical form: h is the largest probability of selecting an action for which $\rho(h|\mathbf{U}) \geq T$; the lower reliability curve ρ° is conditioned by more uncertainty than ρ'.

We can also express these principles in the following way. First, let reliability be represented by the function $\rho(h|\mathbf{U}) = r(h|\mathbf{U})/w(h|\mathbf{U})$, where ρ is assumed to be a monotonically decreasing function of h, the exact shape of which is conditional on $\mathbf{U}$. We can also refer to ρ as a reliability curve because it is implied directly from a corresponding

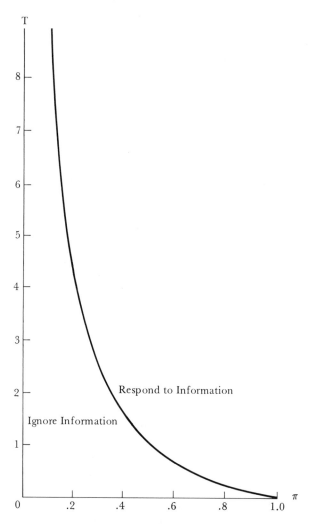

Figure 4.6b. The tolerance limit. The figure shows how $T = \ell/g \cdot (1 - \pi)/\pi$ varies as a function of π, for constant ℓ/g (in this case $\ell/g = 1$). The resulting curve is a boundary of minimum reliability that must be met before responding to information will benefit an agent. Note how rapidly the minimum reliability accelerates as the probability of right conditions (π) drops below .2.

reliability curve drawn in a unit-probability box. The monotonicity assumption formalizes the property that an action's reliability falls as it is selected more frequently. Next, define $\hat{h}(\rho,T)$ as the largest h such that $\rho(h|\mathbf{U}) \geqslant T(\mathbf{U})$. It represents the largest h that satisfies the Reliability

Condition, as jointly determined by the reliability and tolerance-limit curves ρ and T.

Note that the monotonicity of ρ implies that h must fall as T rises, as indicated in principle (a) above. Similarly, (b) implies that h must also fall for given T when there is less reliability ρ. Combining these two effects together yields the following *Reliability Principle*.

> $R1$ $\hat{h}(\rho,T)$ responds inversely to shifts in T and positively to shifts in ρ.

Restating principle (c) we also have

> $R2$ $\hat{h}(\rho,T)$ drops faster as T increases when there is less reliability. More generally, $\hat{h}(\rho,T)$ shifts faster in either direction as T changes when there is less reliability.

Another simple principle describes how T is affected by its major components. The formula $T = (\ell/g)[(1 - \pi)/\pi]$ immediately implies

> $R3$ T increases as either ℓ/g increases or π decreases. For given $\ell/g > 0$, T accelerates to infinity as π drops toward zero.

Principles R1 and R2 can be graphically depicted by drawing the function $\rho(h|\mathbf{U})$ in a diagram with r/w on the vertical axis and h on the horizontal axis, as shown in Figure 4.6a. Different kinds of uncertainty $\mathbf{U} = u(\mathbf{p},\mathbf{e})$ produce particular reliability curves $r/w = \rho(h|\mathbf{U})$. Different tolerance limits are also shown as horizontal lines, the heights of which equal T. These are called T-lines, analogous to those drawn in Figure 4.4. (See Section 4.8.2 for an illustration of curves having the same shape as those in Figure 4.6a.)

Notice that greater uncertainty shifts a reliability curve downward, and greater required reliability shifts a T-line upward. Both of these shifts cause $\hat{h}$ to move closer to the origin, as implied by Principle R1. Note also that the lower reliability curve has a flatter slope than the higher one. Consequently, higher T-lines will more quickly reduce $\hat{h}$ toward zero, in accordance with Principle R2. Figure 4.6b depicts Principle R3. The steeply accelerating curve represents a boundary of minimum reliability that must be met before an agent will benefit from reacting to information about when to select an action.

Implications can be obtained from Principles R1 – R3 by introducing assumptions about how the uncertainty variables $(\mathbf{p},\mathbf{e})$ cause shifts in the T-lines or the reliability curves of individual actions, thereby shifting the intersection point between ρ and T that determines the maximum probability bound, $\hat{h}(\rho,T)$. The analytical structure of $\hat{h}(\rho,T)$ is similar to traditional microtheory, in which market price equilibrates at the maximum exchangeable quantity given by the intersection of market demand and supply. Analysis then proceeds by determining how the intersection point changes in response to variables that shift the market demand and supply curves. A few illustrations of this general approach for $\hat{h}(\rho,T)$ are discussed next.

4.5 Some brief illustrations in microeconomics

I now present applications of Principles R1, R2, R3 to certain areas of microeconomics. My intent is to briefly suggest possibilities of significance potentially broader than that of the initial examples themselves – and at the same time to draw from situations in the common background of analysts trained in economics.

4.5.1 The law of demand

First, consider a topic raised in an earlier paper (Heiner 1983). Suppose h_x refers to the probability of purchasing a commodity x. If something happens to increase the required reliability (T_x) for buying x, then $\hat{h}_x$ will drop (Principle R1), thus further constraining h_x so that a person can benefit from continued purchases. This might result from a variety of factors. For example, a person learns that he or she has diabetes and thus noticeably reduces the likelihood of appropriate conditions for sugar intake (i.e., π_x drops so that T_x rises by Principle R3).

Another possibility is that the money price of x (denoted by P_x) rises, so that the right conditions for buying x are defined relative to a higher opportunity cost of forsaken commodities. This will lower the chance of right conditions for buying x and also tend to increase the ℓ/g ratio.[12] These effects will raise T_x by Principle R3, thus reducing $\hat{h}_x$ by Principle R1.

Whatever factors might produce a rise in T_x the implication is clearly that the frequency of purchasing x will drop as T_x rises. This implication is essentially the Law of Demand for consumer behavior. However, it does not depend on compensating to maintain constant real income (so that qualification for income effects is no longer needed).

On the other hand, the Slutsky equation of traditional theory suggests that preference conditions exist in which a Giffen response (denoted by G) is preferred to buying less at higher prices (i.e., there is a

---

[12] This is a special case of a general result: Increasing the average performance attainable without selecting an action will raise the required reliability for selecting that action.

positive probability, $\pi_G > 0$, of the right situation for a G-response). However, $\pi_G > 0$ does not necessarily imply that a person can reliably detect when G-responses are appropriate. Rather, the person must try to decipher the conditions from available information (for example, whether the income effect is sufficiently negative to outweigh the pure substitution effect).

Now suppose π_G is small, as already suggested by the Slutsky equation for goods that absorb a small fraction of a consumer's income. This implies (by Principle R3) that G-responses must be very reliable. Consequently, a consumer's reliability curve $\rho G(h_G | U)$ may be bounded below T_G (so that $\hat{h}_G = 0$ is implied). If this is the case, Giffen behavior will never (or very infrequently) be observed even though π_G is bounded above zero.

Note that these conclusions follow without assuming that agents maximize with respect to their preferences or that they even *have* well-defined preferences. Instead, it is basically preference uncertainty that makes changes in the reliability required for purchasing individual goods a key determinant of behavior. Consequently, a clear response pattern is implied precisely when preference uncertainty is permitted to affect consumer decisions.[13]

4.5.2   Complements, substitutes, and arbitrage

Another simple pattern involves complements and substitutes. For example, consumers usually switch among close substitutes toward those with lower prices. Similarly, consumers shift away from goods if they are highly complementary to other goods whose prices have risen. Conventional theory would interpret these reactions by saying that consumers are responding optimally to complementary or substitution relationships between different commodities. Another interpretation is suggested by Principles R1 – R3.

There may be great uncertainty about the best way of modifying purchases of other goods in response to a different price of a specific good x. However, certain goods may be close substitutes in that, under most conditions, the consequences from using them will be (almost) the same as the consequences from using x. When the price of x rises, this

---

[13] An agent may even have to discipline his reaction to self-perceived tastes in order to reduce h (as in the case of a diabetic turning away candy that he would otherwise much enjoy). A person's preferences thus cease to have a privileged status that always defines what should be maximized. Rather, they become simply another information source that may or may not reliably direct how to act (see Heiner 1985).

This also applies to any other self-perceived information source, such as an agent's expectations or subjective probability beliefs. See also Cohen and Axelrod (1984); and Slovic and Lichtenstein (1983, pp. 602–13).

means consumers will usually benefit from shifting purchases toward them irrespective of how x might be used or what conditions might affect the results from different uses of x. Consequently, the likelihood of right situations for switching toward such goods is relatively high when the price of x rises (i.e., the probability of right conditions for switching, denoted by π_s, is close to 1.0 for such goods).

As π_s approaches closer to 1.0, agents need not be as reliable about detecting when to switch (Principle R3), thereby increasing $\hat{h}_s$ (Principle R1). At some point, a noticeable pattern may emerge in which switching between certain goods typically occurs in response to changes in their relative prices. Analogous argument also implies that a noticeable reaction pattern will emerge between certain complementary goods (i.e., goods that do not require agents to decipher when their complementary properties can be trusted to guide action).

Think of this also in terms of arbitrage opportunities made available by discrepancies in relative prices. Such opportunities are part of a very large set of potentially beneficial switching possibilities that may be available at any moment. However, for very similar or physically identical goods, the chance of right conditions for switching to lower-priced ones will be close to 1.0. Therefore, Principles R1 and R3 imply that (out of all the available switching possibilities) a noticeable pattern will emerge in which agents become alert and respond relatively quickly to price differentials between sufficiently similar goods. (Note that price arbitrage is one of the few empirical regularities besides the Law of Demand that has been singled out as a major "law" of market behavior.)[14]

4.5.3   Status quo demand rigidities

Now consider ways of responding to price changes for which the required reliability is *not* low (as in the preceding section). For example, a person might respond to higher meat prices by systematically changing his or her diet toward fish and poultry items. In addition, suppose there is greater uncertainty in making purchasing decisions that are more remote or distant from an agent's previous consumption pattern.[15] If so, Principle R1 implies that the probabilities of various ways of reacting

---

[14] For a few references on the traditional analysis of arbitrage (the "law of indifference") and on the effects of substitutes on demand elasticity, see Hicks (1939, p. 49); Jevons (1871, pp. 49, 98); Hirshleifer (1980, pp. 44–8, 171); Wicksell (1938, pp. 34, 52); and Wicksteed (1933, pp. 715, 719, 836).

[15] The traditional interpretation of this response would say that a person switches to the most preferred alteration in his original diet. The new interpretation would not assume consumers always act in the most preferred way, but instead would consider the reliability of different ways of responding.

to price changes will drop as they involve larger deviations from previous spending patterns. Consequently, revised purchases (at least initially, see the next example) will be biased toward the consumption pattern chosen before prices changed. This tendency was unexpectedly but systematically noticed in recent demand experiments by Battalio *et al.* (1981); Kagel *et al.* (1980, 1978); Battalio *et al.* (1973); and Ayllon and Azrin (1968).

Next, suppose that the chance of right circumstances for shifting away from certain commodities (denoted by π_s) quickly drops as shifts become larger. Required reliability for shifting from these goods will thus be very high (Principle R3). Suppose also that consumers cannot achieve such reliability without regular experience with revised consumption patterns. Using R3 and R1 successively implies that $\hat{h}_s$ will quickly drop for larger shifts. This will produce a predictably inelastic response to price changes for these goods. Only the gradual accumulation of new experience (permitted if $\hat{h}_s \neq 0$) can change the situation. If this is possible, R1 implies the reverse trend in $\hat{h}_s$ over time, thereby producing a noticeably more elastic but delayed reaction.[16]

Finally, note a key feature of the above examples: the role played by the status quo spending pattern in comparison with other potential consumption patterns. This is a symptom of a more general implication that agents are noticeably sensitive to information that defines their local frame of reference in the environment. Other symptoms have been increasingly recognized in the risk-behavior literature,[17] and related possibilities are suggested in the next two sections.

4.5.4   Short- and long-run supply behavior

In traditional production theory, short-run response typically means that firms respond while holding certain inputs fixed. Their long-run

[16] For empirical illustrations about the demand for water and other goods, see Alchian and Allen (1977, pp. 64–7); Hirshleifer (1980, pp. 134–5). For tables of related short-and long-run consumer demand elasticities, see Kohler (1982, pp. 100–5).

[17] Note in particular the "framing effects" studied experimentally by Kahneman and Tversky (1979, 1981, 1982). Two features have a close parallel: (1) Subjects are strongly predisposed to encode information about probabilistic options in terms of a reference point usually describing their local situation before choosing (such as their current wealth or income); (2) an interpersonal regularity often occurs where the direction of such framing effects is the same for a large fraction of subjects (i.e., most people have similar "risk preferences" in these situations; see Sections 4.5.5–4.5.7). Related preference behavior is also studied by Slovic and Lichtenstein(1983); Slovic and Tversky (1974); Grether and Plott (1979); Hamm (1979); Allais (1953); Fischoff, Slovic, and Lichtenstein (1980); Ellsberg (1961); McCord and de Neufville (1983); and Prague *et al.* (1980). See also Edwards (1961, 1962); Fellner (1961); Hershey, Kunreuther, and Schoemaker (1982); Hogarth (1975); Kunreuther et al. (1978); Lindman (1971); and Weber (1982).

adjustment consequently unfolds as more inputs are varied. Thus, the distinction between short and long run simply reflects a dynamic lag pattern of successively adjusting more inputs over time. However, standard production theory does not explain the more basic pattern of fixed and variable inputs. For example, could an automobile firm substantially benefit by timing the completion of a major retooling phase for small cars to coincide with an increased demand for them because of higher gasoline prices?[18] How might uncertainty affect this kind of advance reaction to future price increases?

Suppose the price of a good x changes, and a firm must determine how to respond (or, prospectively, the firm must decide when to react to its own expectations of future price changes). Let $i = 1, \ldots, n$ index the inputs used to produce x. Suppose the right situations to adjust certain inputs are dependent on future contingencies more remote than those on which other inputs depend (say retooling with new machinery requires a longer payback period than hiring part-time labor over the weekend). Thus, different "amounts" of the future (denoted f_i) must be correctly anticipated to avoid mistakenly adjusting particular inputs. Assume there is greater uncertainty in deciphering more of the future. The uncertainty in adjusting each input i is thus a positive function of its corresponding anticipation period f_i, viz., $U_i = u_i(f_i)$ (where the other $\mathbf{p}$ and $\mathbf{e}$ variables of $u(\mathbf{p},\mathbf{e})$ are suppressed to highlight this relationship). This in turn implies the reliability ρ_i, of adjusting input i will drop (by Principle R1), so that the net relationship between f_i and ρ_i is negative, denoted by $\rho_i(\bar{f_i})$.

In order to benefit from reacting to (past or expected) price changes, the probability of adjusting each input (denoted by h_i) is bounded by $\hat{h}_i(\rho_i, T_i)$, which drops as ρ_i falls and T_i increases (Principle R1). Thus, less reliability from longer f_i causes h_i to drop. Moreover, there will be zero chance of adjusting certain inputs if their reliability curves, $r/w|_i = \rho_i(h_i|U_i)$, are bounded below their respective tolerance limits, T_i. This is more likely for inputs with long anticipation periods if most price rises are temporary, because the likelihood of durable price increases (i.e., the chance π_i of the right situation for adjusting these inputs) is

---

[18] It is sometimes argued that adjustment costs (for example, see Alchian and Allen 1977, pp. 246–58) explain which inputs are varied and which are temporarily held fixed. However, adjustment costs serve only to increase the potential gain from appropriately adjusting (or preparing to adjust) inputs ahead of time (as in the retooling example), rather than responding after an event has occurred. This is especially the case if delayed response often requires higher-cost, quicker-adjustment methods in order to capture temporary profit opportunities before they are dissipated. For a traditional discussion about the dynamic response of consumers, see Alchian and Allen (1977, pp. 62–3).

then small. Consequently, smaller π_i will steeply increase the required reliability for adjusting these inputs (by Principle R3).

Suppose that if a price change lasts for a while, the conditions producing it are more likely to be durable. Thus, the π_i probabilities are increasing over time, thereby reducing the tolerance limits T_i (Principle R3). To represent this, let $t_x = t(\Delta p_x)$ denote how long a price change Δp_x has lasted, and write T_i as a negative function of t_x, $T_i(\bar{t}_x)$.

This will produce a dynamic pattern of delayed input adjustments, as governed by $\hat{h}_i[\overset{+}{p}_i(\bar{f}_i),\ T_i\ (\bar{t}_x)]$. The probability of adjusting each input decreases with f_i, dropping to zero for f_i beyond a certain length. Thus, soon after p_x rises, only some of the inputs adjust. However, if the price change lasts, successively more inputs will respond as more $\hat{h}_i$ probabilities rise above zero. Consequently, a larger supply response cumulates over time.

4.5.5　Sensitivity to information about nonlocal contingencies

Consider the general possibility of information that is increasingly distant in some dimension from an agent's immediate experience or from its local environmental situation. For example, distance might refer to the future (as in the production case above), or to distance from previous behavior patterns (as in status quo demand rigidities). Another measure of distance might involve the number of agents whose interactions extend beyond the local experience of an agent (yet nevertheless affect the consequences resulting from different actions). Still another measure of distance might reflect the relative infrequency of certain events (i.e., rare events are increasingly nonlocal to agents' normal experience).

Whatever the interpretation, we can represent these measures as a vector of distance variables, denoted by **d**. These variables form a subset of the **(p,e)** variables that determine the type of uncertainty involved in selecting particular actions. For simplicity, suppress the other determinants and write u**(p,e)** as a function of **d** only, denoted by $U = u(\mathbf{d})$. Suppose also that uncertainty increases with each element of **d** (i.e., there is greater uncertainty in deciphering how to respond to nonlocal contingencies). Greater uncertainty will in general reduce the reliability of behavior, so that reliability becomes a negative function of **d**, as indirectly given by $\rho(h|u(\mathbf{d}))$ (i.e., greater **d** increases u, which in turn reduces ρ). Again for simplicity, let us suppress all the determinants of ρ except the negative relationship between ρ and **d**, written simply as $\rho(\bar{\mathbf{d}})$.

Now substitute $\rho(\mathbf{d})$ into $\hat{h}$. We then have $\hat{h}(\rho(\mathbf{d}),T)$, which governs the likelihood of responding to information about nonlocal events or relationships. Principle R1 implies that responding will become less likely (for given T) as d increases in some dimension (i.e., greater d reduces p, which by R1 in turn reduces $\hat{h}$).

The preceding sections discussed a few symptoms of this pattern, as evidenced in how consumers and producers react over time to price changes. Another symptom is the noticeable tendency of people not to insure against large but rare disasters.[19] Such disasters are exactly those that are remote to an agent's local experience. The resulting uncertainty will further constrain the reliability of responding to information about which rare events to insure against. Thus, by Principle R1, people are less likely to respond to information that refers to increasingly rare but conceivable events.[20]

4.5.6 Recurrent preference patterns as behavioral regularities implied from uncertainty

Suppose an agent has repeated opportunities to react to information about future contingencies. These contingencies may or may not turn out to be beneficial. However, as they become more remote into the future, it becomes increasingly difficult to detect ahead of time whether the net effect will be favorable or not. Consequently, by Principle R1, agents will become increasingly insensitive to future events as those events become more temporally remote (i.e., the likelihood of current responses to information about the future will drop off, as governed by $\hat{h}_t(\rho(d),T)$).

We can measure the insensitivity implied by $\hat{h}_t(\rho(d),T)$ in a special stylized context. An agent is given the opportunity to relinquish one unit of a commodity in return for a given amount of the same commodity in the future. Let λ_t denote the amount that would be received at time t in the future if the offer is accepted. Conditions may exist in which the agent would benefit from accepting less than one unit (i.e., $\lambda_t < 1$) of the commodity in the future (say, when the commodity will unavoidably decay if not consumed).[21] However, suppose that the chance of such circumstances arising is small, given a number of potentially fruitful opportunities for investing units of the commodity.

This means that the probability of right circumstances, π_t, for accepting $\lambda_t < 1$ is correspondingly small, which in turn implies (by Principle R3) that the required reliability for accepting $\lambda_t < 1$ is relatively high.

[19] See Kunreuther, et al. (1978); Arrow (1981); and Heiner (1983, pp. 576–8). See also n. 17 for related behavioral symptoms.
[20] See Heiner (1983, pp. 576–7).
[21] See Irving Fisher's "hard tack" and "figs" examples (1970, pp. 35, 186–92).

Consequently, if the right conditions for accepting $\lambda_t < 1$ are also difficult to detect, then Principle R1 implies the corresponding response probability is close to zero (i.e., the probability of accepting $\lambda_t < 1$ is bounded by $\hat{h}_t(\rho,T) \cong 0$). Therefore, a person is very likely to refuse $\lambda_t < 1$. In traditional language we might describe this by saying a person will very likely prefer one unit of the commodity now to $\lambda_t < 1$ in the future, or simply that people will usually have positive time preference.

Now think of this from a new perspective. Time preference no longer enters the picture as an assumption about how people typically prefer, but instead as a behavioral regularity induced by a certain type of uncertainty (in this case uncertainty in deciphering how future events will affect the return from investing currently available commodities). Thus, instead of simply describing a certain behavior pattern in the form of a preference relation, we may be able to derive those patterns from an appropriate specification of uncertainty.[22]

4.5.7   Deriving time preference and liquidity preference

I now briefly suggest one way to develop such implications. If a person is likely either to accept or to reject the option of λ_t, we will say he or she is not indifferent. Indifference means a probability of acceptance close to one-half (i.e., $h_t \cong \frac{1}{2}$).[23] Let $\hat{\lambda}_t$ represent the minimum value of λ_t such that $h_t \geqslant \frac{1}{2}$. For the type of uncertainty described above, $\hat{\lambda}_t$ must exceed one so long as t is not close to zero (that is, for some $\delta > 0$, $\hat{\lambda}_t > 1$ for all $t \geqslant \delta$). In traditional language $\hat{\lambda}_t$ represents a person's marginal rate of substitution between one unit of a good now and $\hat{\lambda}_t$ units at time t in the future (i.e., the rate at which he is indifferent or equally likely to choose between one unit now and $\hat{\lambda}_t$ units later).

Recall that h_t is bounded by $\hat{h}_t(\rho,T)$. Thus, $\hat{\lambda}_t$ also depends on ρ and T, and is accordingly written $\hat{\lambda}_t(\rho,T)$. Principles R1 – R3 can thus be used to deduce implications about the properties of $\hat{\lambda}_t$. For example, R1 implies that $\hat{\lambda}_t$ is an increasing function of variables (such as the **(p,e)** variables) that either raise T or lower ρ. Without going into further detail, let me briefly suggest two properties of $\hat{\lambda}_t(\rho,T)$.

[22] The most widely assumed preference regularity in economics is self-interest. It is also implied from uncertainty in deciphering nonlocal social interdependencies involving other persons outside the agent's reliable sphere of interpersonal experience (see Heiner 1983, n. 32). Closely related are kinship-helping strategies and other altruistic traits widely observed in both human and animal societies [see Alexander and Borgin (1978); Hirshleifer (1982); Maynard Smith (1964); and Trivers (1971)].

[23] A fifty-fifty chance of picking an option is the standard behavioral definition of indifference in psychology. See, for example, Coombs, Dawes, and Tversky (1970, pp. 156–62).

(1) As already discussed, there is less reliability in detecting when to accept a given amount λ_t as more remote future contingencies are involved (i.e., ρ is a negative function of t, denoted $\rho(\bar{t})$). Thus, R1 implies that $\hat{\lambda}_t(\rho(t),T)$ is also an increasing function of t. That is, in order to maintain a chance of acceptance of at least 50 percent, more of the good in question will be necessary the longer into the future its possession is deferred. We can also describe this general pattern in the form of a discount rate by solving the following equation for r_t:

$$1 = \hat{\lambda}_t(\rho,T)e^{-r_t t}.$$

In traditional language, r_t represents an agent's personal rate of time preference.

(2) Now suppose that the future amount λ_t is itself variable. Letting μ_t denote the average amount received at time t and σ_t^2 denote the variance around μ_t, we can define $\hat{\mu}_t(\rho,T)$ as the minimum average amount necessary to maintain the probability of accepting an uncertain deferred amount (over the guarantee of one unit now) at or above one-half (i.e., the minimum μ_t such that $h_t \geq \frac{1}{2}$). As before, $\hat{\mu}_t$ is a positive function of T and a negative function of ρ, so that determinants of ρ and T will also affect $\hat{\mu}_t$. For example, suppose it is more difficult to determine when to accept a deferred amount as more volatile environmental factors affect that amount. If this is the case, ρ will be a negative function of the variance σ_t^2 produced by these volatile factors, denoted by $\rho(\sigma_t^{\bar{2}})$. Principle R1 then implies $\hat{\mu}_t(\rho(\sigma_t^2),T)$ is positively related to σ_t^2 (i.e., higher σ_t^2 reduces ρ, which in turn increases $\hat{\mu}_t$).[24] We thus derive a positive behavioral relationship between $\hat{\mu}_t$ and σ_t^2 instead of having to assume such a relationship in the form of liquidity preference.[25]

4.5.8 Punctuated learning and dynamics

Finally, I briefly discuss the dynamic reaction to changing environmental conditions (see also Heiner 1983, pp. 582–3). A key property is produced by the transition point at which the reliability curve just reaches the tolerance limit (i.e., when $\rho[0|u(\mathbf{p},\mathbf{e})] = T(\mathbf{p},\mathbf{e})$, so that $\hat{h} > 0$ is implied for small upward shifts in ρ or downward shifts in T, or both). The basic property is the following:

[24] The greater uncertainty produced by a higher variance, δ_t^2, reduces the reliability of savings-investment decisions, thus reducing the probability of acceptance for any given mean return μ_t (Principle R1). Consequently, in order to maintain the probability of acceptance at 0.5 or higher, μ_t must be larger as δ_t^2 increases.
[25] See Tobin (1958); Markowitz (1952); and Fama (1976).

Changes in the environmental variables **e** may cause an action's reliability curve or its tolerance limit to shift; causing them to "cross over" each other from their initial positions. If this happens, $\hat{h}$ will switch between allowing and severely restricting the likelihood of selecting that action (i.e., $\hat{h}$ will switch between $\hat{h} > 0$ and $\hat{h} = 0$). Consequently, a relatively sudden "switching" between different behavior patterns may occur. (Heiner 1983, p. 582)

This switching pattern is depicted in Figure 4.6a, in which $\hat{h}$ suddenly switches between zero and a strictly positive level as a reliability curve and T-line cross over each other. This is implied as long as the reliability curves have the qualitative shape shown (a flat or almost flat segment as $h \rightarrow 0$), which is a generic property of these curves under certain conditions. (See Section 4.8.2 for a brief discussion of this topic.)

Now introduce Principle R2 into the analysis. The lower reliability curve in Figure 4.6a corresponds to greater uncertainty in detecting when to select an action. Note the longer flat segment and the generally flatter slope compared with the higher reliability curve (conditioned by less uncertainty). These features will increase both the amplitude and speed of switching produced in the neighborhood of a crossover point.

A variety of applications can be analyzed by combining the switching property with Principle R2. Only a few are mentioned here:[26] (a) dynamic reaction of consumers and producers to price changes (as discussed in sections 4.5.3 – 4.5.4); (b) switching between buying and selling strategies in stock and commodity-futures markets; and (c) volatile "Keynesian" investment behavior; (d) hysteresis effects in which the switching point is path dependent – dependent on the history of environmental conditions and on the behavior patterns chosen before a switching point occurs.

These properties also affect the dynamic response to information. If agents are dealing with little uncertainty, they will continually adjust to new information, thereby producing relatively smooth marginal adjustment in behavior (the type of behavior often assumed in conventional choice theory). On the other hand, high uncertainty may produce complete insensitivity to certain types of ongoing information (for example, see the remarks in Section 4.6 about the DNA molecule).

Between these two extremes, behavior will neither continually adjust to nor completely ignore new information. Rather, the general pattern will be a "punctuated" sensitivity: first little reaction as new information accumulates, then a relatively quick but delayed response. Agents will thus not be equally and continually alert to all information. Instead,

---

[26] See Heiner (1983, pp. 582–3). On Keynesian investment behavior, see the *General Theory*, chaps. 11–13, 15; also Leijonhufvud (1968, pp. 282–314).

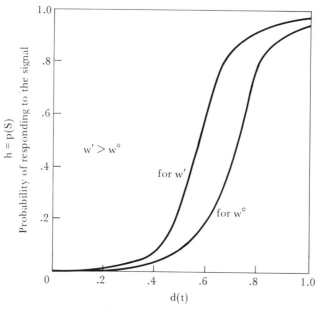

Figure 4.7a. Dynamic effects of an increasingly reliable signal. The curves show the likelihood of responding to a signal (in a standard signal-detecting experiment) for increasing values of the signal-to-noise ratio d. Each curve is defined for a particular false-alarm rate, $w = p(S|n)$. The S-shaped curvature is a generic property of such curves (see Green and Swets 1974, pp. 130–40, 191–7; Egan 1975, pp. 81–7). Note that d is written as a function of time t to indicate the temporal effects implied if it was increased over a sequence of experiments. Each curve would then represent the dynamic reaction to an increasingly reliable signal over time (as might be produced by gradually cumulating experience with a new technical innovation).

they will display a punctuated alertness to changing information (i.e., they will not be continually alert to information, but instead will notice only those trends in information that last a sufficient length of time). Transitory information may consequently be ignored, even if it contains extremely reliable indicators of when to selectively modify behavior. Figure 4.7 illustrates one class of examples. It compares the type of punctuated learning curve implied from a signal-detection experiment with a typical S-shaped innovation curve used to show the dynamic spread of new inventions.[27]

[27] See Griliches (1957, p. 190); also Mansfield (1961).

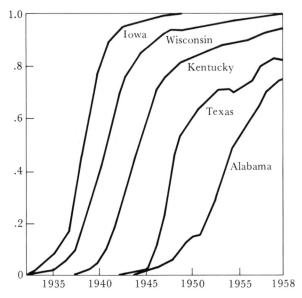

Fraction of total corn acreage in different states
planted with a new form of hybrid seed.

Figure 4.7b. Empirical innovation-diffusion curves. The curves show
a new form of hybrid seed spread in use over time in the states indicated. Note the punctuated or S-shaped diffusion pattern. *Source*: Griliches (1960, p. 276).

4.6   Brief comparison with information costs and rational
expectations

I now briefly compare the reliability model with two recent topics in
neoclassical theory: information costs and rational expectations.

4.6.1   *Ignoring costless information*

Consider a basic feature of information-cost theory. It assumes that,
except for the cost of obtaining information, agents would behave as if
they had perfect knowledge. Thus, without information costs, agents
will behave just as modeled in the older perfect-information models.

In contrast, the reliability model implies that agents will not necessarily benefit from responding to more information – and this is true irrespective of whether potential information may be costly to obtain. For
example, costlessly available information may be ignored if the behavior resulting from its use violates the Reliability Condition. This possi-

bility is still consistent with positive information costs substantially affecting behavior. However, it suggests that the more fundamental determinant of behavior is the reliability of selecting individual actions (which may depend on the cost of obtaining information on how to behave). We can thus think of information costs as additional factors that affect the reliability of behavior. This may even refer to decisions about whether to incur information costs or not, as discussed next.

4.6.2   The reliability of search behavior

Although information-cost theory drops the assumption of full information, it still assumes agents can determine the expected benefits and costs needed to decide how much information to obtain (i.e., there is no uncertainty about these costs and benefits). Consequently, agents are assumed to be perfectly reliable in deciding when and how long to engage in search activities.

The reliability model suggests another possibility. Search activities are simply particular elements in an agent's behavioral repertoire, which (like any other potential action) may or may not be reliably selected. The reliability of such activities will thus also be governed by the (p,e) variables, and Principles R1 – R3 can be used to analyze how the probability of searching for information will change under different conditions.[28]

4.6.3   Ignoring metalevel information

Consider another interpretation of this issue. One might say that agents mistakenly respond to information because they lack still other information about how to respond correctly. Or one might say that miscomparing the costs and benefits from searching simply reflects the costs of obtaining information about these costs and benefits. Thus, one can always refer to some additional or metalevel information needed to determine how to use any given set of information. By optimizing subject to the costs of obtaining the metalevel information, the analysis collapses into the conventional framework.

[28] A simple illustration involves consumers searching for lower prices. Principles R3 and R1 imply that the probability of searching will increase for items whose mean price is not a small fraction of a consumer's income or wealth. Stigler (1966, pp. 1–4) has a traditional demand-theory discussion of this. For a sampling of the search and information-cost literature, see Alchian (1969); Gould (1974); Lippman and McCall (1976a,b,c, 1979); McCall (1965, 1971); Rothschild (1973, 1974); Rothschild and Stiglitz (1976); Diamond and Rothschild (1978); Stiglitz (1969); Stigler (1961,1966); and Williamson (1979).

However, the reliability theory suggests a general result that denies this possibility. Consider the following example. A person is uncertain about the costs and benefits of a particular search opportunity. He or she might try to resolve this uncertainty by obtaining information about the expected costs and benefits over a number of similar search opportunities at different points in time or over a number of different agents facing the same search opportunity at different locations. If there is still uncertainty about these expected values, the person could try to average them over different types of search opportunities that might arise or over different environmental factors that might reshuffle the mix of search opportunities likely to occur. Even this second level of averaging may fail to resolve the uncertainty about the expected costs and benefits from searching, thus forcing the agent into successively higher levels of averaging. Note also that each additional stage involves averaging over conditions increasingly remote from the agent's local experience.

Therefore, consider a hierarchy of information levels in which each level provides information about how to use the next lower level of information but in which higher levels are increasingly distant in some dimension from an agent's local experience. Suppose also, as discussed in Section 4.5.5, that uncertainty increases as information involves more nonlocal events or relationships. Principle R1 then implies that the chance of agents responding to each information level (denoted by h_i, corresponding to the ith level) will become smaller and smaller as successive levels become more nonlocal. At some point as we go to successively higher metalevels, the reliability curves for responding to each information level will drop below their corresponding tolerance limits (so that for some level j, $\hat{h}_i = 0$ for all $i \geq j$). Thus, agents will ignore information for all levels beyond a certain point. In this way, the reliability model closes itself by cutting off the possibility of an infinite regress to higher metalevels of information.

4.6.4   Modeling cyclical patterns in business activity

The Rational Expectations Hypothesis has recently been used to model cyclical patterns in business activity. A key example is Lucas's 1975 paper ("An Equilibrium Model of the Business Cycle"), which concludes with the following intuitive summary (p. 1140) of its main theme:

[A]gents are well aware that the economy goes through recurrent "cycles" which distort perceived rates of return. [However], the transitory nature of real investment opportunities forces them to balance the risk of incorrectly responding to spurious price signals against the risk of failing to respond to meaningful signals.

Now think of this in terms of the reliability of behavior, as measured by the conditional probabilities $r(h \mid U)$ and $w(h \mid U)$. These probabilities can also be interpreted in terms of Type 1 and Type 2 errors in statistics. The null hypothesis represents favorable situations for selecting an action; the alternate hypothesis represents unfavorable situations for selecting it. Type 1 errors intuitively represent *excluded benefits* from failing to respond under favorable conditions, whereas Type 2 errors refer to *included mistakes* from still responding under unfavorable conditions. The probabilities of these two types of errors (denoted by t_1 and t_2) are related to r and w, viz., $r = 1 - t_1$ and $w = t_2$.

In general, therefore, the reliability ratio r/w also equals $(1-t_1)/t_2$ (meaning one minus the chance of excluded benefits relative to the chance of included mistakes). Lucas's statement above describes a particular interpretation of $(1-t_1)/t_2$ in which the right time to react to price movements occurs when they result from genuine changes in real investment opportunities and are not nominal price changes indirectly produced by purely monetary disturbances. That is, agents must try to detect the right from the wrong time to deviate from otherwise appropriate patterns of response to price information. The uncertainty involved in accomplishing this task depends on their ability to distinguish "meaningful" from "spurious" price signals, especially given the "transitory nature of real investment opportunities."

Note that Lucas also says agents are "forced" to balance the "risk" or likelihood of excluded benefits against included mistakes. This is consistent with the idea of reliability curves; namely, agents are limited to certain attainable combinations, $r = 1 - t_1$ and $w = t_2$. However, the existence of such a reliability curve does not depend on agents having any special abilities in forming expectations or in deciphering complex market interdependencies. Irrespective of the type of uncertainty involved (including inability to infer probability distributions), Principles R1–R3 can still be used to analyze how agents respond to market information (for example, to information that might signal when to engage in various investment, employment, or other exchange activities). Consequently, we may be able to analyze such possibilities without rational expectations and related assumptions, as discussed next.

4.6.5 Are "island" economies or rational expectations necessary for business cycles?

Lucas's paper first shows that cyclical effects cannot arise in a standard neoclassical growth model that incorporates rational expectations (Section 2 of his paper). Consequently, a more complex market environment is introduced in which agents randomly jump between a continuum of informationally isolated markets (called island markets). These separated islands are needed to counter the agents' rational-expectation abilities. Thus, the model starts by giving agents rational-expectation skills (enabling them to behave as Bayesian statisticians), and then introduces a specially constructed island economy in order to prevent these skills from thwarting the model's purpose of producing aggregate cyclical patterns.

Analogous conclusions also apply to more recent rational-expectations models. The newer models focus on the distinction between temporary and permanent changes in real exchange opportunities.[29] As in Lucas's model, the agents' rational-expectation abilities must be countered by some type of subtlety in the economy. The newer models drop island markets in favor of a random structure of temporary versus more durable changes in real variables. ("Spurious price signals" now refers to the temporary changes and "meaningful price signals" to the permanent changes.) In both the older and newer models, therefore, the essential problem boils down to uncertainty in detecting meaningful from spurious price information.

The general problem thus becomes one of uncertainty in using market information to guide real exchange activities, where uncertainty can arise from whatever combination of the (p,e) variables might apply in different contexts. Given this realization, we can use the reliability model to investigate how agents react to ongoing price information (but without necessarily using rational expectations and related assumptions). Recall that reliability curves can exist regardless of the kind of uncertainty involved and even if agents' statistical and expectation abilities are severely limited. Thus, Principles R1 – R3 can be used to analyze how agents respond to ongoing price movements.

For example, Principle R1 implies that greater uncertainty (in detecting genuine from spurious price signals) reduces the probability that agents will deviate from their normal response patterns to ongoing price movements. Or conversely, agents are more likely to stick to their normal response patterns even though price changes may not result from real factors in the economy.[30] Consequently, greater uncertainty increases the likelihood that purely nominal disturbances will generate

---

[29] For example, see Brunner, Cukierman, and Meltzer (1980); Cukierman (1979, 1980); Gertler (1981, 1982). For illustrations of earlier rational-expectation models, see Abel, et al. (1979); Barro (1976); Fischer (1977); Grossman (1977); Lucas (1972, 1975, 1977, 1981); Sargent (1976a,b, 1977, 1979); and Sargent and Wallace (1973, 1975).

[30] The Austrian trade-cycle theory also depends on a similar process in which agents stick to normal investment reaction patterns as interest rates are affected by credit expansion through the banking system. See Hayek (1933; also 1935, 1939).

serially correlated repercussions in investment and other exchange activities, thereby producing more systematic and recurrent cyclical patterns.[31]

4.7   Conclusion: a broader perspective

I conclude with a broader perspective about the modeling issues raised in the paper. Figure 4.8 will help motivate this perspective.

The figure depicts a sample of the broad spectrum of behavior-generating mechanisms or agents that have evolved in nature. At one end of the spectrum are the kind of agents usually envisioned in economics. In particular, human agents are endowed with highly developed cognitive faculties. Such agents may use their thinking abilities to purposefully seek self-perceived goals, while in the process adjusting to expected future conditions. They may even be capable of making new discoveries and harnessing these discoveries in the continued pursuit of their goals.

However (without diminishing the significance of these mental traits), there is also systematic evidence that human behavior is not uniformly governed by conscious mechanisms. The language of habits, rules of thumb, drives, passions, and the like is also pervasively connected with human decision making. In fact, only a relatively small fraction of people's conduct is informed by explicit self-awareness of its intended purpose.[32] Note in addition that signal-detection ROC curves are also produced in a tacit manner (i.e., people cannot fully articulate

---

[31] Note the contrast with Lucas's statement quoted at the beginning. The above conclusion also holds when uncertainty increases beyond simple "risk" to include Knightian features (where agents cannot assign probabilities to all events). Thus, more persistent business cycles are implied in exactly the case in which Lucas claimed "economic reasoning will be of no value."

[32] A brief sample of the extensive investigations related to this issue includes Michael Polanyi's (1962, 1967, 1969) theory of tacit knowledge, Sigmund Freud's (see 1961, 1962) theory of the subconscious, and James Gibson's (1966, 1977, 1979) studies of human perceptual systems and his theory of affordances. References related to Polanyi's work include Nisbett and Wilson (1977); Siegman (1978); and Solomon (1977). For related references in cognitive psychology, see Anderson (1980); Anderson, Kline, and Beasley (1980); Bransford and Franks (1971); Chomsky (1980); Crowder (1976); Geschwind (1980); Glucksberg and McCloskey (1981); Hayes-Roth (1977); Healey (1975); Jones (1962); Klahr, Langley, and Neches (1983); Larkin, et al. (1980); Lenat and Harris (1978); Lindsay and Norman (1977); Miller, Galanter, and Pribram (1960); and Townsend (1974). For references related to Freud's work, see Dixon (1971); Kahneman (1973); Koffka (1928); Kramer (1963); Mandler (1975); Neisser (1976); Nisbett and Wilson (1977); Sartre (1953); Siegman (1978); Solomon (1977); and Treisman and Geffen (1967). For references related to Gibson's work, see Hamlyn (1977); Navon (1977); Palmer (1975); Chase and Simon (1973); and Cooper and Podgorny (1976). For related material on information processing in hierarchically organized biological systems, see Miller (1978, pp. 89–202) and Simon (1969).

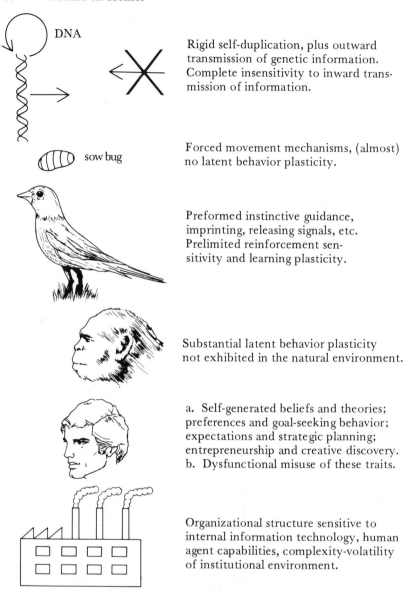

Figure 4.8. A spectrum of agents and decision-problems.

how they make the sequence of choices that collectively generate these patterns).

When we consider other species, tacit behavior mechanisms are manifest everywhere. The general pattern is one of increasingly rigid, preprogrammed behavior elicited without the use of conscious mental design.[33] An extreme version is displayed by the DNA molecule. Its structure enables it to transmit genetic information outward to a cybernetic molecular process that converts the information into larger biological systems. However, the molecule's structure also prevents inward transmission of chemical signals from altering the genetic information stored for future outward transmissions.[34]

Of the entire spectrum of evolved behavior mechanisms, only a small fraction use conscious mental processes. In a metaphorical sense, nature has been a master designer of tacitly generated behavior, with only limited attempts at designing consciously self-aware processes. In these latter cases, tacit mechanisms still substantially affect behavior (even regulating in part how the more conscious elements are used).[35]

This does not imply that conscious elements will have a negligible impact on behavior, as demonstrated by the very emergence of human society from its primitive beginnings. Nevertheless, the general pattern evidenced in nature suggests the systematic importance of developing a conceptual framework that can naturally represent and accommodate the diverse range of behavioral mechanisms that have evolved, including those responsible for the ongoing development of human society.[36]

On the other hand, theorizing in economics largely stems from the idea of agents consciously maximizing in their pursuit of self-perceived

[33] On instinctive behavior and related issues in evolutionary ecology and ethology, see Alcock (1979); Brown and Herrnstein (1975, pp. 31–60); Lorenz (1981); McFarland (1982); Miller (1978); Pianka (1978); and Tinbergen (1951).

[34] On the information structure of the DNA molecule, see Monod (1972, pp. 104–17) and Watson (1976, pp. 203–47, 281–302). Recent experiments in antibody mechanisms have shown quasi-Lamarkian transfer of information to the DNA genome. However, even this appears consistent with exclusive outward transmission between successive phenotype generations (the "central dogma" of molecular biology). On this, see pages 91–9 of Maynard Smith (1982).

[35] For an analysis of constraints on human intelligence and the evolution of language and consciousness see Konner (1982); Grether and Wilde (1982); Hattiangadi (1973); Hayek (1979); Jaynes (1976); Jerison (1973); Koffka (1928); March (1978); Mandler (1975); Mayr and Provine (1980); Neisser (1976); Piaget (1952); Pilbean (1972); Premack (1983); Rozin (1976); Simon (1969, 1955, 1959, 1979a, 1979b); Newell and Simon (1972).

[36] This includes not only the behavior of individual persons within different societies but also the recurrent patterns in economic, legal, and political institutions, as well as cultural norms, which have been instrumental in the development of human civilization. See Heiner (1983, pp. 573–4, 580–2); Hayek (1973, 1978, 1979); Buchanan (1975, 1977); Schotter (1981), Campbell (1982); and Ullmann-Margalit (1978).

goals. This is not meant to imply that real agents always act in this manner, or that they are even capable of conscious maximization. Rather, standard theory conceives of agents as if they choose in this way. Nevertheless, such a limited analytical perspective can have a great impact on how formal models are constructed and used.[37]

Now think of these issues in terms of the reliability theory. No particular type of behavioral mechanism (conscious maximizing or otherwise) is singled out in motivating its formal ingredients. Instead, a general relationship is modeled in which uncertainty affects the reliability of administering more flexible patterns of behavior. Particular kinds of uncertainty are characterized by the (p,e) variables. For example, the p variables can be used to describe different types of agents, along with the perceptual capabilities of these agents. Together with the e variable, they determine the reliability curves for selecting behavior in response to information or signals potentially encountered by an agent. These curves are combined with the Reliability Condition, $r/w > T$, to determine the likelihood that particular actions will be selected under different conditions (including the dynamic response to changing conditions).

In addition to these analytical features, recall certain possibilities suggested in the preceding discussion. In particular, suppose we didn't need to assume agents always maximize in light of their preferences or even that they have well-defined preferences. Suppose we could instead derive behavior patterns that otherwise would be assumed in the form of preferences or that would arise only if preferences are uncertain. Suppose we didn't need to assume agents can foresee all potential future events, or formulate determinate probability beliefs, or list all possible courses of action they might select. Finally, suppose we could use probability and optimizing concepts, but without any tendency thereby to ignore the agents' true decision capabilities.

These possibilities fit within a general theme I have discussed elsewhere, namely, that uncertainty (rather than maximizing as such) is the basic source of regularity in behavior. We may thus have much to gain by broadening our analytical horizon to incorporate uncertainty determinants in a natural way, especially in situations in which agents are unable to assess probability information in the manner assumed in conventional risk and utility theory. If this is the case, the modeling con-

---

[37] For example, on what types of assumptions are introduced, on how these assumptions and other modeling tools are used, on the nature of the problems and questions suggested by using these assumptions and tools, etc. For a recent analysis of the methodology of conventional choice theory, see Caldwell (1982) and McCloskey (1983).

cepts suggested in this chapter may fruitfully enhance our ability to understand and investigate behavior.

4.8 Appendix

4.8.1 Derivation of the reliability condition

The Reliability Condition is here briefly derived. See Heiner (1983) for further motivation and interpretation of the condition.[38]

Recall that $V_U(A)$ represents the average performance if actions are selected from repertoire $A = A' - \{a\}$, conditional on the uncertainty $U = u(\mathbf{p,e})$. Recall also that $R \subset S^*$ and $W = S^* - R$ are the right or wrong conditions for selecting an action, $a \in A'$ (where performance will rise or fall, respectively, compared with selecting actions only from A).

Let V_1 and V_2 represent the performance of repertoire A under R and W respectively; that is, $V_1 = V_U(A|R)$ and $V_2 = V_U(A \mid W)$. Thus, if action a is selected under conditions R, (rather than choosing from A), average performance will increase from V_1 to a higher level, denoted by $V_3 = V_U(a|R)$. The resulting gain in performance is denoted by $g = V_3 - V_1 > 0$. Similarly, performance will drop from V_2 to a lower level, denoted by $V_4 = V_U(a|W)$, if a is mistakenly selected under conditions W. The resulting loss in performance is denoted by $\ell = V_2 - V_4 > 0$. Finally, recall the following definitions from Section 4.3: $r = p(a|R)$, $w = p(a|W)$, $\pi = p(R)$, $1 - \pi = p(W)$. In addition we also have $1 - r = p(A|R)$ and $1 - w = p(A|W)$.

Now the basic question is whether an agent (given uncertainty $U = u(\mathbf{p,e})$, so that $r < 1$ and $w > 0$) can benefit from reacting to information about when to select an action rather than other choosable actions. That is, when will average performance (over potential situations in S^*) from also choosing action a improve compared with staying exclusively within repertoire A; so that $V(A \cup \{a\}) > V(A)$? From the above we have

$$V(A \cup \{a\}) = \pi[rV_3 + (1 - r)V_1] + (1 - \pi)[wV_4 + (1 - w)V_2] \quad (A1)$$
$$V(A) = \pi V_1 + (1 - \pi)V_2. \quad (A2)$$

Recalling that $g = V_3 - V_1$ and $\ell = V_2 - V_4$ and subtracting (A2) from (A1) obtains, by rearranging,

$$V(A \cup \{a\}) - V(A) - g\pi r - \ell(1 - \pi)w. \quad (A3)$$

---

[38] For an axiomatization of the Reliability Condition under general mathematical conditions, see Heiner (1984).

Equation (A3) implies the following result, which establishes the Reliability Condition,

$$V(A \cup \{a\}) > V(A) \text{ if and only if } \frac{r}{w} > \frac{\ell}{g} \frac{(1-\pi)}{\pi}. \tag{A4}$$

Note that for simplicity the above derivation used a standard von Neumann-Morgenstern value function to calculate (A1) and (A2). However, the same formula for (A3) (and thus the Reliability Condition A4) still holds if the recent nonexpected utility theories of Machina (1982), Chew(1983), Fishburn (1983), and others are used instead. A precise demonstration of the latter is given in Heiner (1984).

4.8.2   A two-step reliability illustration

Suppose the right and wrong conditions, R and W, for selecting an action are correlated with a signal, denoted by s. The signal is always normally distributed with variance $\delta^2 = 1$. However, its mean shifts from $\mu_1 = 0$ to $\mu_2 = 1$, with the former corresponding to R and the latter to W. Assume the agent uses a decision rule in the following form: select the action only if $s \le z$ (otherwise – if $s > z$ – don't select the action), for some given z between ∞ and $-\infty$. The variable z is thus a cutoff value or decision point for selecting an action in response to observing s.[39]

Deciding in this way indirectly determines the conditional probabilities of responding under R and W, as implied by the cutoff point z. These probabilities thus depend on z and are denoted by $r(z)$ and $w(z)$, respectively. Varying z will produce an ROC or reliability curve.

In addition, suppose the agent has difficulty in detecting which value of s is actually observed, where his or her perceived s is denoted by s'. In this case, s' will sometimes be mistakenly perceived to be above z when s is actually below z, and vice versa. We thus have a secondary detection task of determining whether s is above or below z. Let r' denote the chance of correctly detecting whether s is above or below z, and w' denote the chance of mistakenly detecting where s places relative to z. That is, $r' = p(s' \le z \mid s \le z) = p(s' > z \mid s > z)$ and $w' = p(s' \le z \mid s > z) = p(s' > z \mid s \le z)$.

---

[39] For each value of s, the ratio of the two density functions forms a "likelihood ratio," denoted by $L(s)$. An equivalent decision criterion is then to respond whenever $L(s) \ge L(z)$. As $z \to -\infty$, $L(z) \to \infty$, so that the corresponding probabilities $r(z)$ and $w(z)$ both approach zero for successively higher $L(z)$. See Ferguson (1970, pp. 206–12); Blackwell and Girshick (1979, pp. 218–22); DeGroot (1970, pp. 239–40, 244–7); Egan (1975, pp. 20–8). For related material on various hypotheses and significance tests, see Jeffreys (1961, pp. 245–368) and Zellner (1979).

These probabilities determine the reliability of the secondary detection task, as measured by the reliability ratio r'/w'. The net reliability ratio for selecting an action over the two steps (of first setting the cutoff point z, and then detecting how s compares to z) is given by the formula,

$$\rho''(z,r'w') \equiv \frac{r''}{w''} - \frac{r(z)\mathrm{r}' + [1 - r(z)]w'}{w(z)\mathrm{r}' + [1 - w(z)]w'}. \qquad (A5)$$

Rearranging (A5) obtains,

$$\rho''(z,\rho') = \frac{r(z)\,(\rho' - 1) + 1}{w(z)\,(\rho' - 1) + 1}, \qquad \text{where } \rho' = \frac{r'}{w'}. \qquad (A5')$$

The probabilities $r(z)$ and $w(z)$ both approach zero as z becomes smaller. Thus, the structure of (A5') implies that, for any given $\rho' = r'/w'$, ρ'' rises to a maximum (at some z, denoted z^*) beyond which lower values of z will reduce ρ'' toward 1.0. Consequently, the agent can no longer benefit from reducing z. Rather, it can only maintain the maximal value of $\rho''(z^*,\rho')$ by using a random device to decide whether to select the action once $s' \leqslant z^*$ or $s' > s^*$ is perceived. (This will have an equal proportionate effect on both r'' and w'', so that ρ'' remains constant).[40]

Figure 4.9 shows the resulting net reliability curves (over the two steps involving z and ρ' for a few selected values of $\rho' = (9, 99, 999, \infty)$. These values also correspond to particular values of r' (the chance of correctly determining whether s satisfies the first step); $\rho' = (9, 99, 999, \infty)$ corresponds to r' on the order of $(.9, .99, .999, 1.0)$,[41] respectively. Thus, for example, $\rho = 999$ means a 99.9 percent chance of correctly perceiving the first step.

Note that Figure 4.9 has three key features. (1) Perfectly detecting the first step (i.e., $\rho' = \infty$) produces a reliability curve that is unbounded as $h \rightarrow 0$. This follows from standard statistical theory of the likelihood-ratio test (and is implied for most common distributions besides the normal).[42] (2) However, the net reliability over both steps is severely

---

[40] Setting a cutoff value z as indicated in the example is the best decision procedure (for most common distributions such as the normal) in that it maximizes $r(z)$ for any given value of $w(z)$ produced by a particular selection of z; see Blackwell and Girshick (1979, pp. 200–6); Ferguson (1967, pp. 198–242). Consequently, any means of further reducing h (beyond that implied by z^*) by reducing the acceptance zone will only reduce ρ'' below $\rho''(z^*,\rho')$. The only way of reducing h while maintaining ρ'' at its highest value is to respond randomly to $s' \leqslant z^*$ (with probability λ). This will produce a constant ratio, $\lambda r''/\lambda w'' \equiv \rho''(z^*,\rho')$ for all $0 \leqslant \lambda \leqslant 1$.

[41] These calculations assume, for convenience, that $r' + w' = 1$. In the more general case, $r' + w' = \lambda$ for $0 \leqslant \lambda \leqslant 2$, so that $r' = \rho'\lambda/(1 + \rho')$.

[42] An unbounded reliability ratio is implied for distributions with monotone likelihood ratios (such as normal, binomial, negative binomial, Poisson, gamma, beta, hypergeometric, uniform). See Ferguson (1967, pp. 206–12).

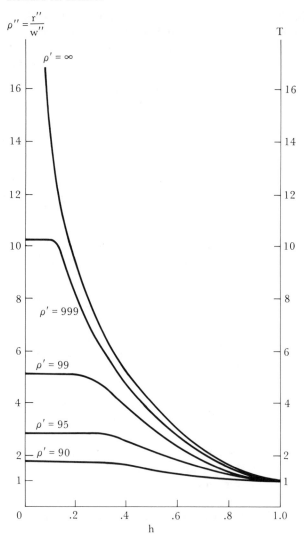

Figure 4.9. A (two-step) family of reliability curves: $\rho = \infty$ means the first-step cutoff point is perfectly detected; otherwise the reliability of the second step is given by $r'/w' = \rho'$. Note how severely $\rho' < \infty$ limits the new reliability, ρ'', achievable over both steps.

constrained unless the first step is perceived with extreme reliability. For example, even $\rho' = 999$ (or $r' = .999$) will still bound ρ'' below 11.0 as $h \rightarrow 0$. (3) For all finite ρ', the net reliability curve will have a flat segment where it intersects the vertical axis. This is not always true in more general cases than illustrated here. However, it can be shown that all bounded reliability curves (produced through however many intermediate steps and irrespective of the type of statistical connections between each stage) must begin with a concave-shaped segment (meaning the second derivative of the net reliability curve is nonnegative) that is approximately flat under most conditions.

Finally, consider another possibility. Experiments systematically show that the reliability of detecting a signal quickly drops as the signal becomes increasingly rare[43] (i.e., as it occurs less frequently). Consequently, the net reliability of responding to otherwise extremely reliable but infrequent signals may nevertheless be severely limited (especially if the reliability of these signals is contingent on a subtle mixture of conditions which is only rarely satisfied). Without going into details, we can show that commonly used statistical distributions[44] often will not produce a reliable signal unless an unlikely cutoff value is set (meaning a value of z for which the chance of observing $s \le z$ is small). Consequently, the net reliability of responding to signals generated by these distributions will often be severely constrained, even though the reliability of these signals (if perfectly observed when they occur) is usually unbounded as $h \to 0$.[45]

4.8.3 A marginal reliability condition that incorporates maximizing tools

The Reliability Condition, $r/w > T$, must be satisfied if an agent is to benefit from allowing a positive probability ($h > 0$) of selecting an action. That is, it determines the range of response probabilities between zero and $\hat{h}$ (see Section 4.4) for which the change in average performance, $V(A \cup \{a\}) - V(A)$, is positive. If the reliability curve for an action is not bounded below its tolerance limit, we can then ask where in the interval $(0,\hat{h})$ the gain in performance will be maximized. To obtain a simple answer, proceed as follows:

Let $\Delta V = V(A \cup \{a\}) - V(A)$ denote the change in performance, and

---

[43] See Green and Swets (1974, pp. 268–9, 332–6). In addition, see Parasuraman and Davies (1976); Adams (1963); Alluisi, Coates, and Morgan (1977); Baddeley and Colquhoun (1969); Craig and Colquhoun (1977); Howell, Johnson, and Goldstein (1966); Mackworth (1970); Swets (1977); Vickers, Leary, and Barnes (1977); Davenport (1969); Moray and O'Brien (1967); Loeb and Binford (1968); Milosević (1974); Colquhoun (1961); Davies and Tune (1969); Broadbent (1953); Mackworth (1964, 1968); Montague, Webber, and Adams (1965); Taub and Osborne (1968); Ware, Baker, and Druckner (1964).

[44] See n. 38.

[45] Even if there is no difficulty in perceiving a decision point (even one unlikely to be satisfied), a very small response probability is still often necessary to raise the reliability above 20 for the commonly used statistical distributions (as mentioned in n. 38).

assume $\hat{h} > 0$. Recall that the conditional response probabilities r and w are both functions of h, and that these functions are conditional on $\mathbf{U} = u(\mathbf{p},\mathbf{e})$. Consequently, ΔV also varies with h, with the functional relationship conditional on $u(\mathbf{p},\mathbf{e})$. It is thus written $\Delta V[h|u(\mathbf{p},\mathbf{e})]$. Note also that $\Delta V[h|u(\mathbf{p},\mathbf{e})] > 0$ for all $0 < h < \hat{h}$.

Now differentiate ΔV with respect to h (where the resulting derivatives are denoted with a dot above the corresponding variables), and set $\dot{\Delta V} = 0$ to obtain the first-order conditions for maximizing ΔV. Using expression (A3), this implies[46]

$$\dot{\Delta V} = g\pi\dot{r} - \ell(1 - \pi)\dot{w} = 0. \tag{A6}$$

By rearranging (A6) we obtain the "marginal" analogue to $r/w > T$; namely,

$$\frac{\dot{r}}{\dot{w}} = T = \frac{\ell}{g} \cdot \frac{1 - \pi}{\pi}. \tag{A7}$$

I will call (A7) the *Marginal Reliability Condition* to distinguish it from the inequality already developed, $r/w > T$. It intuitively means that an agent will benefit from more frequently selecting an action up to the point where the increase in the likelihood of correct selections ($\dot{r}$) relative to the increase in the likelihood of mistaken selections ($\dot{w}$) just equals the tolerance limit (T), or minimum required reliability for selecting that action.

We can also represent the condition using ROC curves in a unit probability box (see Figure 4.4). It corresponds to that point along an ROC or reliability curve at which the *tangent* slope just equals the slope of a particular T-line. This point will usually be closer to the origin than the point at which the T-line intersects a reliability curve (corresponding to $\dot{r}/\dot{w} = T$ rather than $r/w = T$).

No further discussion about the Marginal Reliability Condition is pursued here, except for the following brief remarks.

(1) As with $\hat{h}$ in Section 4.4, we can define h^* as the largest h such that $\dot{r}(h|\mathbf{U})/\dot{w}(h|\mathbf{U}) \geq T$, which will be a function of $\mathbf{U}$ and T, denoted by $h^*(\mathbf{U},T)$. The (strict) monotonicity of $r/w = \rho(h|\mathbf{U})$ implies $\dot{r}/\dot{w}$ is also (strictly) monotonic; that $(h^* < \hat{h})$ $h^* \leq h$; and that $(\dot{r}/\dot{w} < r/w)$ $\dot{r}/\dot{w} \leq r/w$ for all $0 < h \leq 1$. Finally $h^*(\mathbf{U},T)$ also retains the properties described by Principles R1 and R2. Thus, the implications discussed in the text (see Sections 4.4 and 4.5) remain valid whether h^* or $\hat{h}$ is used.

---

[46] This assumes that varying h has a negligible effect on the environment and on the reliability of selecting other actions in A, so that (g,ℓ,π) are constant. A more complicated result (still with the same qualitative properties) is implied if these elements also change with h.

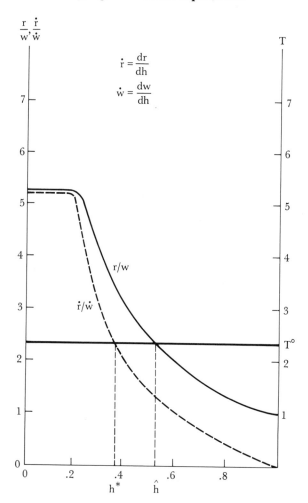

Figure 4.10. The marginal reliability curve. The broken line is the marginal reliability curve corresponding to a particular reliability curve taken from Figure 4.9. Note that $h^* < \hat{h}$, and that both curves have the same qualitative shape.

(2) We can also represent these relationships graphically. An example is shown in Figure 4.10, which adds the corresponding marginal reliability curve to one of the reliability curves shown in Figure 4.9.

(3) Detecting changes in r and w may itself be a difficult perceptual task. One reason (as already discussed) is that an agent may have difficulty in distinguishing conditions R and W, so that the probabilities r

and w are themselves uncertain. Even if they can be estimated, another problem arises. The very fact that r and w are probabilities means that they have stable values only over a long sequence of trials. Thus, changes in r and w cannot be reliably estimated from a small sample of ongoing experience. Consequently, the dynamic behavior of h may not closely track movements in h^* caused by changes in U or T, even though it may still be bounded within the interval $(0, \hat{h})$.

The main text, therefore, emphasized the use of $\hat{h}$ as a first (but robust) approximation for analyzing behavior (and one whose qualitative properties are typically the same as h^*). Under certain conditions, h^* may enable us to obtain more refined implications.

(4) The foregoing discussion briefly sketches how one might incorporate maximizing tools into the reliability model. Recall, however, a crucial difference from traditional optimization theory already discussed in Section 4.2. The Marginal Reliability Condition, $\dot{r}/\dot{w} = T$, does not assume agents have special decision capabilities of any kind, nor is any "as if" interpretation needed to justify its use. Rather, it is conditional on whatever kinds of perceptual limitations might be described by the p variables. This may include factors that severely limit an agent's ability to maximize in the traditional sense (or to assign probabilities to potential events). Thus, we can disassociate the use of maximizing tools with any tendency to abstract from agents' true decision capabilities.

References

Abel, A., R. Dornbusch, J. Huizingor, and A. Marcus. 1979. "Money Demand During Hyperinflation." *Journal of Monetary Economics* 5:97–104.

Adams, J. A. 1963. "Experimental Studies of Human Vigilance." *United States Air Force ESD Technical Documentary Report.* No. 63-320.

Alchian, Armen A. 1950. "Uncertainty, Evolution, and Economic Theory." *Journal of Political Economy* 58:211–21.

————. 1969. "Information Costs, Pricing, and Resource Unemployment." *Western Economic Journal* 7:109–28.

Alchian, Armen A., and William Allen. 1977. *Exchange and Production: Competition, Coordination, and Control.* 2d ed. Belmont, Calif.: Wadsworth.

Alcock, John. 1979. *Animal Behavior: An Evolutionary Approach.* Sunderland, Mass.: Sinauer Associates.

Alexander, Richard, and G. Borgin. 1978. "Group Selection, Altruism, and the Levels of Organization of Life." *Annual Review of Ecology and Systematics* 9:449–75.

Allais, Maurice. 1953. "Le Comportement de l'Homme Rationnel devant le Risque: Critiques des Postulats et Axiomes de l'Ecole Américaine." *Econometrica* 21:503–46.

Alluisi, E. A., G. D. Coates, and B. B. Morgan. 1977. "Effects of Temporal Stressors on Vigilance and Information Processing." In *Vigilance: Theory, Operational Performance, and Physiological Correlates.* ed. R. R. Mackie. New York: Plenum.

Anderson, J. R. 1980. *Cognitive Psychology and Its Implications.* San Francisco: Freeman.

Anderson, J. R., P. J. Kline, and C. M. Beasley. 1980. "Complex Learning Processes." In *Aptitude, Learning and Instruction.* ed. R. E. Snow, P. A. Federico, and W. E. Montague. Vol. 2. Hillsdale, N. J.: Erlbaum.

Arrow, Kenneth J. 1951. "Alternative Approaches to the Theory of Choice in Risk-Taking Situations." *Econometrica* 19:404–37.

1981. "Risk Perception in Psychology and Economics." *Economic Inquiry* 20:1–9.

Axelrod, Robert. 1984. *The Evolution of Cooperation.* New York: Basic Books.

Ayllon, T., and N. H. Azrin. 1968. *The Token Economy: A Motivational System for Therapy and Rehabilitation.* New York: Appleton-Century-Crofts.

Baddeley, A. D., and W. P. Colquhoun. 1969. "Signal Probability and Vigilance: A Reappraisal of the Signal-Rate Effect." *British Journal of Psychology* 60:169–178.

Baldwin, R. D., D. Chambliss, and A. D. Wright. 1962. "Target Detectability as a Function of Target Speed, Noise Level, and Location." *Journal of Applied Psychology* 46:26–30.

Barro, Robert J. 1976. "Rational Expectations and the Role of Monetary Policy." *Journal of Monetary Economics* 2(1):1–32.

Battalio, Raymond C., et al. 1973. "A Test of Consumer Demand Theory Using Observations of Individual Purchases." *Western Economic Journal* 11:411–28.

Battalio, Raymond C., John H. Kagel, Howard Rachlin, and Leonard Green. 1981. "Commodity Choice Behavior with Pigeons as Subjects." *Journal of Political Economy* 81:67–91.

Blackwell, David and M. A. Girshick. 1979. *Theory of Games and Statistical Decisions.* New York: Dover.

Bransford, J. D., and J. J. Franks. 1971. "The Abstraction of Linguistic Ideas." *Cognitive Psychology* 2:331–50.

Broadbent, D. E. 1953. "Noise, Paced Performance, and Vigilance Tasks." *British Journal of Psychology* 44:295–303.

Brown, Roger and Richard Herrnstein. 1975. *Psychology.* Boston: Little, Brown.

Brunner, Karl, Alex Cukierman, and Allan Meltzer. 1980. "Stagflation, Persistent Unemployment and the Permanence of Economic Shocks." *Journal of Monetary Economics* 6:467–92.

Buchanan, James M. 1975. *The Limits of Liberty: Between Anarchy and the Leviathan.* Chicago: University of Chicago Press.

1977. *Freedom In Constitutional Contract.* College Station: Texas A&M University Press.

Caldwell, Bruce J. 1982. *Beyond Positivism: Economic Methodology in the Twentieth Century.* London: Allen and Unwin.

Campbell, Jeremy. 1982. *Grammatical Man: Information, Entropy, Language, and Life.* New York: Simon and Schuster.

Cannon, D. S. 1970. "Human Signal Detection of Fixed Ratio Reinforcement Schedules." *Diss. Abst. Internat.* 31(3-B):1530.

Chase, W. G., and H. A. Simon. 1973. "The Mind's Eye in Chess." In *Visual Information Processing,* ed. W. G. Chase. New York: Academic Press.

Chew, Soo Hong. 1983. "A Generalization of the Quasilinear Mean with Applications to the Measurement of Income Inequality and Decision Theory Resolving the Allais Paradox." *Econometrica* 51:1065–92.

Chomsky, Noam. 1980. "Rules and Representations." *Behavioral and Brain Sciences* 3:1–61.

Christ, R. E. 1969. "Effects of Pay-Off and Probability on Recall of Multi-Symbol Displays." *Journal of General Psychology* 80, 81–92.

Cohen, Michael D., and Robert Axelrod. 1984. "Coping with Complexity: The Adaptive Value of Changing Utility." *American Economic Review* 74:30–42.

Colquhoun, W. P. 1961. "The Effect of 'Unwanted' Signals on Performance in a Vigilance Task." *Ergonomics* 4:41–52.

Coombs, Clyde H., Robyn M. Dawes and Amos Tversky. 1970. *Mathematical Psychology.* Englewood Cliffs, N.J.: Prentice-Hall. 1970.

Cooper, L. A., and P. Podgorny. 1976. "Mental Transformation and Visual Comparison Processes: Effects of Complexity and Similarity." *Journal of Experimental Psychology: Human Perception and Performance* 2:503–14.

Craig, A., and W. P. Colquhoun. 1977. "Vigilance Effects in Complex Inspection." In *Vigilance: Theory, Operational Performance, and Physiological Correlates,* ed. R. R. Mackie. New York: Plenum.

Crowder, R. G. 1976. *Principles of Learning and Memory.* Hillsdale, N.J.: Erlbaum.

Cukierman, A. 1979. "Rational Expectations and the Role of Monetary Policy: A Generalization." *Journal of Monetary Economics* 5:213–30.
     1980. "The Effects of Wage Indexation on Macroeconomic Fluctuations: A Generalization." *Journal of Monetary Economics* 6:147–70.

D'Amato, M. R. 1970. *Experimental Psychology: Methodology, Psychophysics, and Learning.* New York: McGraw-Hill.

Davenport, W. G. 1969. "Vigilance for Simultaneous Auditory and Vibrotactile Signals." *Australian Journal of Psychology* 21:159–66.

Davies, D. R., and G. S. Tune. 1969. *Human Vigilance Performance.* New York: American Elsevier.

DeGroot, Morris H. 1970. *Optimal Statistical Decisions.* New York: McGraw-Hill.

Diamond, Peter, and Michael Rothschild. 1978. *Uncertainty in Economics.* New York: Academic Press.

Dixon, N. F. 1971. *Subliminal Perception: The Nature of a Controversy.* London: McGraw-Hill.

Edwards, Ward. 1961. "Behavioral Decision Theory." *Annual Review of Psychology* 12:473–98.
     1962. "Subjective Probabilities Inferred from Decisions." *Psychological Review* 69:109–35.

Egan, James P. 1967. *Signal Detection Theory and Psychophysics: A Topical Bibliography.* Washington, D.C.: National Academy of Sciences.
     1975. *Signal Detection Theory and ROC Analysis.* New York: Academic Press.

Ellsberg, Daniel. 1961. "Risk, Ambiguity, and the Savage Axioms." *Quarterly Journal of Economics.* (August):643–94.

Emmerich, D. S. 1968. "Receiver-Operating Characteristics Determined under Several Interaural Conditions of Listening." *Journal of the Acoustical Society of America* 43:298–307.

Fama, Eugene F. 1976. *Foundations of Finance: Portfolio Decisions and Securities Prices.* New York: Basic Books.

Fellner, William. 1961. "Distortion of Subjective Probabilities as a Reaction to Uncertainty." *Quarterly Journal of Economics* 75:670–90.

Ferguson, Thomas S. 1967. *Mathematical Statistics: A Decision Theoretic Approach.* New York: Academic Press.

Fischer, Stanley. 1977. "Long-Term Contracts, Rational Expectations and the Optimal Money Supply Rule." *Journal of Political Economy* 85(1):191–206.

Fischhoff, Baruch, Paul Slovic, and Sarah Lichtenstein. 1980. "Knowing What You Want: Measuring Labile Values." In *Cognitive Processes in Choice and Decision Behavior,* ed. Tom S. Wallstren. Hillsdale: Erlbaum.

Fishburn, Peter C. 1983. "Transitive Measurable Utility." *Journal of Economic Theory* (August).

Fisher, Irving. 1970. *The Theory of Interest.* New York: Augustus M. Kelley.

Freud, Sigmund. 1962. *Standard Edition of the Complete Psychological Works of Sigmund Freud.* Vols. 1–16. London: Hogarth.

Gertler, Mark. 1982. "Imperfect Information and Wage Inertia in the Business Cycle." *Journal of Political Economy* 90:967–87.

    1981. "Long-Term Contracts, Imperfect Information, and Monetary Policy." *Journal of Economic Dynamics and Control* 3:197–216.

Geschwind, N. 1980. "Neurological Knowledge and Complex Behaviors." *Cognitive Science* 4:185–194.

Gibson, James. 1977. "The Theory of Affordances." In *Perceiving, Acting, and Knowing,* ed. R. E. Shaw and J. Bransford. Hillsdale: Erlbaum.

    1979. *The Ecological Approach to Visual Perception.* Boston: Houghton Mifflin.

    1950. *The Perception of the Visual World.* Boston: Houghton-Mifflin.

    1966. *The Senses Considered as Perceptual Systems.* Boston: Houghton-Mifflin.

Glucksberg, S., and M. McCloskey. 1981. "Decisions About Ignorance: Knowing That You Don't Know." *Journal of Experimental Psychology: Human Learning and Memory* 7:311–25.

Gould, J. P. 1974. "Risk, Stochastic Preference and the Value of Information." *Journal of Economic Theory* 8(1):64–84.

Green, David M., and John A. Swets. 1974. *Signal Detection Theory and Psychophysics.* New York: Robert Kriegur.

Grether, David M., and Charles R. Plott. 1979. "Economic Theory of Choice and the Preference Reversal Phenomenon," *American Economic Review* 69: 623–38.

Grether, David M., and Louis L. Wilde. 1982. "Consumer Choice and Information: New Experimental Evidence on the Information Overload Hypothesis." Social Science Working Paper 459. Pasadena: California Institute of Technology.

Griliches, Zvi. 1957. "Hybrid Corn: An Exploration in the Economics of Technical Change." *Econometrica* 25:501–22.

    1960. "Hybrid Corn and the Economics of Innovation." *Science* 132:275–80.

Grossman, S. J. 1977. "The Existence of Futures Markets, Noisy Rational Expectations, and Informational Externalities." *Review of Economic Studies* 44(3):431–50.

Hamlyn, D. W. 1977. "The Concept of Information in Gibson's Theory of Perception." *Journal for the Theory of Social Behavior* 7(1):5–16.

Hamm, Robert MacG. 1979. "The Conditions of Occurrence of the Preference Reversal Phenomenon." Ph.D. dissertation, Harvard University.

Hattiangadi, Jagdish. 1973. "Mind and the Origin of Language." *Philosophy Forum* 14.

Hayek, Friedrich A. 1933. *Monetary Theory and the Trade Cycle.* London: Macmillan.

    1935. *Prices and Production.* London: Routledge and Keegan Paul.

    1939. *Profits, Interest, and Investment.* London: Routledge and Sons.

    1973. "The Changing Concept of Law." In *Law, Legislation and Liberty.* Vol. 1. Chicago: University of Chicago Press.

    1978. "Competition as a Discovery Procedure." In *New Studies in Philosophy, Politics, Economics and the History of Ideas.* Chicago: University of Chicago Press.

    1979. "Three Sources of Human Values." In *Law, Legislation and Liberty.* Vol. 3. Chicago: University of Chicago Press.

Hayes-Roth, B. 1977. "Evolution of Cognitive Structures and Processes." *Psychological Review* 84:260–78.

Healy, A. F. 1975. "Coding of Temporal-Spatial Patterns in Short-Term Memory." *Journal of Verbal Learning and Verbal Behavior* 14:481–95.

Heath, Richard A. 1977. "The Effects of Payoff on Attention in a Bisensory Signal Detection Task," *Australian Journal of Psychology* 29:143–50.

Heiner, Ronald A. 1983. "The Origin of Predictable Behavior." *American Economic Review* 73:560–95.

1984. "On Reinterpreting The Foundations of Risk & Utility Theory." Provo, Utah: Brigham Young University.

1985. "Experimental Economics: Comment." *American Economic Review* 75(1): 260–63.

Hershey, John C., Howard C. Kunreuther, and Paul J. Schoemaker. 1982. "Sources of Bias in Assessment Procedures for Utility Functions." *Management Science* 28:936–54.

Hey, John D. 1979. *Uncertainty in Microeconomics.* New York: New York University Press.

1981. "Are Optimal Search Rules Reasonable? And Vice Versa? (And Does It Matter Anyway?)." *Journal of Economic Behavior and Organization* 3:47–70.

1982. "Search Rules for Search." *Journal of Economic Behavior and Organization* 3:65–81.

Hicks, John R. 1939. *Value and Capital.* London: Oxford (Clarendon Press).

Hirshleifer, Jack. 1982. "Evolutionary Models in Economics and the Law: Cooperation Versus Conflict Strategies." *Research in Law and Economics* 4:1–60.

1980. *Price Theory and Applications.* 2d ed. Englewood Cliffs, N.J.: Prentice-Hall.

Hogarth, R. M. 1975. "Cognitive Processes and the Assessment of Subjective Probability Distributions." *Journal of the American Statistical Association* 70, 271–94.

Howell, W. C., W. A. Johnston, and I. L. Goldstein. 1966. "Complex Monitoring and Its Relation to the Classical Problem of Vigilance." *Organizational Behavior and Human Performance* 1:129–50.

Jaynes, Julian. 1976. "Consciousness," and "The Origin of Civilization." In *The Origin of Consciousness in the Breakdown of the Bicameral Mind.* Boston: Houghton Mifflin.

Jeffreys, Harold. 1961. *Theory of Probability.* 3d ed. London: Oxford University Press.

Jerison, Harry J. 1967. "Activation and Long-Term Performance." *Acta Psychologica* 27:373–89.

1973. *Evolution of the Brain and Intelligence.* New York: Academic Press.

Jevons, William S. 1871. *Theory of Political Economy.* London: Routledge and Sons.

Jones, J. E. 1962. "All-or-None Versus Incremental Learning." *Psychological Review* 69:156–60.

Kagel, John H., et al. 1978. "Experimental Studies of Consumer Demand Using Laboratory Animals." *Economic Inquiry* 13:22–39.

Kagel, John H., Raymond C. Battalio, Howard Rachlin, and Leonard Green. 1980. "Demand Curves for Animal Consumers." *Quarterly Journal of Economics* 96:1–16.

Kahneman, D. 1973. *Attention and Effort.* Englewood Cliffs, N.J.: Prentice-Hall, Inc.

Kahneman, D., and Amos Tversky. 1979, "Prospect Theory: An Analysis of Decision Under Risk." *Econometrica* 47:263–91.

1981. "The Framing of Decisions and the Psychology of Choice." *Science* 211:453–58.

1982. "The Psychology of Preferences." *Scientific American* 246:160–73.

Keynes, John M. 1936. *The General Theory of Employment, Interest, and Money.* New York: Harcourt, Brace and Company.

Killeen, Peter R. 1982. "Learning as Causal Inference." In *Quantitative Analysis of Behavior: Discriminative Properties of Reinforcement Schedules,* ed. M. L. Commons and J. A. Nevin. Vol. 1. Cambridge: Harper and Row (Ballinger).

Klahr, D., P. Langley, and D. Neches, eds. 1983. *Self-Modifying Production System Models of Learning and Development.* Cambridge, Mass.: Bradford Books/MIT Press.

Knight, F. H. 1933. *Risk, Uncertainty, and Profit.* Boston: Houghton-Mifflin.

Koffka, K. 1928. *The Growth of the Mind.* 2d ed. New York.

Kohler, Heinz. 1982. *Intermediate Microeconomics: Theory and Applications.* Palo Alto, Calif.: Scott, Foresman.

Konner, M. 1982. *The Tangled Wing: Biological Constraints on the Human Spirit.* New York: Basic Books.

Kramer, E. 1963. "Judgment of Personal Characteristics and Emotions from Nonverbal Properties of Speech." *Psychological Bulletin.* 60:408–20.

Kunreuther, Howard et al. 1978. *Disaster Insurance Protection.* New York: Wiley.

Kydland, Finn E., and Edward C. Prescott. 1977. "Rules Rather than Discretion: The Inconsistency of Optimal Plans," *Journal of Political Economy,* 85:473–91.

Larkin, J. H., J. McDermott, D. P. Simon, and H. A. Simon. 1980. "Models of Competence in Solving Physics Problems." *Cognitive Science* 4:317–45.

Leijonhufvud, Axel. 1968. *On Keynesian Economics and the Economics of Keynes.* New York: Oxford University Press.

Lenat, D. B., and G. Harris. 1978. "Designing a Rule System that Searches for Scientific Discoveries." In *Pattern-Directed Inference Systems,* ed. D. A. Waterman and F. Hayes-Roth. New York: Academic Press.

Lindman, Harold R. 1971. "Inconsistent Preferences Among Gambles." *Journal of Experimental Psychology* 89:390–97.

Lindsay, P. H., and D. A. Norman. 1969. "Short-Term Retention During a Simultaneous Detection Task." *Perception and Psychophysics* 5:201–5.

1972. *Human Information Processing: An Introduction to Psychology.* New York: Academic Press.

1977. *Human Information Processing: An Introduction to Psychology.* New York: Academic Press.

Lindsay, P. H., M. M. Taylor, and S. M. Forbes. 1968. "Attention and Multi-Dimensional Discrimination," *Perception and Psychophysics,* 4:113–117.

Lippman, S. A., and J. J. McCall. 1976a. "Job Search in a Dynamic Economy." *Journal of Economic Theory* 12(3):365–90.

1976b. "The Economics of Job Search: A Survey. Part I: Optimal Job Search Policies." *Economic Inquiry* 14(2):155–89.

1976c. "The Economics of Job Search: A Survey. Part II: Empirical and Policy Implications of Job Search." *Economic Inquiry* 14(3):347–68.

Loeb, M., and J. R. Binford. 1968. "Variation in Performance on Auditory and Visual Monitoring Tasks as a Function of Signal and Stimulus Frequencies." *Perception & Psychophysics* 4:316–66.

Lorenz, Konrad. 1981. *The Foundation of Ethology.* New York: Springer-Verlag.

Lucas, Robert E., Jr. 1975. "An Equilibrium Model of the Business Cycle." *Journal of Political Economy* 83:1113–44.

1972. "Expectations and the Neutrality of Money." *Journal of Economic Theory* 4:103–24.

1977. "Understanding Business Cycles." In *Stabilization of the Domestic and International Economy,* ed. Karl Brunner and Allan H. Meltzer. Carnegie-Rochester Conferences on Public Policy. *Journal of Monetary Economics* 5:7–29.

1981. *Studies in Business Cycle Theory.* Cambridge: MIT Press.

McCall, J. J. 1965. "The Economics of Information and Optimal Stopping Rules." *Journal of Business* 38:300–17.

1971. "Probabilistic Microeconomics." *The Bell Journal of Economics and Management Science* 2:403–33.

McCloskey, Donald N. 1983. "The Rhetoric of Economics." *Journal of Economic Literature* 21:481–517.

McCord, Mark R., and Richard de Neufville. 1983. "Utility Dependence on Probability: An Empirical Demonstration." Technology and Policy Program, MIT.

MacDonald, Ronald R. 1976. "The Effect of Sequential Dependencies on Some Signal Detection Parameters." *Quarterly Journal of Experimental Psychology* 28:643–52.

McFarland, David. 1982. *The Oxford Companion to Animal Behavior.* New York: Oxford University Press.

McNicol, D. 1972. *A Primer on Signal Detection Theory.* London: Allen and Unwin.

Machina, Mark. 1982. "Expected Utility Analysis Without the Independence Axiom." *Econometrica* 50:277–323.

Mackworth, J. F. 1964. "The Effect of Intermittent Signal Probability Upon Vigilance." *Canadian Journal of Psychology* 17:82–89.

———. 1968. "Vigilance Arousal and Habituation." *Psychology Review* 75:308–22.

———. 1970. *Vigilance and Attention.* Harmondsworth: Penguin Books.

Mandler, G. 1975. "Consciousness: Respectable, Useful and Probably Necessary." In *Information Processing and Cognition: The Loyola Symposium,* ed. R. Solso. Hillsdale, N.J.: Erlbaum.

Mansfield, Edwin. 1961. "Technical Change and the Rate of Imitation." *Econometrica* 29:741–66.

March, James G. 1978. "Bounded Rationality, Ambiguity, and the Engineering of Choice." *Bell Journal of Economics* 9:587–608.

Markowitz, H. 1952. "Portfolio Selection." *Journal of Finance* 7:77–91.

Maynard Smith, John. 1964. "Group Selection and Kin Selection." *Nature* 201:1145–7.

Maynard Smith, John, ed. 1982. *Evolution Now: A Century After Darwin.* San Francisco: W. H. Freeman.

Mayr, Ernst, and W. Provine. 1980. *The Evolutionary Synthesis: Perspectives on the Unification of Biology.* Cambridge: Harvard University Press.

Miller, James G. 1978. *Living Systems.* New York: McGraw-Hill.

Miller, G. A., E. Galanter, and K. H. Pribram. 1960. *Plans and Structures of Behavior.* New York: Holt, Rinehart, and Winston.

Milosević, S. 1974. "Effect of Time and Space Uncertainty on a Vigilance Task." *Perception & Psychophysics* 15:331–4.

Monod, Jacques. 1972. *Chance and Necessity.* New York: Random House (Vintage Books).

Montague, W. E., C. E. Webber and J. A. Adams. 1965. "The Effects of Signal and Response Complexity on 18 Hours of Visual Monitoring." *Human Factors* 7:163–72.

Moray, N., and T. O'Brien. 1967. "Signal Detection Theory Applied to Selective Listening." *Journal of the Acoustical Society of America* 42:765–72.

Navon, D. 1977. "Forest Before Trees: The Precedence of Global Features in Visual Perception." *Cognitive Psychology* 9:353–83.

Neisser, U. 1976. *Cognition and Reality: Principles and Implications of Cognitive Psychology.* San Francisco: W. H. Freeman and Company.

Nevin, J. A. 1969. "Signal-Detection Theory and Operant Behavior. A Review of David A. Green and John A. Swets' *Signal-Detection Theory and Psychophysics.*" *Journal of the Experimental Analysis of Behavior* 12:475–80.

———. 1982. "Psychophysics and Reinforcement Schedules: An Integration." In *Quantitative Analysis of Behavior: Discriminative Properties of Reinforcement Schedules,* ed. M. L. Commons and J. A. Nevin. Vol. 1. Cambridge: Harper and Row (Ballinger).

Newell, A., and Herbert Simon. 1972. *Human Problem Solving.* Englewood Cliffs, N.J.: Prentice-Hall.

Nisbett, R. E., and T. D. Wilson. 1977. "Telling More Than We Can Know: Verbal Reports on Mental Processes." *Psychological Review* 84(3):231–59.

Palmer, S. E. 1975. "Visual Perception and World Knowledge: Notes on a Model of Sensory-Cognitive Interaction. In *Explorations in Cognition*, ed. D. A. Norman and D. E. Rumelhart. San Francisco: Freeman.

Parasuraman, Raja, and D. Roy Davies. 1976. "Decision Theory Analysis of Response Latencies in Vigilance." *Journal of Experimental Psychology: Human Perception and Performance* 2:578–90.

Piaget, J. 1952. *The Origins of Intelligence*. New York: International Universities Press.

Pianka, Eric R. 1978. *Evolutionary Ecology*. 2d ed. New York: Harper & Row.

Pilbean, D. 1972. *The Ascent of Man: An Introduction to Human Evolution*. New York: Macmillan.

Polanyi, Michael. 1962. *Personal Knowledge: Towards a Post-Critical Philosophy*. New York: Harper and Row.

1967. *The Tacit Dimension*. London: Routledge and Kegan Paul.

1969. "The Republic of Science: Its Political and Economic Theory." In *Knowing and Being*, ed. Marjorie Grene. Chicago: University of Chicago Press.

Prague, John W., Dan J. Laughhunn and Roy Crum. 1980. "Translation of Gambles and Aspiration Level Effects in Risky Choice." *Management Science* 26:1039–60.

Premack, David. 1983. *The Mind of an Ape*. New York: Norton.

Rothschild, M. 1973. "Models of Market Organization with Imperfect Information: A Survey." *Journal of Political Economy* 81(6):1283–1308.

1974. "Searching for the Lowest Price when the Distribution of Prices is Unknown." *Journal of Political Economy* 82:689–711.

Rothschild, M., and J. E. Stiglitz. 1976. "Equilibrium in Competitive Insurance Markets: An Essay on the Economics of Imperfect Information." *Quarterly Journal of Economics* 90(4):629–49.

Rozin, P. 1976. "The Evolution of Intelligence and Access to the Cognitive Unconscious." In *Progress in Psychobiology and Physiological Psychology*, ed. J. A. Spague and A. N. Epstein. Vol. 6. New York: Academic Press.

Sargent, Thomas J. 1976a. "A Classical Macroeconomic Model for the United States." *Journal of Political Economy* 84(2):207–37.

1976b. "Rational Expectations and the Theory of Economic Policy." *Journal of Monetary Economics* 2:169–83.

1977. "The Demand for Money During Hyperinflation Under Rational Expectations: I." *International Economic Review* 18:59–82.

1979. *Macroeconomic Theory*. New York: Academic Press.

Sargent, Thomas J., and Neil Wallace. 1975. " 'Rational' Expectations, the Optimal Monetary Instrument, and the Optimal Money Supply Rule." *Journal of Political Economy* 83:241–54.

1973. "Rational Expectations and the Dynamics of Hyperinflation." *International Economic Review* 14(2):328–50.

Sartre, J.-P. 1953. *Being and Nothingness*, trans. H. E. Barnes. New York: Washington Square Press. (Originally published as *L'Etre et le Néant* in 1943.)

Schotter, Andrew. 1981. *The Economic Theory of Social Institutions*. New York: Cambridge University Press.

Schulman, A. I. and G. Z. Greenberg. 1970. "Operating Characteristics and Apriori Probability of the Signal." *Perception and Psychophysics* 8:317–20.

Shackle, G. L. S. 1969. *Decision, Order, and Time in Human Affairs*. 2d ed. Cambridge: Cambridge University Press.

1972. *Epistemics and Economics: A Critique of Economic Doctrines*. Cambridge: Cambridge University Press.

Siegman, A. W. 1978. "The Tell-Tale Voice: Nonverbal Messages of Verbal Communication." In *Nonverbal Behavior and Communication*, ed. A. W. Siegman and S. Feldstein. Hillsdale, N.J.: Erlbaum.

Simon, Herbert. 1955. "A Behavioral Theory of Rational Choice." *Quarterly Journal of Economics* 69:99–118.

1959. *Administrative Behavior: A Study of Decision-Making Processes in Administrative Organization*. 2d ed. New York: Macmillan.

1969. *The Sciences of the Artificial*. Cambridge: MIT Press.

1979a. *Models of Thought*. New Haven: Yale University Press.

1979b. "Rational Decision Making in Business Organizations." *American Economic Review* 69:493–513.

Slovic, Paul, and Amos Tversky. 1974. "Who Accepts Savage's Axiom?" *Behavioral Science* 19:368–73.

Slovic, Paul, and Sarah Lichtenstein. 1983. "Preference Reversals: A Broader Perspective." *American Economic Review* 73:596–605.

Solomon, R. C. 1977. *The Passions: The Myth and Nature of Human Emotion*. Garden City, N.Y.: Anchor Press.

Stigler, George J. 1961. "The Economics of Information." *Journal of Political Economy* 69:213–25.

1966. *The Theory of Price*. 3d ed. New York: Macmillan.

Stiglitz, J. E. 1969. "Behavior Towards Risk with Many Commodities." *Econometrica* 37(4):660–67.

Swets, J. A. 1964. *Signal Detection and Recognition by Human Observers*. New York: Wiley.

1977. "Signal Detection Theory Applied to Vigilance." In *Vigilance: Theory, Operational Performance, and Physiological Correlates*, ed. R. R. Mackie. New York: Plenum.

Tanner, T. A., R. W. Haller, and R. C. Atkinson. 1967. "Signal Recognition as Influenced by Presentation Schedules." *Perception and Psychophysics* 2:349–58.

Tanner, T. A., J. A. Rauk, and R. C. Atkinson. 1970. "Signal Recognition as Influenced by Information Feedback." *Journal of Mathematical Psychology* 7:259–74.

Taub, H. A., and F. H. Osborne. 1968. "Effects of Signal and Stimulus Rates on Vigilance Performance." *Journal of Applied Psychology* 52:133–38.

Tinbergen, Niko. 1951. *The Study of Instinct*. London: Oxford University Press.

Tobin, James. 1958. "Liquidity Preference as Behavior Toward Risk." *Review of Economic Studies* 25:65–86.

Townsend, J. T. 1974. "Issues and Models Concerning the Processing of a Finite Number of Inputs." In *Human Information Processing: Tutorials in Performance and Cognition*, ed. G. H. Kantowitz. Hillsdale, N.J.: Erlbaum.

Treisman, A. M., and G. Geffen. 1967. "Selective Attention: Perception or Response?" *Quarterly Journal of Experimental Psychology* 19:1–17.

Trivers, Robert L. 1971. "The Evolution of Reciprocal Altruism." *Quarterly Review of Biology* 46:35–58.

Ullmann-Margalit, Edna. 1978. *The Emergence of Norms*. New York: Oxford University Press.

Vickers, D., J. Leary, and P. Barnes. 1977. "Adaptation to Decreasing Signal Probability." In *Vigilance: Theory, Operational Performance, and Physiological Correlates*, ed. R. R. Mackie, New York: Plenum.

von Neumann, John and Oskar Morgenstern. 1944. *Theory of Games and Economic Behavior*. Princeton: Princeton University Press.

Ware, J. R., R. A. Baker, and E. Druckner. 1964. "Sustained Vigilance II. Signal Detection for Two-Man Teams During a 24-Hour Watch." *Journal of Engineering Psychology* 3:104–10.

Watson, James D. 1976. *Molecular Biology of the Gene.* 3d ed. Menlo Park, Calif.: W. A. Benjamin.

Weber, R. 1982. "The Allais Paradox, Dutch Auctions, and Alpha-Utility Theory." Evanston, Ill.: Northwestern University.

Wicksell, Knut. 1938. *Lectures on Political Economy.* New York: Macmillan.

Wicksteed, Philip. 1933. *The Common Sense of Political Economy.* Vol 2. London: Routledge and Sons.

Williamson, Oliver E. 1979. "Transactions-Cost Economics: The Governance of Contractual Relations." *Journal of Law and Economics* 22:233–61.

Zellner, Arnold. 1979. "Posterior Odds Ratios for Regression Hypotheses: General Considerations and Some Specific Results." Graduate School of Business, University of Chicago, Invited paper at the December 1979 Meeting of the Econometric Society.

CHAPTER 5

The evolution of rules

ANDREW SCHOTTER

5.1   Introduction

There are basically two views of institutions. In the first, which I shall call the rules view, social or economic institutions are seen as sets of rules that constrain individual behavior and define the social outcomes that result from individual action. This view is most closely associated with the work of scholars belonging to what I shall call the design and implementation school of social institutions. The focus of attention here is on the possibility of designing sets of rules or game-forms (to use Gibbard's terminology) that, when imposed on a set of social agents, leads to prespecified equilibrium outcomes. Investigators in this school typically ask questions of the following sort.

1. Does an allocating mechanism (a set of rules) exist that gives selfish individuals an incentive to report their true willingness to pay for a public good? (See for example Groves and Loeb 1975; Clarke 1971; Tideman and Tullock 1976.)
2. Do strategy-proof voting or allocating mechanisms exist? (Gibbard 1973; Satterthwaite 1975; Moulin 1980; Dasgupta, Hammond, and Maskin 1979.)
3. What set of rules forms an optimal constitution for agents to use in making public choices or conducting macroeconomic fiscal (tax) policy? (Buchanan and Tullock 1962; Brennan and Buchanan 1981.)
4. Do allocating mechanisms exist that define games whose equilibria (be they Nash, Bayesian Nash, or dominant strategy) define outcomes in (or identical to) the choice set that would be defined in a perfect-information world where all technologies are known and a social-choice function has been agreed upon? (Hurwicz 1979; Schmiedler 1980; Maskin 1978.)

Throughout this literature, social institutions are planned and designed mechanisms given exogenously to or imposed upon a society of agents. Institutional change is a process of social engineering that takes place through the manipulation of the rules.

The other view of social institutions, which I shall call the behavioral view, is represented by Menger (1963 [1883]), Hayek (1973), Schotter (1981), and Williamson (1975), among others, all of whom look at social institutions not as sets of predesigned rules, but rather as unplanned and unintended regularities of social behavior (social conventions) that emerge "organically" (to use Menger's term). Institutions are outcomes of human action that no single individual intended to occur. The behavioral approach retains the concept of equilibrium, at least in the work of Schotter and Williamson. What changes is the view of how these social institutions are created – they emerge or evolve spontaneously from individual maximizing or satisficing behavior instead of being designed by a social planner. The object of analysis is not the rules of social conduct but rather the conventions of social behavior that evolve as social agents repeatedly face the same types of social problems. The rules are not as important as the behavioral regularities that players establish given the rules.

This chapter investigates the endogenous or organic creation of equilibrium sets of rules (or social institutions viewed as sets of rules). In that sense it incorporates elements of both the rules view and the behavioral view. On the one hand, it is interested in the rules of social conduct rather than the endogenous conventions of social behavior that are created given these rules. To that extent its concerns are similar to those of the rules view. On the other hand, the chapter addresses evolutionary questions in the spirit of the behavioral view. How did the rules of conduct with which we run our social and economic lives (the rules of the game) come into being or emerge as the unintended product of individual action? What types of rules could emerge as equilibrium sets of rules for society to adhere to?

I will proceed as follows. In Section 5.2 I will present an analysis of the process of equilibrium rule-selection. This involves asking which set of rules – which subset of the physically feasible set of rules – a group of rational agents will select and adhere to if they repeatedly face the same types of problems. The rules, once emerged, will constrain the behavior of our agents throughout the lifetime of their social interaction. Section 5.2 presents a static analysis of this question; in Section 5.3, I outline what a dynamic view of the process might look like and present three simple propositions. Finally, in Section 5.4, I offer some concluding remarks.

5.2   A theory of rules and rule-selection

5.2.1   Organic or endogenous rule-creation

Social institutions – understood as sets of abstract rules that constrain the behavior of economic agents and define for them payoffs that depend on their behavior – emerge in a variety of ways. Some, like the International Monetary Fund, the United Nations, the Federal Reserve Bank of the United States, the system of statute law, and others are designed and created *ex nihilo* by a social planner or board of planners. Others, like conventions of war, the terms of implicit contracts, the legal concept of common or customary business practices, emerge in an unintended manner without any conscious will directed toward their creations. They emerge, as Hayek says, by human action but not by human design. If one takes a look at the second type of social institution, however, one sees that for a given social situation the set of rules that evolves to govern the actions of the agents engaged in that situation almost always involves only a subset of the feasible set of strategies available to the agents. In other words, the set of rules we create and adhere to involves a tacit agreement to limit our actions or strategies and not avail ourselves of all possible strategies. The rules brand some strategies as illegal or taboo. The question we ask in this section is: How do these tacit constraints on our behavior emerge and become recognized as *the* legitimate set of rules for our conduct?

Consider the creation of rules of war. Say that two countries (or many countries) are likely to engage in wars repeatedly over their (possibly infinite) lifetimes. Further, assume that they have at their disposal a war technology that will allow them to fight these wars using nuclear arms, chemical warfare, conventional arms, and so on. Now, despite this breadth of available capabilities, wars are often fought with each side availing itself of only a subset of these strategies. Rules of war are established (although not necessarily codified and agreed to formally) that govern how wars will be fought; and these rules are adhered to over time. They are equilibrium sets of rules from which no side wishes to deviate.

Our task here is to present a theory that will identify which set or subset of rules will form this kind of stable rules-set for the agents.[1]

---

[1] There is an obvious parallel between this situation and that of two duopolists who compete with each other repeatedly over time. If they can compete using price, quality, advertising, etc. as strategies, we can ask about the equilibrium set of rules for the market and about how the firms will compete.

120   **Andrew Schotter**

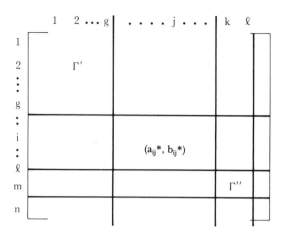

Figure 5.1. The primitive game.

Consider, then, a game that is to be played repeatedly by a set of agents *I*. As I've already suggested, this game might be thought of as a war to be fought over and over by two countries – or any similar situation of social interaction among two or more players. Let us say that the finite set of physically feasible or technologically possible strategies for player *i* is $S_i, i = 1, \ldots ,n$, with $S_i = S_j$ for all $i, j \in I$. Finally, let *P* be the payoff function defining a payoff for each player as a function of the strategy choice made by every player. With *I* as the set of players, *S* as the set formed from the product from 1 to *n* of all the S_i, and *P* as the payoff function, we can define a game in normal form:

$$\Gamma = (I, S, P).$$

Γ is a game that is to be played repeatedly over an infinite horizon. We can assume that each player wants to maximize his mean payoff over his lifetime[2] (which we assume to exist) or

$$\Pi_i = \lim_{T \to \infty} \left[\frac{1}{T} \sum_{t=1}^{T} P_{it} \left(s_{it}, s_{jt} \right) \right] \qquad i = 1, \ldots ,n,$$

where s_{it} is player *i*'s strategy choice in period *t* and P_{it} is *i*'s payoff in period *t*. We will call Γ the *primitive game*, since, as we will see, it will contain the largest possible set of strategies available to the player. Γ is depicted in Figure 5.1. We will call ψ the game defined when Γ is

---

[2] We could introduce discounting. But since the flavor of the analysis would not be changed by its introduction and it would complicate our discussion, I have chosen the undiscounted case.

repeated infinitely many times and Π_i, $i = 1, \ldots, n$, is used to evaluate the outcomes for the agents.

5.2.2   Mode structures

Many times, when people interact repeatedly with one another in a gamelike situation (be it two duopolists competing, two countries fighting wars, or a worker and an employer in an employment relationship), they establish recognizable modes of behavior each of which is consistent for a given player with a particular set of actions by the other players.

For instance, firms in an industry can recognize when their competitors are engaging in cutthroat competition and when they are basically behaving collusively or in a live-and-let-live manner. In these circumstances, certain actions are viewed as consistent with particular modes of behavior, whereas others are not. Hence, in oligopolistic industries, a sudden increase in the advertising of one firm may be viewed as disrupting a comfortable mode of behavior for the industry, and retaliation and price wars may result.

In this section, we are interested in discovering which mode or modes of behavior will emerge as the equilibrium mode in situations in which the same set of agents repeatedly interact with each other. To investigate this question, consider the primitive game depicted in Figure 5.1. From this game a series of subgames can be defined by simply eliminating certain pure strategies from the primitive game. For instance, in Figure 5.1 we see that subgame Γ' can be defined if the players limit their strategy sets to include only the first g pure strategies, and game Γ'' can be defined if player 1 limits his or her strategy set to pure strategies ℓ and m and player 2 limits his or her strategy set to k and ℓ. Each of these subgames corresponds to a different mode of behavior in which the players constrain themselves to using only a subset of the strategy set available to them. Now, players may be able to distinguish certain modes of behavior on the part of their opponents but may be incapable of distinguishing others. For instance, if $\mathcal{P}$ is the set of all subgames that could be formed from Γ, then we can define $G \subset \mathcal{P}$ as the game-set – the set of subgames or modes of behavior that the players can distinguish.

As an example, consider the two-person prisoners' dilemma game depicted in Figure 5.2. (We will always use the convention of making player 1 the row chooser and player 2 the column chooser.) In this game, we can easily identify certain modes of behavior. These are shown in Figure 5.3. First, we can identify a competitive mode in which players do not restrict themselves but play the entire primitive game. We can also pick out a cooperative mode, in which each player limits

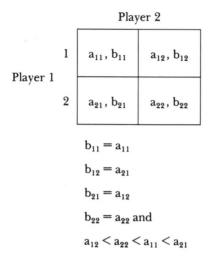

Player 2

$b_{11} = a_{11}$

$b_{12} = a_{21}$

$b_{21} = a_{12}$

$b_{22} = a_{22}$ and

$a_{12} < a_{22} < a_{11} < a_{21}$

Figure 5.2. A two-person prisoners' dilemma game.

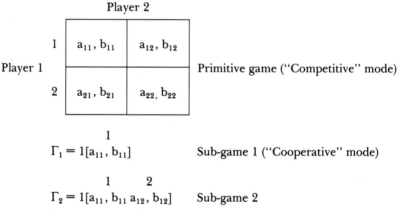

Player 2

Primitive game ("Competitive" mode)

$\Gamma_1 = 1[a_{11}, b_{11}]$ Sub-game 1 ("Cooperative" mode)

$\Gamma_2 = 1[a_{11}, b_{11} \; a_{12}, b_{12}]$ Sub-game 2

Figure 5.3. A mode structure.

himself to playing only strategy 1. Together, these two modes might constitute one *mode structure*. If in addition we included subgame Γ_2 (although this one is hard to explain without attributing altruistic behavior to player 1), the mode structure would be finer than the two-game structure because its game-set includes the other game-set as a proper subset.

Basically, the role of the mode structure is to help the players characterize one another's actions as belonging to a recognizable mode of behavior. For instance, in the prisoners' dilemma game just discussed, cooperative behavior was associated with game Γ_1 whereas "competitive" behavior was associated with the primitive game. If either player ever introduces strategy 2 into the game, he or she breaks the cooperative mode and, in this case, competitive behavior follows – that is, all players abandon all restrictions on their behavior. The mode structure, then, is a mapping that associates each mode of behavior with a subgame of Γ; and the set of subgames thus defined is called the game-set G. This game-set is assumed to be common knowledge (in the sense of Aumann 1976) among the players in the game. To begin our analysis, let us assume that the primitive game Γ is always contained in G (that is, it is always recognizable – possibly as a competitive or cutthroat mode of behavior) and that its Nash equilibrium (assumed unique) is not Pareto optimal. Now, we know from Nash (1950) that each subgame Γ_ℓ in G has at least one Nash equilibrium. Call it n_ℓ, and assume for the moment that it is unique. Also, denote the associated payoff vector as

$$P_\ell = (P_1(n_\ell), \ \ldots \ ,P_n(n_\ell)).$$

Denote the set of Nash equilibria associated with all games in G by N_G and the set of payoffs by Π. In many cases it may turn out that there exist Nash equilibria in N_G whose payoffs are Pareto superior to the Nash-equilibrium payoff associated with the primitive game. If this is so, then the game-theoretical problem is to determine which mode of behavior will form the dominant mode or, more specifically, which subgame in G will be tacitly agreed upon as the dominant game to be played repeatedly. We will call this game the *steady-state game*, since, once agreed to, it will be played indefinitely and will be policed by a simple supergame equilibrium strategy.

It is the rules of this steady-state game that will dictate how social intercourse will be carried out in the strategic situation under investigation. Hence, if one defines a social institution as nothing more than an abstract set of rules, our analysis aims to explain the type of social institution, or the set of possible social institutions, that could evolve to help govern behavior in repeated situations of this type.

5.2.3 The static solution

It may seem odd to specify a static solution-concept for what seems to be an obviously dynamic game. This is easily explained, however, by remembering that the game-theoretical problem our players face is the selection of one subgame of G as the steady-state game and that our aim is to determine which subgame or set of subgames could emerge (from

$$\Gamma_1 = 1\,[5,5]$$

$$\Gamma_2 = \begin{array}{c|cc} & 1 & 2 \\ \hline 1 & 5,5 & 1,7 \\ 2 & 7,1 & 3,6 \end{array}$$

$$\Gamma_3 = \begin{array}{c|ccc} & 1 & 2 & 3 \\ \hline 1 & 5,5 & 1,7 & 1,1 \\ 2 & 7,1 & 3,6 & 2,2 \\ 3 & 4,0 & 4,4 & 4,1 \end{array}$$

$$\Gamma = \begin{array}{c|cccc} & 1 & 2 & 3 & 4 \\ \hline 1 & 5,5 & 1,7 & 1,1 & 1,13 \\ 2 & 7,1 & 3,6 & 2,2 & 0,12 \\ 3 & 4,0 & 4,4 & 4,1 & 1,4 \\ 4 & 3,4 & 2,5 & 1,3 & 0,8 \\ 5 & 19,0 & 1.8,1 & 16,0 & 2,2.5 \end{array}$$

Figure 5.4. The game-set G.

some unspecified dynamic process) as a stable social institution. There-fore, in the static phase of our theory, we will be interested in the set of subgames that will be stable in some sense or constitute a solution. We will not worry about the process that leads us there.

To proceed, let us specify an example. Consider the primitive game Γ in Figure 5.4, a two-person variable-sum game that is to be repeated infinitely. Along with subgames Γ_1, Γ_2, and Γ_3, this game displays a mode structure that identifies the game-set G (as depicted in Figure 5.4). What this game-set implies is that the rules of conduct existing between these two players are such that there are only four identifiable modes of behavior – one game per mode. There is no common mode of behavior that identifies a game such as:

$$\Gamma_4 = \begin{array}{c|ccc} & 1 & 2 & 3 \\ \hline 1 & 5,5 & 1,7 & 1,1 \\ 2 & 7,1 & 3,6 & 2,2 \\ 3 & 4,0 & 4,4 & 4,1 \\ 4 & 3,4 & 2,5 & 1,3 \end{array}.$$

This implies that if player 1 ever introduces the use of strategy 4, the game would immediately become Γ, the primitive game, and not Γ_4. This is so because the mode structure is simply not fine enough to allow players to distinguish between Γ and Γ_4. Hence, when a player intro-duces the use of strategy 4, the other player has no idea whether player 1 plans to limit himself or herself to the first four strategies or actually intends to play Γ.

The various modes of behavior might have names associated with them. For instance, game Γ_2 may be associated with what the players call a cooperative mode of behavior, and Γ_3 may have some other name.

The primitive game will always be associated with competitive behavior because it puts no restrictions on the strategies used – an all-out war with no holds barred would be an example.

Now, with a nondegenerate mode structure and the game-set G, the relevant question is: which game – Γ_1, Γ_2, or Γ_3 – in G will be agreed upon as the steady-state mode of behavior? In other words, which subset of games in G will contain the steady-state game?

To answer this question, we need some definitions. Let Γ_j be a subgame of Γ in G (that is to say, a recognizable subgame), and let P_j^* be the set of payoffs associated with the (possibly many) Nash equilibria of Γ_j. Likewise, let Γ_k be another subgame of Γ in G, and let P_k^* be the set of Nash equilibria for Γ_k. We say that Γ_j dominates Γ_k if

1. both Γ_k and Γ_j are in G and
2. there exists a payoff vector $\beta_j^* \in P_j^*$ such that, for every payoff vector $\alpha_k^* \in P_k^*$, $\beta_j^* > \alpha_k^*$ (where $>$ indicates a strict vector inequality).

Notice that both Γ_k and Γ_j must be in G in order for the domination relation to be defined. Subgames not in G are not recognizable by the players and therefore cannot be compared. Consequently, the domination relationship is not a complete ordering over all subgames in $\mathscr{P}$.

Put briefly, this definition says that game Γ_j dominates game Γ_k if there exists one payoff β_j^* associated with a Nash equilibrium in Γ_j that is better, player for player, than all the payoffs associated with Nash equilibria in Γ_k.

With these concepts in hand, we can now locate the set of subgames in G such that any game in this set could emerge as the steady-state game or steady-state set of rules for our society. This set will be called the solution set and can be defined as follows:

Definition 1: The Solution Set. A set of subgames Σ in G is a solution set or a set of potential stable steady-state games for the social situation represented by the repeated play of the primitive game Γ if

1. no game $\Gamma_j \in \Sigma$ dominates any other game $\Gamma_i \in \Sigma$;
2. for any game $\Gamma_\ell \in G$ there exists a $\Gamma_k \in G$ that dominates it; and
3. all Nash equilibria of games in Σ are Pareto superior to the Nash equilibrium (assumed unique) of Γ, the primitive game.

Notice what this says. If the players are rational, they would be willing to constrain their strategy sets only as long as such a constriction of their freedom improves their expected payoff. If the primitive game is always available to them, however, they will agree to restrain themselves only if the equilibrium payoff they receive is superior to the Nash-equilibrium payoff associated with Γ. This is condition 3, and it corresponds to an assumption of individual rationality. Condition 1 is basically an internal-stability condition, since it says that rational players will never agree to a steady-state game in Σ if there exists another game in Σ that is better for all of them. Analogously, condition 2 is an external-stability notion, since it says that rational players will not agree to limit their strategy choices to games in Σ if there exists a game outside Σ, but still in G, that is better for all of them. The solution set Σ therefore consists of all games whose Nash equilibria constitute a set of individually rational outcomes that are both internally and externally stable.[3] Each game in Σ is then a candidate steady-state game for our society and represents an alternative standard of behavior for our players to adhere to. Which game in Σ actually is singled out as *the* steady-state game cannot be determined given this static analysis. All we can say is that, whatever that game is, it must be in Σ if our players are rational.

In view of the emphasis elsewhere in this volume on the importance of process modeling, the static solution concept I've just outlined may seem somewhat out of place. Let me try to anticipate some possible criticisms from that direction and offer preemptive rebuttals.

First, one might claim that the type of steady-state game that emerges from my analysis is not unplanned or unintended at all but is rather a coordinated bargaining solution agreed upon explicitly by the agents in the model. This objection, though important, is not totally valid. As I already suggested, the solution concept I have offered is a totally static one. Questions about how a steady-state set of rules emerges are obviously dynamic, and I have left them unmodeled. But the point I'm trying to make is that, if our agents are rational, there are only certain types of steady-state games that, if unintentionally stumbled upon, could be stable. These games, I claim, must be in Σ. Even though social institutions emerge unintentionally, they emerge unintentionally through the actions of rational agents. The question of where this process comes to rest can then be separated from the process that brings it there – and this is what I have attempted to do.

This raises another – and possibly more disturbing – question: Why does the process come to a rest at all? Why does one steady-state game emerge? The answer here, I believe, is empirical and not theoretical. It is my claim that, in situations isomorphic to the repeated game situation that has motivated this discussion, social agents do establish conventional sets of rules for themselves. I have already alluded to rules of war;

---

[3] Game theorists will notice a distinct similarity between the definition of Σ and the von Neumann-Morgenstern solution of a cooperative game. This similarity is no coincidence.

$$\Gamma = \begin{array}{c} \\ 1 \\ 2 \\ 3 \\ 4 \\ 5 \end{array} \begin{array}{|ccc|} 1 & 2 & 3 \\ 8,8 & 7,3 & 4,1 \\ 7,7 & 9,9 & 1,1 \\ 2,6 & 10,10 & 3,2 \\ 9,7 & 14,6 & 4,1 \\ 5,1 & 14,2 & 6,6 \end{array} \quad \text{(Primitive game)}$$

$$\Gamma_1 = \begin{array}{c} 1 \\ 1[8,8] \end{array}$$

$$\Gamma_2 = \begin{array}{c} \\ 1 \\ 2 \end{array} \begin{array}{|cc|} 1 & 2 \\ 8,8 & 7,3 \\ 7,7 & 9,9 \end{array}$$

Figure 5.5. A non-Pareto optimal solution.

but there are other examples as well. Oligopolistic industries have been known to create and adhere to standards of conduct. Baumol (1959) has pointed out that industries sometimes establish a live-and-let-live attitude according to which it becomes bad form to cut prices. For example, the medical profession established bans on advertising long before the American Medical Association (and legislation) formalized them; and doctors adhered to the bans voluntarily (fearing reprisals if they violated them, of course). Finally, one can look at detente between the United States and the Soviet Union as a strategy-restricted steady-state game, the rules of which were violated (at least from the American point of view) by the Soviet invasion of Afghanistan. This list is long, but the point is clear. Social agents are capable of establishing and do establish steady-state games for themselves to play. Many times the process does come to a rest.

The most disturbing criticism that could be made about my analysis, however, might be along the following lines. Even if the equilibrium property *were* granted, why would the resulting steady-state game have to have the Pareto-properties I attribute to it? In other words, how functionalist is this analysis? Here I will accept some blame – but not enough to plead guilty. First, it is true that the solution concept I have offered is laden with talk of Pareto-optimality and thus of efficiency in that sense. Hence, to that extent what emerges seems to be what is efficient. But this is not to say that a Pareto-optimal payoff must result from this analysis. Whether it does depends on how fine the mode structure is, that is, how sophisticated the players are in interpreting the actions of others. Consider the example in Figure 5.5. The Pareto-optimal points are (10,10), (14,6), and (14,2); yet the solution set contains only the point (9.9). Hence, the rules that societies develop need not be Pareto optimal – even though they do in this case define an outcome Pareto superior to the outcomes defined in the world in which the primitive game forms the steady-state game.

Consequently, the fineness of the mode structure, along with the sophistication of the apparatus that allows players to distinguish among their opponents' strategy-choices, will greatly influence the extent to which the final outcome is Pareto optimal. The mode structure, then, is basically an information device that allows players to interpret the actions of their opponents. The finer this structure – the more powerful this information device – the more likely are the players to achieve a Pareto-optimal outcome. In most real-world settings, however, all that we can typically be sure of is that any rules that do emerge will produce outcomes Pareto superior to the outcomes that would have resulted from repeated play of the entire primitive game. (If this were not the case, the rules would not have emerged, since both players would have had an incentive to introduce strategies from the larger primitive game.)

The next question is: How will the resulting steady-state game chosen from Σ be policed or enforced? Obviously, there will be incentives to break the mode of behavior. The answer is that there is one simple form of enforcement arising out of a policing supergame noncooperative equilibrium strategy. It works as follows.

Assume for simplicity that the Nash equilibrium of the primitive game isn't Pareto optimal and that there is a game in the solution set Pareto superior to it. Let Γ_ℓ be one such game and let $n_\ell = (n_{1\ell}, \ldots, n_{n\ell})$ be a Nash-equilibrium strategy n-tuple for Γ_ℓ (and assume it's unique). Finally, let $n = (n_{1\Gamma}, \ldots, n_{n\Gamma})$ be a Nash-equilibrium strategy n-tuple for Γ. An enforcing strategy for a game $\Gamma_\ell \in \Sigma$ is a strategy σ_{it}, $i = 1, \ldots, n$, $t = 1, \ldots$ of the following type:

$$\sigma_{it} = \begin{cases} s_{i1} = n_{i\ell} \\ s_{it} = n_{i\ell} \text{ if } s_{j\tau} = n_{j\ell\tau} \text{ for all } j \neq 1 \text{ and } \tau = 1, \ldots, \tau - 1 \\ s_{it} = n_{i\Gamma} \text{ otherwise,} \end{cases}$$

where s_{it} indicates the strategy-choice that player i makes in period t.

This means that each player will continue to play his or her Nash-equilibrium strategy for the game Γ_ℓ as long as the others do; but as soon as someone defects, all players will play the Nash-equilibrium strategy for the primitive game from then on. This is a supergame Nash equilibrium, with the subgame Γ_ℓ forming the steady-state game.

This is, of course, an extreme policing strategy. It involves all the players; and all must suffer if one defects. (It also assumes that the players can detect one such defection.) Other, less drastic, policing policies can be defined; but we need not complicate our analysis by discussing them here. The point remains that, once social agents violate the established steady-state rules of conduct, they risk the possibility of throwing society into the harsh world represented by the repeated play of the primitive game. Since this is worse for all of them, the threat of having to live in a world where people place no restrictions on their behavior polices the current steady-state game. In situations of war, countries many times refrain from, say, germ warfare simply because they know that today's war is not the last they will ever fight – and that it may even be better to lose this war than to win if winning means having to fight future wars with distasteful weapons.

5.3   Toward a dynamic solution

If one tried to specify a dynamic process that would describe how these steady-state games actually emerged, he or she would have a difficult time. However, I will outline in this section one possible *scenario* upon which we could build such a dynamic process. (I emphasize the word scenario to make clear that this is by no means a theory.)

Consider a game-set G, which, as we know, must include the primitive game Γ. Since we can't assume that any convention of behavior exists on the first play of the game, let's assume that the primitive game is played at time 0. For convenience, we will also assume that each subgame in G has a unique Nash equilibrium in pure strategies. (Nonuniqueness or mixed-strategy equilibria would complicate the analysis considerably and deflect us from our main point here.)

Now, if there exists a subgame Γ_k in G in which the payoffs are Pareto superior to the payoffs defined by the Nash equilibrium of the primitive game, we can expect some player to signal his or her willingness to play that game by choosing its Nash-equilibrium strategy (that is to say, by restraining his or her choices in Γ). Since the game-set is common knowledge and the players assumed rational, this signal is unambiguous proof of intention – the player signaling is doing so at a cost to himself or herself. Moreover, the subgame's Nash equilibrium is Pareto superior to the Nash equilibrium of the primitive game. Hence, we can expect the other players eventually to follow our player's lead (after possibly exploiting and being punished by that player for a while). Once this new game Γ_k is established, however, it may not endure. For instance, let's say that there exists another game Γ_ℓ that fulfills two conditions: (1) that either $\Gamma_\ell \supset \Gamma_k$ (i.e., the strategy-set of Γ_ℓ contains the strategy-set of Γ_k) or neither $\Gamma_\ell \supset \Gamma_k$ nor $\Gamma_k \supset \Gamma_\ell$; and (2) that the Nash equilibrium of Γ_ℓ is better for at least one player than the Nash equilibrium of Γ_k. If such a game exists, we can expect the players who would benefit to signal their intention to play Γ_ℓ by choosing their components in its Nash equilibrium. If this behavior persists, we can expect the remaining players to choose their best response in Γ_ℓ and to bring about its Nash equilibrium. Now we are at Γ_ℓ. Again, two things can change this. Either there exists a subgame of $\Gamma_n \subset \Gamma_\ell$ that is in G and whose Nash equilibrium is Pareto superior to Γ_ℓ; or there exists a game Γ_n for which either $\Gamma_n \supset \Gamma_\ell$ or neither $\Gamma_n \supset \Gamma_\ell$ nor $\Gamma_\ell \subset \Gamma_n$ and for which the Nash equilibrium of Γ_n is better for at least one player. These benefited players will then signal their intention to play Γ_n; and if they persist, the society will move to Γ_n. And the process continues.

Although much of this process is left unspecified, the intuition behind it is that if, at any time t, our players find themselves playing a subgame in G whose Nash equilibrium is Pareto superior to that of the game being played, then group rationality would dictate that the current game eventually be abandoned in favor of the subgame. On the other hand, if the current game does not contain such a subgame, but there exists another game in G whose Nash equilibrium is better than that of the current game for at least one player, then individual rationality would dictate a switch if the benefited players are persistent. (Remember, in a nondiscounted iterated game, any finite period is inconsequential to the players' mean payoffs; so players can be expected to be persistent.) These movements among games will furnish the basis of the domination relation we will soon define.

Before doing that, it is important to point out the asymmetric way we treat the domination of games by other games – asymmetric in respect of whether the dominated games are or are not strict subgames of the game under consideration. In order for a game Γ_ℓ to dominate a game Γ_k when $\Gamma_\ell \subset \Gamma_k$, it must be that the Nash equilibrium of Γ_ℓ is Pareto superior to the Nash equilibrium of Γ_k. This requirement is not imposed if $\Gamma_\ell \not\subset \Gamma_k$. The reason is simple. If players are already using strategies in Γ_k, the only reason they will stop using them is if doing so increases their payoff. Hence, when $\Gamma_\ell \subset \Gamma_k$, each player must benefit before all players will stop using strategies in Γ_k – otherwise they will persist with Γ_k. Therefore, we need the Pareto-superiority condition. When $\Gamma_\ell \not\subset \Gamma_k$, if there exist strategies in Γ_ℓ that improve any player's payoff, nothing prevents such a player from using one of those advantageous strategies. Hence, it does not make sense to impose the Pareto-superiority condition here; individual rationality is enough to allow Γ_ℓ to dominate Γ_k.

Where will the process stop? To discuss the resting point of the process, we must redefine the dominance relationship used in our static theory to take account of our discussion above. To do this we need the following definition.

Let Γ_ℓ and Γ_k be two subgames in G. We say that Γ_ℓ dominates Γ_k if

1. both Γ_k and $\Gamma_\ell \in G$ and either
2. $\Gamma_\ell \subset \Gamma_k$ and the payoffs associated with the Nash equilibrium of Γ_ℓ is Pareto superior to the Nash equilibrium of Γ_k; or
3. either $\Gamma_\ell \supset \Gamma_k$ or neither $\Gamma_\ell \supset \Gamma_k$ nor $\Gamma_k \subset \Gamma_\ell$ but there exists at least one player i and a Nash-equilibrium strategy in Γ_ℓ for i such that i's payoff at the Nash equilibrium of Γ_ℓ is better for i than his or her Nash-equilibrium payoff in Γ_k.

A solution set is then a set of subgames in G such that

1. no game in G dominates any other and
2. for every game not in G there exists a game in G that dominates it.

Although these definitions sound familiar, the dynamic theory has consequences different from those of the static theory outlined above. For instance, of the following propositions, the first is true only for the dynamic theory.

Proposition 1: If a set of games exists that is a solution, that set must contain only one subgame.

Proof: This follows from the definition of domination, since, for any two games, either part 2 or 3 of the definition must be true. Hence, we can never have internal stability.

Proposition 2: If the Nash equilibrium of Γ (the primitive game) is Pareto optimal, it is a solution.

Proof: According to domination, if we are to move from Γ to a subgame $\Gamma_\ell \subset \Gamma$, then Γ_ℓ can dominate Γ only if it has a Nash equilibrium that is Pareto superior to that of Γ. But this cannot be – by assumption. Hence, Γ is externally stable; and, by the domination argument, Γ dominates all other games. So it must be the unique solution.

Proposition 3: If a subgame $\Gamma_k \in G$ is a solution to a game, then its Nash equilibrium must be Pareto superior to the Nash-equilibrium payoff of all other subgames in G.

Proof: If the Nash-equilibrium payoffs in Γ_k were not Pareto superior to the Nash equilibrium of all other games in G, then Γ_k would be dominated and hence not a solution.

Remark: Notice that this does not mean that the solution to the game

132   Andrew Schotter

must be Pareto optimal in Γ. Again, the mode structure may not be fine enough to allow this to happen.

5.4   Conclusion

In this chapter I have depicted social institutions as sets of rules that evolve or emerge from the repetitive play of an underlying game by a group of rational agents. My emphasis has been on the set of rules that is capable of furnishing conventions of behavior for our agents to adhere to. The important point to realize is that rational social agents, through a process of individual utility maximization, can evolve sets of rules by which to conduct their lives. These rules may mean each player "voluntarily" restricts his or her strategy space. The set of rules that evolves defines what I have called the steady-state game; and such a game defines the rules of social interaction for the society. Although the analysis presented here can by no means be considered a theory of the evolution of rules, I hope that it will provide a first step in thinking about them.

References

Aumann, R. 1976. "Agreeing to Disagree." *Annals of Statistics* 4:1236–9.
Baumol, William J. 1959. *Business Behavior, Value, and Growth.* New York: Macmillan.
Brennan, Geoffrey, and James Buchanan. 1981. *The Power to Tax.* New York: Cambridge University Press.
Buchanan, James M., and Gordon Tullock. 1962. *The Calculus of Consent: Logical Foundations of Constitutional Democracy.* Ann Arbor: University of Michigan Press.
Clarke, E. H. 1971. "Multipart Pricing of Public Goods." *Public Choice* 2:17–33.
Dasgupta, Partha, P. Hammond, and E. Maskin. 1979. "The Implementation of Social Choice Rules: Some General Results on Incentive Compatability." *Review of Economic Studies* 46(2):185–216.
Gibbard, A. 1973. "Manipulation of Voting Schemes." *Econometrica* 41:587–601.
Groves, Theodore, and M. Loeb. 1975. "Incentives and Public Inputs." *Journal of Public Economics* 4:211–26.
Hayek, F. A. 1973. *Law, Legislation, and Liberty.* Vol. 1, *Rules and Order.* Chicago: University of Chicago Press.
Hurwicz, Leonid. 1979. "Outcome Functions Yielding Walrasian and Lindahl Allocations at Nash Equilibrium Points." *Review of Economic Studies* 46(2):217–26.
Maskin, E. S. 1978. "Implementation and Strong Nash Equilibrium." Cambridge: Massachusetts Institute of Technology. Photocopy.
Menger, Carl. 1963. *Problems of Economics and Sociology.* Trans. F. J. Nock. Urbana: University of Illinois Press. [First published in 1883.]
Moulin, H. 1980. "Implementing Efficient, Anonymous and Neutral Social Choice Functions." *Journal of Mathematical Economics* 7:249–69.
Nash, John F. 1950. "Equilibrium Points in n-Person Games." *Proceedings of the National Academy of Sciences of the U.S.A.* 36:48–9.

Satterthwaite, M. 1975. "Strategy-Proofness and Arrow's Conditions: Existence and Correspondence Theorems for Voting Procedures and Social Functions." *Journal of Economic Theory* 10:187–217.

Schmiedler, D. 1980. "Walrasian Analysis via Strategy Outcome Functions." *Econometrica* 48(7):1585–94.

Schotter, Andrew. 1981. *The Economic Theory of Social Institutions.* New York: Cambridge University Press.

Tideman, Nikolaus, and Gordon Tullock. 1976. "A New and Superior Principle for Collective Choice." *Journal of Political Economy* 84:1145–59.

Williamson, Oliver E. 1975. *Markets and Hierarchies: Analysis and Antitrust Implications.* New York: The Free Press.

CHAPTER 6

The tension between process stories and equilibrium models: analyzing the productivity-growth slowdown of the 1970s

RICHARD R. NELSON

6.1 Equilibrium models and process models

Several common themes unite the authors in this volume. A central one is the belief that, in analyzing economic phenomena, it is important to have a solid understanding of the economic processes that generated those phenomena. This may involve a sophisticated appreciation of the institutions that are the molders of these processes. Most of us would go on, I think, to argue that an understanding of processes and institutions should guide formal modeling.

Apparently, this is a minority opinion. Most formal economic analyses ignore process and institutional complexity. The core of the theory that is taught to students and used in formal economic arguments presumes that observed phenomena ought to be interpreted as equilibrium configurations resulting from the consistent maximizing behavior of a collection of economic actors.

Although this sounds, at first listening, like a process characterization, it is not. Theorizing about how economic actors actually go about making their choices has long been ruled out as methodologically inappropriate by a substantial part of the profession. Economic actors behave "as if" they were maximizing. One shouldn't worry about what they are actually doing. Although there are occasional exceptions, as a rule, no one attempts to analyze explicitly how the system gets to an equilibrium. The intellectual strategy of comparative statics ignores the question of what happens along the road and implicitly presumes both that the road leads to an equilibrium and that the time spent in passage is short. Stability analysis is sometimes grafted on in an ad hoc manner.

Sidney Winter and I have proposed that economists ought to pick up the theoretical stick by the other end (Nelson and Winter 1982). Whenever possible, formal economic models ought to be process models.

Equilibrium ought to be defined and analyzed as the steady state or states to which the processes move the system. Put another way, we argue that the conventional style of doing formal equilibrium analysis first and centrally, and then grafting on ad hoc dynamics to explore stability, has got the task exactly backward. Processes of adjustment ought to be what the modeling is all about, with equilibrium appearing as a condition in which no new adjustment is called forth.

Our complaint about the currently fashionable style of *formal* modeling does not mean we believe economists don't theorize about processes and the effects of institutions. If one listens to how economists *talk* about particular events – their origins or their likely effects – one quickly realizes that such talk generally *does* involve a characterization of process. This economists' talk is by no means simple description; indeed, it is not clear what the term "simple description" might mean. Our verbal storytelling focuses on certain variables, certain mechanisms, certain connections, rather than others. Winter and I have argued that this storytelling ought to be recognized as a form of theorizing, which we call appreciative theory.

Appreciative theory is more tailored to the particulars, less rigorous, than formal theory. Formal theory is more general, more analytic, than appreciative theory. Winter and I have proposed that appreciative and formal theorizing are complementary whenever economic understanding is progressing strongly. Appreciative theory, starting from a scan of the data, provides the somewhat vague, but believable, account of what is going on. This account in turn provides a challenge for formal theorizing to come up with models that seem to capture the essence of the verbal theorizing. In turn, exploration of those models, and their sometimes surprising implications, provides new angles from which to look at the data and new directions in which to take appreciative theorizing.

By the same token, a lack of consonance between appreciative theorizing and formal theorizing is an indication that the attempt at understanding is foundering. Appreciative stories, not sharpened by formal models that are consonant with them, can't carry us very far. Econometric analyses, based simply on appreciative theory, are hard to interpret and, like the appreciative theory, soft. Neat formal models that don't capture the core of plausible stories are at best unpersuasive. Econometric analyses based on formal theory that doesn't square with appreciative understanding is likely to lead to results that seem puzzling – or even bizarre – and generally beside the point.

Although appreciative theory is usually about process, the process story certainly can be consistent with, indeed can support, a formal model about equilibrium conditions. The appreciative storytelling can be squared even with the mathematics of orthodox modeling when the stories do not signal a system that is significantly out of equilibrium. But when the process stories are largely about disequilibrium, they are going to be in tension with formal models that presume equlibrium.

The best way to illustrate the interplay between formal and appreciative theorizing is to provide a concrete example. The last few years have seen economists groping to understand the slowdown in the growth of measured productivity that occurred during the 1970s. Here the informal stories are very much inconsistent with prevailing formal analyses, which invariably assume a moving equilibrium. It is my contention that appreciative theory about the productivity-growth slowdown translates much more easily into formal process theory. Constructing such a theory in any detail is obviously beyond the scope of this chapter, but a broad outline may be sufficient to highlight the contrast with conventional formal theory.

In the rest of this chapter I proceed as follows. First, in Section 6.2, I attempt to document the process character of appreciative analyses of the productivity-growth slowdown. Then, in Sections 6.3 and 6.4, I sketch the outlines of a hypothetical evolutionary model of productivity growth and stagnation that captures some aspects of these stories. Section 6.5 provides some guesses as to how this model might work to illuminate various aspects of the puzzle.

6.2   Analyses of the productivity-growth slowdown

The 1950s and 1960s were an era of unprecedentedly high productivity growth in most of the industrialized nations. After 1973 (and somewhat earlier in the United States), productivity growth was significantly slower in virtually all countries. In the United States, output per man-hour hardly grew at all in the late 1970s and early 1980s. It is too early to judge whether the pickup of productivity growth since 1982 is largely a cyclical phenomenon or whether it represents a long-term renaissance. In any case, in the rest of the essay I focus on the slowdown.

At the beginning of this period, and then again more recently, the industrialized nations experienced large jumps in oil prices. In addition, the inflation rate in most countries was significantly higher in this period than during the 1950s and 1960s. Controlling inflation became a central concern of most governments, but those governments found it difficult to spur growth and fight inflation at the same time. By the mid-1970s, unemployment was significantly higher than during the 1960s and, in many countries, reached rates in the early 1980s higher than any since the great depression. During the 1970s, profit rates and the rate of growth of capital stock were depressed relative to the 1960s. Government spending (largely transfer payments) as a fraction of national income was higher in the 1970s than earlier, significantly so in many countries. Toward the end of the 1970s and into the 1980s, governments turned to a variety of measures to protect industries and jobs that were being threatened by failing exports or rising imports. Although the extent of regulation is hard to measure, many analysts have argued that the costs to private business firms increased significantly during the 1970s.

Clearly, a lot of complex, and correlated, phenomena distinguish the period since 1973 from the earlier postwar period. One needs some broad appreciative theory to help sort out these developments into roughly three classes: (1) those that might be considered causes of the productivity slump; (2) those that, although not causative of the productivity-growth decline, ought to be understood as being part of the same syndrome, in the sense of being caused by the same underlying events and mechanisms; and (3) those that are basically unrelated to productivity stagnation and its causes.

I suggested earlier that economic theorizing about concrete events tends, initially at least, to take the form of devising plausible stories qualitatively consistent with the data. Quantitative analysis of the phenomena of course requires more formal theorizing. The appreciative theory and the formal theory ought to be consonant with one another and to work together. I argued above that this has not been the case in our attempts to analyze the productivity-growth slowdown.

There are at least three different, but not mutually exclusive, appreciative theories of the productivity-growth slowdown. One is about price shocks and the events they set in train. A second is about the effects on productivity growth of the macroeconomic environment of the 1970s. A third is about the effects of institutional change.

There are a number of stories about how the first, and later the second, energy–price shock knocked the system out of equilibrium. After the energy–price hike, variable factor proportions were out of equilibrium given the existing capital stock, and firms had to substitute away from energy-intensive inputs. Moreover, the energy–price shocks made earlier investment decisions look bad in many industries, in the sense that different kinds of equipment would have been bought had the pattern of prices been anticipated. In these cases, old plants often had to be junked or significantly revamped. It has also been suggested that the energy–price shock required that firms significantly reorient their research and development (R&D) efforts and learn how to do new kinds of R&D. The proposition here is that the energy–price shocks not only rendered obsolete much of physical capital but also made obsolete the R&D experience of companies that earlier had been successful in innovating.

This complex story has been drawn from the accounts of Hudson and Jorgenson (1978); Baily (1981); Berndt and Wood (1979), and other scholars. Not all would agree with all parts of it. The broad story may be basically right or basically wrong. But note, in any case, that the discussion – the appreciative theory – is about disequilibrium and the response of an economic system to a large unforeseen price shock.

A second set of stories is concerned with the connections between productivity stagnation and the difficulties that governments have had in managing inflation and unemployment. Some of these accounts – that put forth by Angus Maddison (1982), for example – also involve the oil–price shocks. A synthetic story would read this way. The energy–price shocks generated inflationary pressures and balance-of-payments problems. This induced governments to fight inflation and control the hemorrhaging balance-of-payments accounts through tight monetary and fiscal policies. This led to a slowdown in investment and to increases in unemployment. Because of new labor-market institutions, however, unemployment has been much less effective in driving down wage bargains and prices than it once was; and economic slack has been much less effective in purging economic inefficiencies. Productivity growth has been deterred in the short run by growing slack, and in the medium run by the investment slowdown. In some versions of the story, slow growth and lower investment have fed back to deter or make difficult technological advance.

Again, the story, or various parts of it, may be a good characterization of what has happened; or it may be a poor one. But it is clear that the story involves disequilibrium in a fundamental way. Still other stories, not inconsistent with the ones above, have focused on institutional change. Thus it has been proposed that, over the decade of the 1960s, governments came to play a much more intrusive role in industrial economies, making the advance of productivity more costly and structural adjustment to shocks more difficult. Extensions of environmental and safety regulations are one part of the story. Another part is the shifting of labor away from manufacturing industry into government-ally provided services such as education and health – together with rising tax rates to pay for these services. Still another part is the widening and deepening of governmental mechanisms and contractual arrangements that decouple access to goods and services from earned income. Government programs to protect industries and jobs further ossify resource allocation. As a result of all this, incentives for investment were dampened, pressures toward efficiency were diminished, and more fat and rigidity was built into the system.

This point of view is consistent with the diagnosis of Britain's poor performance presented by Bacon and Eltis (1976). Lindbeck (1974) has written similarly about the demise of the Swedish welfare state. A number of Americans – MacAvoy (1979) is a prominent example – are part of the chorus. Mancur Olsen (1982), with his propositions about the natural tendencies of democracies to make their economies increasingly protected and rigid, presents the story in its most sweeping form. Note that this story, like the other ones, is about process. Also, to come to grips with this story requires paying attention to institutional detail and changes in institutions.

All of these stories have a certain plausibility. They conform, at least roughly, with large parts of the pattern of observed changes. That is not surprising – because, like most appreciative theory, these theories were put together largely by scholars who were concerned with the phenomena, who were looking at the data, and who were trying to come up with an explanation that seemed basically to fit. It is true that parts of these stories were suggested by the scholars' understanding of, and adherence to, the body of formal theory learned by most members of our profession as a union card for entering it. I would argue strongly, however, that these accounts as I have described them stem largely from puzzling over the phenomena themselves rather than from thinking about the phenomena as an arena for testing some general tenets of prevailing theory. And the stories are relatively loose, not bound by the restrictions of formal theory.

That is why it is so hard to test these theories of the productivity-growth slowdown. They were carefully crafted to fit the data qualitatively and are not well specified quantitatively. Also, they place special importance on the particularities of the situation in question. This is why further abstraction and generalization is so important. Only by more abstraction does one buy degrees of freedom.

However, the formal theory that has been used to harden the qualitative analyses of the productivity-growth slowdown abstracts away not just the details but the fundamentals of the plausible appreciative theories. Let me remind you of the basic outlines of neoclassical growth theory, which lies behind both regression analysis (or the interpretation of the empirical results of such analysis) and growth accounting.

Firms are the key productivity actors, transforming inputs into outputs according to a production function. This production function, which defines the maximum output available with any given quantity of inputs, is determined by the state of technological knowledge. Technological knowledge is implicitly assumed to be public, at least in models based on an industry- or economywide production function. Firms choose a point on their production function to maximize their profits, given product-demand and factor-supply conditions. Generally, these markets are assumed to be perfectly competitive so that the firm treats prices as parameters. Over time, output grows (1) as inputs increase and firms move along their production functions and (2) as technology advances. If we assume differentiability of the production function, profit maximization on the part of the firms, and no externalities, the elasticity of output with respect to any input equals its share of total factor returns, at least for small increments to inputs. The proportional output growth attributable to input growth along the production function equals the sum of share-weighted proportional input growth. The residual (if any) is a measure of production-function shifts, or the change in total-factor productivity, from technological advance.

There is not much room here for price shocks and sluggish responses thereto; for capital made obsolete by incorrectly forecasted events; or for obsolete R&D policies and the need to devise new ones. There is no serious treatment of the possible effects of slack and unemployment on productivity growth – indeed no natural connection with those appreciative theories that stress the importance of the adverse macroeconomic climate. The institutional context is stark. There is no convenient way to deal with regulatory policies or unemployment compensation. Formal theory applied in most analyses of the productivity-growth slowdown is not simply a pruned-down abstracted version of the plausible appreciative theories. The formal theory at best has very little to do with, and at worst is inconsistent with, the appreciative theories.

The result, as I have suggested, has been intellectual disarray and confusion. All quantitative studies that have stuck with the guidelines of the canonical formal theory have come to the conclusion that very little of the slowdown of productivity growth can be attributed to a decline in the rate of growth of quantity or quality of other inputs per worker. Virtually all of it is due to a decline in the rate of growth of total factor productivity. In recent years, total-factor productivity in the United States has actually declined (Denison 1979; Kendrick and Grossman 1980). What to make of that?

Within the formal theory, increases in total-factor productivity have a natural interpretation as the consequences of technological advances. Do declines in total-factor productivity signal technological retrogression? Probably not, if one takes seriously the appreciative stories. Failure of total-factor productivity to grow has to be understood in terms of capital that has become obsolete; R&D strategies that have had to change; a macroeconomic climate and an evolving institutional structure that have made labor-saving innovation harder to implement and structural adjustment more difficult. That is a mouthful of things to say about the likely factors behind the stagnation of total-factor productivity.

And if that collection of problems, or some portion of it, is behind the productivity-growth slump, the formal neoclassical model is not going to be a good tool to guide quantitative research in its attempt to sort out and assign magnitudes to the various sources of the problem. It is not for two reasons. First, total-factor productivity growth is precisely what the theory *doesn't* explain. It is defined as a residual. That wouldn't be a problem if the residual had a natural simple interpretation, as, say, the effect of technological advance. Given that simple interpretation, it seems plausible to graft onto the basic model a simple ancillary model explaining technological advance, say, as the result of R&D spending. Once one backs off from that interpretation, it is not clear what kind of ancillary theory or theories to use. But the key puzzle is why the residual has declined so much.

There is a second and more basic difficulty. Given the above characterization of what has likely been going on, the decomposition of the sources of growth derived from the model – a factor-share-weighted sum of proportional input growth and a residual – loses its convenient analytic interpretation. The former can no longer be argued to represent movements along a production function. The latter then cannot be interpreted as a shift in the production function. Although one can call the index derived by cumulating the residuals "total-factor productivity," the theoretical standing of this index is far from clear. More generally, the conceptualization behind the numbers generated in a growth accounting falls apart.

Put succinctly, models that assume equilibrium are not good instruments for analyzing phenomena that everybody agrees involve disequilibrium in fundamental ways. To analyze such phenomena requires explicit process models. In Section 6.4 I sketch verbally one such model that might be built for exploring analytically at least a few of the more plausible stories about the productivity-growth slowdown. I do not develop the model formally. However, the verbal sketch involves ideas and results from an earlier formal model that Sidney Winter, Herbert Schuette, and I developed (Nelson, Winter, and Schuette 1976). That model was designed to explore the sources of productivity growth back in those happier days when such growth was positive and relatively smooth. I briefly discuss that formal model in the following section.

6.3   An evolutionary model of positive, generally smooth productivity growth

The neoclassical growth model, which continues to be the preferred instrument of the profession for studying patterns of productivity growth, came into fashion in the late 1950s and 1960s when the analytic problem was to explain why productivity growth was proceeding so rapidly. The conclusion that analysts guided by that model drew from the data was that the lion's share of growth of output per worker had to be attributed to growth of total-factor productivity, measured as the residual, with growth of capital and other inputs per worker playing a smaller role.

Largely stimulated by this finding, many economists began to study the processes of technological advance in some detail. Although no broad and general theory of technological advance in all its manifestations was developed, many scholars of technological advance soon came to talk about the processes in a certain coherent manner. Put another way, an appreciative theory of productivity growth fueled by technological advance began to take form. This appreciative theory stressed the uncertainties involved in any attempts to change technologies significantly, and the diversity of approaches that seem to arise naturally in a context of market competition among firms. Some firms bet right or are lucky; others turn out, after the fact, to have laid their chips on the wrong space. A natural consequence, then, of technological advance in a regime of competitive firms is considerable variation among firms at any time in their profitability and in the technologies they are using. Profitable firms tend to grow; unprofitable ones to decline. And, over time, the better of the new techniques expand in relative use as the firms employing them grow and as other firms learn to imitate them. Unprofitable techniques drop out of use through similar but opposite processes. These mechanisms might enable the system to move toward an equilibrium of a neoclassical variety if technological innovation ceased. But continuing technological innovation keeps on jolting the system.

This stylized story is simply inconsistent with neoclassical growth theory. Sidney Winter and I have developed an evolutionary model of economic growth that we think is consistent with the appreciative theory (Nelson and Winter 1982, Part IV).

That model consisted of a number of firms operating in a competitive market environment. At any time, each firm was characterized by its capital stock and the technique it was using. All techniques were of the Leontief variety. The only two factors of production were capital and labor. We assumed that firms always operated their capital at full capacity. Under some market conditions, the result would be positive profits; under other conditions, losses. The investment rule built into our model was, in effect: Plow back all positive profits into investment, and sell off capital (which then disappears) to cover losses.

The long-range dynamic of this model was provided by two stochastic processes that were interpreted as searches. The first process generated novelties or inventions as temporary private knowledge. The second involved a scan of the techniques used by other firms; over the long run, this process made what was private knowledge become public knowledge. When, through either of these processes, a firm found a technique that was more profitable than the one it was using, it immediately and costlessly changed over all of its capital to employ it.

The model was meant to portray the economy as a whole, with Say's Law in effect. We also assumed that the economy faced an upward-sloping labor-supply curve and that, over time, this curve shifted to the right as the labor supply grew. Growth of capital was, of course, endogenous in this model.

The model had a Markovian structure. The system starts with a specified number of firms, the capital stocks in each of them, and the techniques employed by each. Given fixed coefficients and the assumption that all firms always operate at full capacity, this immediately yields output and employment levels in each firm and for the system as a whole. The labor-supply curve determines the wage rate. This immediately determines profits and investment. The individual searches of firms turn up new techniques the profitability of which can be compared with those of the techniques the firms had been using. Firms shift over to techniques that are more profitable. Thus is generated both the capital and the techniques that will be employed next period by each firm. The process begins anew.

This model could generate macroeconomic time-series of outputs, inputs, and factor prices that bore a close family resemblance to the actual time series. The rising capital-labor ratio, associated with an increasing real-wage rate and a roughly constant rate of return on capital, could be interpreted quite tidily within the model. Once the parameters (basic institutions?) were set in a way that encouraged capital to grow faster than the labor supply, wage rates would rise in our model as in the orthodox one. Also as in the orthodox model, rising wage rates in our model make previously unprofitable capital-intensive techniques profitable to adopt, and vice versa. Innovation (the new inventions firms find it profitable to adopt) is nudged in a labor-saving direction, and the capital-labor ratio and output per worker rise. On the other hand, tendencies of the profit rate to rise set in train higher investment rates, which spur demand for labor and quicken the pace at which the wage rate rises, thus driving down the profit rate again. Similar reverse mechanisms are set in train by declines in the profit rate.

Note that the explicit mechanisms built into our formal model are in tune with stories about adjustment. Adjustments can take time, and they can be uncertain in magnitude even when predictable in direction. This suggests that we have a general formal model here that, suitably tailored, might be useful in exploring such questions as how an unexpected large jump in a particular input price – energy – might affect the time path of productivity or related variables. But certain major modifications are needed.

6.4 Toward an evolutionary model to explore the productivity-growth slowdown

My objective in this section is to provide a sketch of an evolutionary model, based on the one described above, within which one can explore a number of the alleged sources of and mechanisms behind the productivity-growth slowdown. The model will be somewhat more complicated than most of the neoclassical ones, but still sufficiently simple so that the workings of its key mechanisms should be transparent.

At this stage of development, the model is most easy to interpret as portraying an industry or a modestly sized piece of an economy, since there are no specific causal lines drawn between income generated in production and demand for the product. However, all of the sales revenues of the companies within the model go either to workers, to material-input suppliers, to bondholders, or to stockholders (either directly or in the form of retained earnings plowed back into investment). The incomes of these groups can be thought of as either saved or spent on the products of the industry in the model. Thus if one doesn't mind that there is no explicit analysis of who is saving when business investment exceeds retained earnings, one can treat this model as one of a macroeconomy. I remark, in passing, that virtually none of the neoclassical macroeconomic models used to study the productivity slowdown contains an explicit analysis of what equalizes savings and investment at the observed levels of output and employment.

In this model, as in the earlier one, all technologies are of the Leontief sort, with fixed proportions and constant returns to scale. There are three factors of production – physical capital, labor, and another input that I will call energy. Capital comes in packets called plants. The capital in any plant embodies a particular technique, and cannot be shifted to another technique. This represents a significant departure from the earlier model, and seems necessary to make sense out of the idea of obsolete capital. There are a number of firms in the economy, each of which owns one or more plants. The plants owned by a firm need not all be of the same type (be designed around the same technique). If operated or maintained, plants last ten periods. However, a firm can abandon a plant short of its natural life span.

A firm has a choice of three levels of operation for any plant that is still operable. The firm may operate it at full capacity. The firm may shut the plant down (or keep it shut) but maintain it. Or, the firm may abandon the plant, in which case there are specific one-time close-down costs. These decisions are made on the basis of calculations using last period's prices. If, at those prices, it is profitable to run a plant, that plant will be operated at capacity. The greater the losses that would be incurred from running the plant at capacity, the more likely it will be shut down but maintained. Firms never choose to scrap a plant that has been in operation the previous period. For plants that are shut down but are being maintained, the probability of scrapping is related to how close to profitable plant operation would be; to maintenance costs; and to close-down costs. This somewhat complex specification seems necessary to encompass the concept of economic slack, and to examine the effects of slack on productivity.

Taken together, the decisions made (probabilistically) by individual firms regarding how they should use their various plants determine the quantity of labor and energy employed and the quantity of output produced. Supply curves for the two variable factors of production and a demand curve for the product of the industry then determine today's prices. The price of new capital equipment is the numeraire in this model.

Today's prices in turn determine the profitability of each firm and of each plant. Some firms will earn more than enough to cover contractual payments (to labor, for energy, for R&D, and to bondholders). Other firms may not be able to cover these contractual costs, and will have to borrow or, alternatively, to declare bankruptcy. The probability of bankruptcy is related to the ratio of the firm's bonded debt to the book value of its maintained or operating capital stock. When a firm goes into bankruptcy, all of its unprofitable plants are scrapped; its profitable plants continue operation; and debt is swapped for equity.

New investment comes in the form of new plants. A firm always knows a number of techniques around which it may choose to build a new plant. It will not invest in a technique, however, unless that technique at prevailing prices yields a rate of return higher than the normal dividend rate. Of the techniques (if any) known by a firm that would yield higher-than-the-normal dividend rate, all investment goes into the one that yields the highest rate of return. Thus, a firm invests in, at most, one new plant each period. The amount invested in that new plant depends on the firm's profit rate, the rate of return that would be earned in that new plant, and firm size. All new investment is financed through retained earnings or the issue of new stock.

The techniques that are known by a firm at any time, and hence that are candidates for investment decision, come from two sources. (From a long-run view, they stem from one source.) There are, first, the techniques embodied in the firm's present operating or maintained plants. There are, second, those techniques that have been identified over the past five years by research and development activities.

The R&D efforts of a firm comprise two different kinds of activities. One of these involves attempts at innovation. Here, a firm can be visualized as drawing a ball from a particular urn each period. The ball may be a blank, representing the failure of R&D to create a technique that works. If a firm does come up with a technique that works, that technique may or may not be profitable; and if it is profitable, it may or may not be more profitable than the firm's best existing technique. Another kind of R&D activity is concerned with learning about the techniques of other firms and learning how to replicate them. This activity is also like drawing from an urn, but the urn is different from the one sampled through R&D aimed at innovation.

There are several different classes of technology; that is, the set of all possible techniques is divided into subsets. I believe it is potentially fruitful to make this assumption for several reasons. First, it enables us to recognize that, for example, nuclear-powered plants, coal-fired plants, and oil-fired plants – all mechanisms used to produce electricity – are located in quite different regions of coefficient space. Thus, I want to capture the idea that significant changes in factor prices will enhance the value of doing R&D on one kind of technology (searching in one bin) versus another. Relatedly, I want a model within which it is possible to recognize that certain scientific or technological developments, perhaps exogenous to the model, can change the value of exploring certain technological routes (bins) relative to others. Thus the semiconductor revolution, in effect, provided the computer designers and manufacturers with a rich new bin of design possibilities to explore; those who got into that bin early did better than those who continued to think about computer design in the old way.

Second, such an assumption lends meaning within the model to the proposition that certain kinds of developments can render obsolete a firm's prevailing R&D strategy. Thus, I assume that, at any time, a firm is either doing R&D, in which case it incurs an R&D cost, or it is not. If it is doing R&D, its attempts at innovation are focused on one kind of technology; that is, the firm is drawing from a particular bin. I also assume that the exploration of what competitors are doing is focused on competitor techniques that are in the same class in which the firm is trying to innovate.

Firms' R&D strategies (whether they are active or not and, if active, the technologies that they explore through R&D) are sticky. In particular, if a firm's R&D this period finds a profitable technique, the firm will, with certainty, continue to search in the same bin next period. If there are no R&D successes this period, there is some probability the firm will stop R&D and some probability it will switch to another bin. The probability of cutting out R&D or shifting bins becomes larger the longer the time since an R&D success. If a firm does shift to exploring another bin, the probability that it shifts to any particular bin is related to the number of new profitable techniques of that type discovered by other firms over the past five periods. Firms that have been doing no R&D may begin to do some. Again, the probability they will begin to search in any particular bin is related to how successful other firms have been in searching in that bin.

6.5   Some conjectures about comparative dynamics

Needless to say, a truly formal model would require a far more rigorous presentation than is appropriate here. But even this rough sketch of a model can be useful for talking through some of the issues surrounding the productivity-growth slowdown. At this level of formalization, of course, one should understand the conclusions as plausible arguments rather than as theorems.

Consider, then, the effect of a significant exogenous jump in the price of energy resulting from a backward shift in its supply curve. There would be an immediate effect on the profits of various plants and firms. Although the economics of all plants would be disadvantaged by the energy–price hike, the cost increase per unit of output would be greater the larger the energy-input coefficient. Other things being equal, energy-intensive plants would be more likely than others to shut down and later be abandoned. Presumably this is what Martin Baily meant when he remarked that the energy–price rise made certain capital obsolete (Baily 1981). Companies that had a lot of their capacity in energy-intensive plants would experience the most severe blow to overall profitability.

What would be the short-run effects on productivity? If the plants that are shut down but maintained have labor-productivity levels equal to or greater than the industry average, shutting them down but keeping a maintenance crew reduces industry-average labor productivity. (This mechanism is the incarnation within the model of Okun's law.) For a variety of reasons, energy-intensive plants are likely to have had above-average levels of labor productivity. Thus, even their abandonment will not bring average productivity back to what it was.

In the short run, physical investment would be affected in two ways. First, both the lower profitability of firms and the lower profitability of a given set of known techniques would tend to push down the total amount of investment. Second, the new plants that are put into place would be less energy intensive and, other things being equal, more labor and capital intensive than would have been the case absent the energy–price shock. Thus, one might osberve that investment is associated with a smaller incremental output-capital ratio than had been the case.

What about R&D and innovation? Assume that, prior to the energy–price shock, virtually all firms had been exploring technologies that were economic as long as energy prices were low. The jump in energy prices would make the typical new technology found through R&D less profitable, just as that shock made less profitable existing plants that, after all, largely embodied techniques that had been won through earlier R&D. In assessing the implications of this sudden drop in the profitability of doing R&D, some firms might decide to cut out R&D entirely. Another response would be to shift the orientation of R&D, to start searching in other bins. As firms began to find R&D strategies that would lead to cost reduction in an era of high energy prices, R&D would become profitable again. And the new technologies brought into operation would tend to be energy saving compared with the ones that had been brought in earlier. Relatedly, to be profitable, these new technologies would not have to save very much, or at all, on labor and capital per unit of output.

In short, this model seems capable of capturing, in a stylized manner, a number of features of the stories about the effects of the energy price shocks on productivity growth. In a more formal version of the model, it would be possible to explore the logic of the relevant relationships more systematically and to develop a better idea of what to look for empirically to see if the conjectured mechanisms are important.

As I've already suggested, the model as sketched here lacks connections flowing from supply to demand; hence, in its present form it isn't suitable for exploring the relationships between the macroenvironment and productivity growth. One can, however, think through the effects within this model of an exogenous falloff in demand for product.

Such a demand shock would set in train many of the same events as the energy–price shock. Indeed, many of the second- and later-round effects of the energy shock look a lot like the direct effects of a demand shock. In both contexts, the falloff in demand for labor puts downward pressure on the wage rate. In both contexts, the falloff in output puts downward pressure on product prices. In both cases, the declines in output take pressure off energy markets. Of course, in the case of an energy–price shock, the initial effect was to boost such prices.

Demand reduction would influence the path of productivity growth through a number of routes. In the short run, this model's version of Okun's law would take effect. Unlike the case of energy–price shocks, in this instance plants that ultimately close down can be expected to have lower-than-average (full-capacity operation) labor productivity; thus the abandoning of capital should act to raise the average productivity of employed workers by more than was the case when the initial disturbance was a jump in the price of energy.

Investment would decline. However, unlike the case of an energy–price rise, in this instance there would be no biasing of new investment toward energy-saving technologies. R&D would become less profitable. Although no change in R&D orientation would be drawn, there might be a decline in R&D activity and the appearance of a decline in R&D productivity simply because investment in newly discovered technologies would be less profitable.

As indicated earlier, some scholars have suggested that the path of causation running from increased slack to diminished physical investment and a falloff in R&D leads further to a long-run erosion of the rate of productivity growth. One important possible mechanism for such a long-run – not simply short-run – effect involves the following specification of the innovation mechanism. The probability distribution of draws for efforts aimed at innovation depends on (1) the character of the firm's best technology (in the relevant class) at the time it was adopted and (2) total accumulated experience (measured in terms of output) with that technology. This would be a specification that combines innovation through R&D with learning by doing or using. In addition to the effects mentioned above, it would appear under this specification that a falloff in demand would then have an additional and possibly more durable effect on productivity growth. The failure of a firm to invest in a new technology that would have been profitable absent the falloff in demand eliminates or delays the opportunity for learning by doing to augment the power of R&D. It would be interesting to explore within this model various empirical concomitants of such an assumption to compare with evidence from experience.

As a final speculative exercise, consider the effect of increased governmental or contractual protection of existing jobs made manifest in a high, if once-and-for-all, cost of closing out a plant. As specified here, this policy would not have an effect upon a firm's decisions to stop producing and to cut employment to the maintenance level. It would have an effect, however, on subsequent decisions as to whether to continue to maintain the plant (partly employing the work force) or to shut it down. The short-run effects of greater incentives to continue some employment would be to make productivity (of employed workers) lower than it otherwise would have been. In the longer run, however, such a policy would deter investment and R&D.

These are, of course, conjectures from a rather informal "formal" model. If the conjectures seem plausible, it is because explicit process models, even when large and complex, can be talked through. Or, from the opposite point of view, they can be designed to formalize and permit exploration of our appreciative stories. That is a great advantage.

References

Bacon, R., and W. Eltis. 1976. *Britain's Economic Problems: Too Few Producers.* London: Macmillan.

Baily, Martin. 1981. "Productivity and the Services of Capital and Labor." Brookings Papers on Economic Activity, no. 1. Washington, D.C.: Brookings Institution.

Berndt, E., and D. Wood. 1979. "Engineering and Econometric Interpretations of Energy-Capital Complementarity." *American Economic Review* 69(3): 342–54.

Denison, E. 1979. *Accounting for Slower Economic Growth: The United States in the 1970s.* Washington, D.C.: Brookings Institution.

Hudson, Edward A., and Dale W. Jorgenson. 1978. "Energy Prices and the U.S. Economy, 1972–1976." *Natural Resources Journal* 18(4): 877–97.

Kendrick, J., and E. Grossman. 1980. *Productivity in the United States: Trends and Cycles.* Baltimore: Johns Hopkins University Press.

Lindbeck, Assar. 1974. *Swedish Economic Policy.* Berkeley: University of California Press.

MacAvoy, Paul. 1979. *The Regulated Industries and the Economy.* New York: W. W. Norton.

Maddison, Angus. 1982. *Phases of Capitalist Development.* Oxford: Oxford University Press.

Nelson, Richard R., and Sidney G. Winter. 1982. *An Evolutionary Theory of Economic Change.* Cambridge: Harvard University Press.

Nelson, Richard R., Sidney G. Winter, and Herbert L. Schuette. 1976. "Technical Change in an Evolutionary Model." *Quarterly Journal of Economics* 90:90–118.

Olsen, Mancur. 1982. *The Rise and Decline of Nations.* New Haven: Yale University Press.

CHAPTER 7

Competition as a process: a law and economics perspective

GERALD P. O'DRISCOLL, JR.

7.1   Competition: two views

There are two radically different theories of competition. And the choice between them has far-reaching implications for the economic analysis of institutions. The still-dominant tradition conceives of competition as a state of affairs or an outcome in which certain well-known marginal conditions (e.g., price equals marginal cost) are fulfilled. More generally, whether a market is competitive or not is decided by the extent to which it satisfies conditions specifiable in advance. Thus, an outcome is "competitive" if it conforms to the predictions of a theoretical model.

At the level of pure theory, these predictions are, of course, merely qualitative and abstract (e.g., no buyer or seller can affect prices by his actions). As a result, however, the judgment about whether a market is or is not competitive is a zero-one decision. That is, a market or industry is either perfectly or less than perfectly competitive. In applications, the criteria are less rigid – but at the cost of translating qualitative into quantitative predictions (e.g., an industry is competitive if the eight largest firms do not control 70 percent of the market). In practice, then, judgment about the competitiveness of a market revolves around the question of the quantitative value of a small number of variables whose "correct" value can be established ex ante. The whole approach is objectionable from a number of perspectives, not the least being its thoroughly institutionless stance. The neoclassical theory of competition is institutionless in the obvious sense of failing to adapt its criteria of competitiveness to relevant institutional differences in various indus-

The views expressed in this chapter are solely the author's and should not be attributed to any part of the Federal Reserve System. I am more than usually indebted to my fellow symposiasts at the two Liberty Fund Symposia on Economics as a Process. I also received useful comments when I presented a version of this chapter at the Claremont Graduate School. James E. Pearce, Mario J. Rizzo, and Lyla H. O'Driscoll each provided assistance at crucial stages in this project. I must, however, single out Richard Langlois for his unstinting help and encouragement.

tries. Indeed, the theory is developed almost without reference to institutions. The case study presented in this chapter is an example of what happens when the complexities of a market are abstracted from in assessing the competitiveness of an industrial practice.

There is also a more profound way in which the traditional static theory of competition ignores the role of institutions. This can best be explained in the course of developing the alternative tradition or approach to the theory of competition. This tradition characterizes competition as a process in time rather than a timeless state of affairs. The process consists in economic agents discovering the very data (e.g., costs) that are assumed given to them in the theory of perfect competition. Hayek (1978, p. 181) has succinctly characterized competition as "a method of discovering particular facts relevant to the achievement of specific, temporary purposes. . . . The benefits of [these] particular facts . . . are in large measure transitory."

Hayek's characterization leads to significantly different criteria for assessing the benefits of competition. It is not how well a market conforms to predicted outcomes that determines its competitiveness. Indeed, almost the opposite is the case: "Competition is valuable *only* because, and so far as, its results are unpredictable and on the whole different from those which anyone has, or could have, deliberately aimed at" (Hayek 1978, p. 180). What recommends competition, then, is the information revealed and the goals achieved, which could not have been known or attained by any other method. The theory of competition as a process focuses on the ability of markets to accomplish what is strictly unpredictable before the process takes place.

The wholly different results of competition constitute an element of surprise not only for economic agents but also for economic theorists. Just as competition inevitably disappoints at least some of the expectations of buyers and sellers, so too it must falsify some of the predictions of theorists about the characteristics of competitive markets. Market participants are engaged in a learning process, in which relevant data are discovered. Similarly, however, theorists can discover which practices are competitive only by observing not by postulating them (see O'Driscoll and Rizzo 1985, chap. 6). Or, to quote Hayek (1978, p. 180) one more time, "[since] we do not know the facts we hope to discover by means of competition, we can never ascertain how effective it has been in discovering those facts that might be discovered."

Historically, the development of a theory of institutions is closely linked to the evolution of the view of competition as a process. For instance, Hayek's conception of the competitive process derives from Carl Menger's work. It was Menger (1963, p. 146) who defined the core problem of the social sciences in terms of the following question: *"How can it be that institutions which serve the common welfare and are extremely significant for its development come into being without a common will directed toward establishing them?"*

For Menger (1963, pp. 158–9), the *theoretical* analysis of price determination is inextricably linked to the answer to his question about the evolution of institutions:

A large number of the phenomena of economy which cannot usually be viewed as "organically" created "social structures," e.g., market prices, wages, interest rates, etc., have come into existence in exactly the same way as those social institutions. . . . For they, too, as a rule are not the result of socially teleological causes, but the unintended result of innumerable efforts of economic subjects pursuing *individual* interest. The theoretical understanding of them, the theoretical understanding of their nature and their movement can thus be attained in an exact manner only in the same way as the understanding of the above-mentioned social structures. That is, it can be attained by reducing them to their elements, to the *individual* factors of their causation, and by investigating the laws by which the complicated phenomena of human economy under discussion here are built up from these elements.

Menger's analysis neatly illustrates the two dimensions of a theory of institutions. On the one hand, it explains theoretically how economic institutions evolve as the unintended consequences of individual maximizing behavior. By a kind of invisible-hand reasoning, individual pursuit of self-interest is seen to produce results that were no part of anyone's intentions. On the other hand, this analysis focuses on how institutions constrain and shape individual behavior in the future. From this theoretical-institutional perspective, to explain only one part of the process would be to offer a one-sided theory.[1]

In the previous quotation, Menger outlined what he called the "compositive method," which is now known as methodological individualism. He saw it as a means of explaining how institutions would evolve spontaneously from social interaction. In contrast to the modern neoclassical approach, however, which takes institutions to be the intended outcomes of a maximizing process, Menger viewed institutions as the unintended consequence of human behavior. In Menger's hands, this method was employed to explain not only the evolution of the price system itself, but also the development of a modern medium of exchange (O'Driscoll 1984b).

In this chapter, I treat organizational innovations both as an instance

---

[1] By this analysis, neoclassical economics and the "old" institutionalism are each only one part of a complete theory. On this point, see Langlois's introductory essay in this volume.

156   Gerald P. O'Driscoll, Jr.

of the competitive process at work and an example of the evolution of economic institutions. The evolution of concrete market institutions and of the rules and practices sustaining these institutions is a process involving organizational innovation (see O'Driscoll 1984a, p. 9). Organizational innovations are perhaps more mundane than the institutional changes on which Menger and Hayek focused, but, nonetheless, they represent useful applications of institutional theory. Moreover, they illustrate the policy relevance of the differences between an institutional and noninstitutional analysis of market institutions.

7.2   Innovation: two views

The static view of competition is, at best, suspicious of organizational innovation. Such innovations almost by definition render the economic landscape different from what is was and, moreover, different from the predictions of standard competitive theory. In practice, such deviations tend to be labeled "anticompetitive" to the extent that they differ from the predictions of this theory.[2]

In contrast, the process theory of competition looks to the institutional basis of organizational innovation. The property-rights structure is a key institutional feature on which a process theory will often focus. In such cases, oganizational innovation is viewed as a response to externalities within a given property-rights structure. Of course, externality arguments are not foreign to modern neoclassical economic theory. Indeed, analysis of externalities is very often the way in which contemporary theory accommodates innovation and institutional change (Demsetz 1967). And certainly the literature on process and institutional analysis would find congenial much of the recent work on transaction costs and externalities.[3]

Two points need to be reiterated here, however. First, by its nature, a process theory of competition can more readily incorporate institutional change. Second, process theory does not force change and inno-

---

[2] Williamson (1981, pp. 1539–40) makes much the same point. He attributes this attitude to the conventional treatment of the firm as *nothing but* a production function rather than as an institution for internalizing externalities. In public policy, this view is instantiated in the "inhospitality tradition" in antitrust economics – a tradition deeply mistrustful of novel corporate practices or of organizational innovations.

[3] Dahlman (1979) demonstrates, however, the pitfalls of the marriage of externality analysis and neoclassical economic theory. As he observes (p. 153), "if it exists, it must be optimal, and if it does not exist it is because it is too costly, so that is optimal too." He rightly rejects this conclusion and even points to an institutional approach in linking transactions costs with imperfect information. He does not, however, develop a full-blown institutional analysis in this article.

vation into the straitjacket of static theory, in which all outcomes are the product of an explicit maximization procedure aiming at these outcomes (O'Driscoll and Rizzo 1985, chap. 6). Process theory is a particularly appropriate vehicle for understanding evolutionary processes that involve, at least in part, the unintended consequences of human action. With these caveats in mind, we can examine innovation and change in the property-rights framework.

Coase (1960) demonstrated that the type of property rule helps determine whether externalities will be Pareto-relevant or not. Mere observations of physical features of the environment tell us nothing about their economic significance. Consider, for instance, a polluted lake. In a world of well-specified property rights and low transaction costs, we could infer that the preferred use of the lake is as a dumpsite. Absent one of the assumptions, we might have reason to suspect that resources are not being put to their highest-valued use. In either case, however, the mere observation that the lake is polluted provides no warrant for interventionist public policy. A given practice or behavior may be consistent or inconsistent with standard economic norms. We can make a reasoned judgment only if we systematically analyze observed outcomes in the light of the relevant legal and property rules.

Monopoly theory virtually ignores the Coasean insight. Behavior is characterized as competitive or anticompetitive almost without regard to the structure of property rights. No longer acceptable in the externality literature, this practice persists in the industrial organization field. Monopoly theory thus remains a backward area of economics for failing to incorporate a property-rights analysis (O'Driscoll 1982). This theoretical lacuna has profound implications for public policy.

Antitrust policy seeks to foster competitive outcomes by legislation and regulation. Advocates believe that economic intervention can protect and promote competition. This position may be defensible if competition is defined in terms of equilibrium conditions in a static model. The position of antitrust advocates is more suspect if one defines competition as a process. Some of the inherent tension in antitrust policy has become evident in recent debates over regulating professional associations.

Since the publication of Kessel's (1958) article on price discrimination in medicine, economists have been sensitive to the potential for monopolistic practices by professional associations. These *private* associations exercise *state* powers delegated to them. They have restricted entry, suppressed competitive behavior, and raised the prices of services supplied by members. State medical boards restricted entry by using their power to accredit medical schools and to certify hospitals. The

158   Gerald P. O'Driscoll, Jr.

Hippocratic Oath was invoked to ban "unethical" practices, such as advertising. "Reasonable fees" have been established by county medical organizations. By thus restricting supply and setting fees, physicians were able to raise prices and increase their incomes above levels that would have prevailed under competition.

A number of restrictive practices, such as professional advertising bans, are now history. In recent years, cases have been successfully prosecuted against these practices.[4] The delegation of police powers to private individuals has not been directly attacked, however. Only particular manifestations of this power have been opposed. For example, the various state boards overseeing medical practices remain in operation. If ever there was a legitimate use of antitrust statutes, it would be in prosecuting these state and local restrictions on competition. Political realities and constitutional questions perhaps preclude this possibility, but economic realities do not thereby disappear. The power of professional organizations *effectively* to restrict competition derives from their use of governmental power.

A cartel of producers, be it a steel or a physicians' cartel, will attempt to raise prices as long as expected costs decrease more rapidly than expected revenue. What producers may want to do and what they can accomplish are, however, two very different things. To the degree that a cartel successfully raises prices, to that degree it creates incentives for individuals to undermine the cartel. Maintaining the cartel price and output quotas is a public good, and cheating results in private gain. Economic theory applicable to such situations is well developed but often forgotten when cartel pricing is the issue.

We are dealing with an n-person prisoners' dilemma game. The smaller n, the easier it may be to effect the initial agreement. Even for industries composed of a small number of producers, the cartelists will quickly begin the process of undermining the agreement. It is the interloper problem, however, that often presents a cartel with its greatest threat. The original number of participants becomes irrelevant. Whatever the initial size of n, it tends to infinity with the formation of a cartel. This happens with varying speeds in individual cases. To a substantial degree, this variation depends on institutional factors. It is these factors that make for interesting law-and-economics analysis. Nonetheless, history bears out the theoretical predictions of the simple model in a

---

[4] *Goldfarb* v. *Virginia State Bar*, 421 U.S. 773, 44 L.Ed.2d 572 (1975), 95 S.Ct. 2004 and *National Society of Professional Engineers* v. *United States*, 435 U.S. 679, 55 L.Ed.2d 637 (1978), 98 S.Ct. 1355.

strikingly large proportion of the cases.[5] This is particularly true when one does not limit oneself to contemporary events and the recent past for case studies.

In what follows, I describe a cartel without a legal mechanism for enforcing the agreement as a voluntary cartel. The success of a voluntary cartel depends on individual behavior that cannot be compelled (and often not even monitored). The voluntary cartel must somehow transform the incentive to *expand* output into a commitment to *restrict* output. The hypothesis presented here asserts that, in the absence of legal enforcement, there is no mechanism for accomplishing this transformation.

Nineteenth-century railroad pools never numbered more than seven participants, usually fewer. They broke down with embarrassing speed and regularity, *save* when state railroad commissions enforced their provisions. Likewise, in this century voluntary cartels have consistently turned to government to police cartel agreements (Kolko 1965, 1967; Weinstein 1968). One apparently crucial factor in Anglo-American history is the fact that contracts to enforce a cartel were either void or unenforceable at common law (Hilton 1966, pp. 91–92). Cartel contracts could be neither self-policed nor enforced in the courts. This contrasts sharply, of course, with public policy and public law in Germany, which fostered collusive agreement and cooperation among competitors.

Particularly in the Progressive era, unsuccessful voluntary cartels adopted political solutions. Firms sought regulatory commissions to stabilize their respective industries. The Interstate Commerce Commission was the model. In any case, federal regulation was nearly always preferred. In an increasingly national economy, firms naturally preferred uniformity of regulation. Additionally, state and local regulatory commissions were far more likely to come under the influence of interests outside the industry, like that of consumers (Kolko 1967, pp. 5–6, 130, 161–3, 173–4).

This analysis leads one to predict the demise of anticompetitive arrangements in which no governmental institutions supporting the prac-

---

[5] Recent work by Schotter (1981) suggests that transactors caught in such a game can, if the game is repetitive, devise mechanisms and contracts to extricate themselves from the dilemma. Because of the interloper problem, however, the cartel game is even more complex than the standard prisoners' dilemma case. Even if existing members of the cartel know the rules, interlopers will not play by these rules. Only by breaking or threatening to break them can the interloper be admitted to the game and share in the spoils. And the cartel's buying one interloper off only *enhances* the likelihood that another will do likewise (as long as expected quasi-rents are positive).

tices exist. It further makes one skeptical of regulation to ensure competition, since this can so readily provide the needed support (if not by design then by capture). By extension, this analysis tends to make one more tolerant of apparently restrictive practices if no governmental support mechanism is evident. This is exactly the kind of case examined in the next section.

All the considerations about the instability of cartels are particularly telling in the case of most professions. The problem of large numbers will typically preclude even forming an agreement, save in small towns. Professionals are closer to the situation of farmers than to that of most manufacturers. For this reason and others, the professions have relied extensively on political solutions. The latter typically involves lobbying for the establishment of state boards to oversee quality.

Among other things, such boards virtually always raise the human-capital requirements for practicing a profession. They do so partly by establishing educational and training requirements. Some of these regulations arguably were originally intended to ensure quality control. Nonetheless, a requirement for additional formal training raises the cost of entry. Such entry restrictions surely make professional care more expensive, but do not ipso facto improve that care. To suppose otherwise would be to judge a policy by its expressed intent rather than by demonstrated results.

Requirements for formal training are particularly effective in excluding interlopers. Consider the topic of this chapter's case study, health care. This can be accomplished either through self-medication, which is highly restricted by prescription codes, or through low-cost providers of professional care. A relatively few alternative sources of health care have succeeded in establishing themselves. Midwifery, chiropractic, podiatry, and optometry come to mind. All have had to fight on a state-by-state basis for the right to practice. Cases are still being fought in some states for some of these professions.

Even when these alternative providers have successfully carved out a niche for themselves, physicians have nonetheless succeeded in sharply delimiting the scope of the care provided. Dentists can treat diseases of the mouth, but not the same or similar diseases occurring in other parts of the body. Podiatrists can treat disorders of the feet, but not of the hands or even the leg.

None of this should be taken as minimizing the importance of ensuring the quality of medical care and other professional services. Indeed, this problem is the core of my analysis of the *Maricopa* case. To anticipate my conclusion, regulatory policies have prevented competition in health care. And antitrust policy is suppressing those competitive forces that are operating.

7.3   The Maricopa case

The Maricopa Foundation for Medical Care was a nonprofit corporation composed of physicians, osteopaths, and podiatrists practicing in Maricopa County (which encompasses Phoenix, Arizona). Approximately 1,750 doctors, about 70 percent of the total practitioners, were members. Participating doctors had no financial interest in the foundation.

The foundation performed three functions. First, it established a schedule of maximum fees that participating doctors agreed to accept as payment in full for patients insured under an approved plan. There were various approved plans offered by different insurance companies; Maricopa itself did not provide insurance. Second, the foundation reviewed the medical necessity and appropriateness of treatment provided by its members to insured patients. Third, it drew checks on the accounts of insurance companies. Maricopa received a small fee (4 percent of premiums collected) for handling claims, and, indeed, was classified as an "insurance administrator" by the Arizona Department of Insurance.

It was the first function that led to a suit under Section 1 of the Sherman Antitrust Act.[6] The case was effectively decided at the Supreme Court level on a point of law. In the majority opinion, Justice John Paul Stevens held that Maricopa had instituted a price-fixing agreement:

In this case the rule is violated by a price restraint that tends to provide the same economic rewards to all practitioners regardless of their skill, their experience, their training, or their willingness to employ innovative and difficult procedures in individual cases. Such a restraint may also discourage entry into the market and may deter experimentation and new developments by individual

---

[6] *Arizona* v. *Maricopa County Medical Society,* 457 U.S. 332, 73 L.Ed.2d 48 (1982), 102 S.Ct. 2466. [In what follows, citations to this decision are given in page numbers only.] The Pima County Foundation was also originally a party to the suit but was subsequently dismissed by consent. Since writing this chapter, I have become aware of articles by Hall (1982) and Leffler (1983) on this case. It would be beyond the scope of this discussion to comment in detail on these two papers. I found Hall's analysis to be consistent with the thesis presented here. Our conclusions, both as to law and as to economics, are basically the same. I believe that Leffler has given insufficient attention to the questions of why insurers and consumers would have wanted to participate in the Maricopa plan. His analysis suffers as a result. Both papers clearly merit more attention, however, as does *Maricopa* itself.

entrepreneurs. It may be a masquerade for an agreement to fix uniform prices, or it may in the future take on that character. (61)

The facts support a very different interpretation. To see this, however, one must look at all three functions together. Stevens's opinion adopted the stance that Maricopa was engaged in a price-fixing scheme, and, for some peculiar reason, was engaged in the ancillary business of processing insurance claims and verifying the medical necessity of operations. The Court offered no objection to either of the latter two functions. But, as I argue below, the three functions were inextricably linked. Moreover, the linkage did not involve a price-fixing scheme but the provision of two jointly supplied economic goods: cost containment and quality assurance.

Consider first the insurance companies' perspective. Certainly insurance companies may contract out the processing of claims and paperwork generally. It is doubtful, however, that a nonprofit medical foundation founded by doctors would be the low-cost provider of these services. It is likely, however, that a group of doctors might possess expertise in monitoring the necessity of medical procedures and the quality of care provided to patients. Moreover, containing costs and monitoring the appropriateness of medical treatment are complementary goods. In supplying two goods, however, Maricopa had to control two variables or dimensions, price and quality. If Maricopa controlled only prices, which constituted cost containment from the insurers' perspective, doctors would have an incentive to cut back on quality. Or they might attempt other subterfuges, like requiring a larger number of perfunctory office visits for a given treatment – a procedure not unknown in workman's compensation cases.

As evidenced by the decision of more than 70 percent to participate, doctors profited by their association with the foundation. Yet each doctor could gain by cheating on the arrangement by charging more for a given quality or quantity of services performed, or by performing unnecessary procedures. Accordingly, Maricopa exercised peer review. This increased the probability that patients were receiving the level of care for which the insurance companies were making payments. Moreover, in providing insurance companies with this assurance, Maricopa was also effectively guaranteeing a median level of care to patients. This, in turn, rationalizes why patients would wish to participate in the program. This latter point is crucial and I return to it shortly.

Cost containment eliminated some underwriting risks. In particular, it lowered the risk that the cost of medical services would exceed some average or expected amount, on the basis of which premiums were constructed. To some extent, of course, insurance companies could reduce these risks by provision for deductibles and by establishing their own maximum-fee schedule. Two considerations would seem to have recommended using Maricopa rather than the alternatives.

First, maximum-fee schedules ordinarily do not eliminate risk but shift it to the insured. This reduces the value of medical insurance to potential purchasers, as well as reducing their demand for medical services. Insurance companies, doctors, and patients could all gain from a genuine reduction in risk. Maricopa provided this by its cost containment and provision of payment in full for all medical care performed by member doctors. As we have seen, this is what led to the maximum-fee schedule.

Mr. Justice Stevens averred that, all other issues aside, insurance companies could have set the allowable fees. He implied that this might have diminished the antitrust objections. He found any efficiency gain from having doctors establish the schedule as merely "theoretical," and that it was likely offset by "the potential or actual power of the foundations to dictate the terms of such insurance plans" (65).

In this passage, Stevens begged all the important questions. First, any power of the foundation to dictate the nature of the insurance plan is without any basis in the facts of the case. As noted in the dissenting opinion, the issue at bar was whether a partial summary judgment should have been entered in the district court. There had only been limited pretrial discovery of facts when the plaintiff entered his motion for partial summary judgment. Accordingly, as Stevens himself noted, the Court had to "assume that the respondents' view of the genuine issues of fact is correct" (57). Yet it would seem that Stevens was surreptitiously attempting to find on the facts at the appellate level with a bit of *dicta*.

Second, there is reason to believe that there were efficiency gains from having doctors establish the fee schedule for the insurance company. In Pima County's plan, which was similar to Maricopa County's, Blue Cross/Blue Shield was a subscribing insurance company. Yet Blue Cross/Blue Shield established its own fee schedules. Either Maricopa's schedule better approximated market conditions or it provided some other economy.

It must be emphasized that Maricopa exercised no entry restrictions. Participation in the plan by physicians and patients alike was purely voluntary. Participating patients could choose to use the services of nonparticipating physicians. In doing so, they gave up the guarantee that all charges would be paid in full. Further, 30 percent of eligible doctors did not join. And finally, participating doctors could continue to see nonparticipating patients and negotiate fees with them. In no sense, then, did the plan control the market or even 70 percent of it. Nor is it reasonable to suppose that Maricopa had the power to dictate to major insurance companies.

The fundamental error in Stevens's opinion is that he failed to distinguish coercion and the power to coerce from contractual agreement, which binds only the parties to the agreement. The majority could not see the importance of voluntariness and, hence, did not understand that licensing already accomplished what they merely feared from Maricopa. The plan attempted to effect an efficiency in an already restricted system of health-care delivery. Justice Lewis F. Powell, Jr., assessed the situation correctly in his dissenting opinion:

The medical care plan condemned by the Court today is a comparatively new method of providing insured medical services at predetermined maximum costs. It involves no coercion. Medical insurance companies, physicians, and patients alike are free to participate or not as they choose. On its face, the plan seems to be in the public interest. (67)

The incentive for patients to participate in the Maricopa plan is surely a crucial issue in this case. Any suggestion of compulsion with respect to the patients is clearly implausible. Yet, as Mr. Justice Powell observed: "The respondents' contention that the 'consumers' of medical services are benefited substantially by the plan is given short shrift" (67). The Court not only ignored this factual issue but presented a novel theory of its own. To wit, in the previously quoted passage Mr. Justice Stevens suggested that consumers would lose under the plan because, in effect, it denied them the possibility of contracting for higher-quality care. In other words, by this theory consumers would be compelled to accept a median level of medical care and could not purchase superior treatment (including novel procedures).

This is exactly what the plan could not and did not do. As long as some physicians remained outside the plan, consumers would have the option of seeking better medical care than the plan was prepared to reimburse them for. Presumably among the 30 percent of the eligible doctors remaining outside the plan, there were some providing superior medical care at premium fees. Patients belonging to the plan would then be responsible for the difference between these premium fees and the maximum allowable rate set in the plan.

This is, of course, precisely the situation in which *everyone* covered by health insurance finds himself. For instance, the patient desiring a private hospital room, but whose own health insurance will pay for no more than the rate for a semiprivate room, must pay the difference.

Stevens's theory simply proves too much. If correct, then every insurance plan would have the effects supposed in his opinion. Again, that opinion confused a contractual agreement between parties with a legal barrier to entry. Specifically, the contract merely specified certain maximum amounts that the plan would reimburse. As with other health plans, the patients remained free to pay additional amounts for what they perceived to be superior care (in whatever dimension).

In fact, patients' behavior can be explained only by their expecting to gain something from participating. And that gain surely lay in the risk reduction and quality assurance provided by the plan. I have thus far emphasized the cost-containment provision of the plan. But the provision of quality assurance was no less important. Consumers often have difficulty in judging the quality of the services or care that they are receiving. There is typically a significant difference in the information possessed by consumers and by producers of professional services. Particularly in health care, the consumer may not always have access to a low-cost mechanism for ascertaining the quality of the care received.

Many consumers would presumably pay for quality-certification services – the equivalent of "Good Housekeeping" reports on purveyors of medical, legal, and other such services. Professionals themselves might even pay for quality certification in order to increase demand for their services. There is, however, a peculiarity to the certification of professional quality. This peculiarity derives from the informational disparity itself. Only professionals will normally be able to provide the certification services.

Again, the provision of medical services is the paradigmatic case. Consumers of medical service can seek a second opinion. This only pushes the problem to a different level. The consumer possesses no more information about the quality of the second opinion than of the first. In another context, Klein (1974 pp. 432–8) has suggested that brand-name capital can serve as a guarantee of quality. Suppliers cheating on quality suffer a loss of future income. Discounted to the present, this shortfall is a loss of brand-name capital.

Group practice in medicine (or law) is a variation on this approach. Deliverers of medical care associated in group practice have incentives to monitor each other. If one member delivers lower-than-expected medical care, then all members of the group suffer. Maintaining standards is a public good. Group practice is a straightforward way of privatizing the good, potentially eliminating any externality at the margin. No one need attend to the standard of the professions as a whole, any more than anyone need plan for the feeding of a large city. Decentralized supervision relying on profit maximization can be more effective.

For various reasons, consumers may feel that the potential loss of brand-name capital is not a sufficient guarantee of quality. They are likely to prefer some independent guarantee, more closely approximating the "Good Housekeeping" model. Though not so independent as Good Housekeeping, the Maricopa Foundation provided this service. And it is this service, together with risk reduction, that must have recommended participation in its plan to consumers.

7.4   Price fixing

I have argued that standards established and enforced by physicians in a voluntary contractual arrangement will be preferred to relevant alternatives by insurance companies and patients alike. This enforcement will be institutionalized and will involve concomitant ancillary restraints. In particular, to be effective, standards must specify quality *and* price. The history of antitrust enforcement suggests that price fixing all but assures antitrust action. Mr. Justice Stevens stated the issue clearly:

> The anticompetitive potential inherent in all price-fixing agreements justifies their facial invalidation even if procompetitive justifications are offered for some. Those claims of enhanced competition are so unlikely as to prove significant in any particular case that we adhere to the rule of law that is justified in its general application. (63)

Judicial hostility to price fixing probably exceeds that found even in the theory of perfect competition. In *Albrecht* v. *Herald Co.*,[7] the Supreme Court forbade a newspaper from setting the *maximum* price at which its distributors could resell the newspaper. In that case, it is clear that neither collusion nor monopolization was involved. The newspaper's owner was concerned that the retail price of the newspaper be uniform within a market. Thus, even when agreements to fix price might pass the muster of standard economic theory, they have been condemned in the courts.[8]

Nonetheless, this caveat aside, the courts basically view the setting of prices as does the static theory of competition. This is the simple world of atomistic decision makers, possessing complete knowledge of the structure of the problem that they face. The world is sparsely populated by institutions. Indeed, when institutions or contractual restraints are observed, there is a presumption against them. Actual markets are composed, however, of a web of complex and interrelated institutions and rules. In some cases, these institutions and rules keep individuals

---

[7]   390 U.S. 145 (1968).
[8]   For an excellent analysis of *Albrecht*, see Posner (1976, pp. 157–9).

from falling into costly prisoners' dilemma-type problems. More generally, in a world of structural uncertainty and concomitant information complexity, cooperative behavior may be the only solution with survival value. Viewed as a process, competition may be consistent with such behavior and institutional forms. Analyzed in terms of the theory of perfect competition, this behavior and these institutions will appear to be inherently anticompetitive. *Maricopa* illustrates the differences in policy implications of adopting a conception of competition as a state of affairs over that of competition as a process.

There has been some tentative theoretical analysis of price fixing that casts doubt on the strong conclusions of conventional theory. Dewey (1979) has suggested distinguishing between competitive and anticompetitive sharing of price information. The latter is part of restrictionist and cartelizing schemes to raise prices and profits. The former can lower the costs of discovering the competitive price to individual firms. In the competitive case, sharing of price information reduces the variance of prices rather than increasing their average level. Dewey accordingly suggests a tolerant attitude toward sharing price information among competitors. O'Driscoll and Rizzo (1985, chap. 7) suggest some criteria for distinguishing the competitive and anticompetitive cases.

From the perspective of the static theory of competition, it is difficult to rationalize Dewey's position. In that analysis, prices are data and firms need not expend resources in discovering them. If we add a stochastic element, firms experience parametric uncertainty. Nothing yet suggests the need for cooperative behavior. If, however, firms are uncertain about the structure of the problem, then we can be less sure of orthodox conclusions about such behavior.

If my analysis is correct, then the doctors in the *Maricopa* case were not engaged in collusion or any other anticompetitive practice. To the degree that the foundation affected prices, it lowered the variance rather than raised the average level. It is the variance not the level of prices that creates the underwriting risk examined here. And it was in reducing that risk that the foundation served the insurance companies and consumers alike.

As noted above, antitrust law treats price fixing as an offense that is illegal per se. Economic analysis should not, however, be decided by its own version of *stare decisis*. Though perhaps weak on legal grounds, Mr. Justice Powell showed economic insight when he argued that a per se rule should be applied only after "carefully considering substantial benefits and procompetitive qualifications. This is especially true when the agreement under attack is novel, as in this case." (71)

In this regard, Mr. Justice Powell's dissent was at least as effective a

168   Gerald P. O'Driscoll, Jr.

rebuttal to conventional antitrust economics as it was to the Court's interpretation of legal doctrine.

I believe the Court's action today loses sight of the basic purposes of the Sherman Act. As we have noted, the antitrust laws are a "consumer welfare prescription." *Reifer v. Sonotone Corp.*, 442 U.S. 330, 343, 60 L Ed 2d 931, 99 S Ct 2326 (1979). In its rush to condemn a novel plan about which it knows very little, the Court suggested that this end is achieved only by invalidating activities that *may* have some potential for harm. But the little that the record does show about the effect of the plan suggests that it is a means of providing medical services that in fact benefits rather than injures persons who need them.

In a complex economy, complex economic arrangements are commonplace. It is unwise for the Court, in a case as novel and important as this one, to make a final judgment in the absence of a complete record and where mandatory inferences create critical issues of fact (73).

References

Coase, Ronald H. 1960. "The Problem of Social Cost." *Journal of Law and Economics* 3 (October):1–44.
Dahlman, Carl. 1979. "The Problem of Externality."*Journal of Law and Economics* 22:141–62.
Demsetz, Harold. 1967. "Toward a Theory of Property Rights." *American Economic Review* 57(2):347–59.
Dewey, Donald. 1979. "Information, Entry, and Welfare: The Case for Collusion." *American Economic Review* 69(4):587–94.
Hall, Thomas D. 1982. "Physician Maximum Fee Reimbursement Agreements: *Arizona v. Maricopa County Medical Society." Emory Law Journal* 31:912–71.
Hayek, Friedrich A. 1978. "Competition as a Discovery Procedure." In *New Studies in Philosophy, Politics, Economics and the History of Ideas.* Chicago: University of Chicago Press.
Hilton, George. 1966. "The Consistency of the Interstate Commerce Act." *Journal of Law and Economics* 9:87–113.
Kessel, Reuben A. 1958. "Price Discrimination in Medicine." *Journal of Law and Economics* 1:20–53.
Klein, Benjamin. 1974. "The Competitive Supply of Money." *Journal of Money, Credit, and Banking* 6:423.
Kolko, Gabriel. 1965. *Railroads and Regulation, 1877–1916.* Princeton: Princeton University Press.
 1967. *The Triumph of Conservatism.* Chicago: Quadrangle.
Leffler, Keith. 1983. "*Arizona v. Maricopa County Medical Society:* Maximum-Price Agreements in Markets with Insured Buyers." *Supreme Court Economics Review* 2:187–211.
Menger, Carl. 1963. *Problems of Economics and Sociology.* Trans. Francis J. Nock; ed. Louis Schneider. Urbana: University of Illinois Press.
O'Driscoll, Gerald P., Jr. 1982. "Monopoly in Theory and Practice." In *Method, Process, and Austrian Economics: Essays in Honor of Ludwig von Mises,* ed. Israel M. Kirzner. Lexington, Mass.: D. C. Heath.
 1984a. "Expectations and Monetary Regimes." *Economic Review* (September):1–11.
 1984b. "Carl Menger and Modern Economics." Photocopy.

O'Driscoll, Gerald P., Jr., and Mario J. Rizzo. 1985. *The Economics of Time and Ignorance.* Oxford: Basil Blackwell.

Posner, Richard A. 1976. *Antitrust Law: An Economic Perspective.* Chicago: University of Chicago Press.

Schotter, Andrew. 1981. *The Economic Theory of Social Institutions.* New York: Cambridge University Press.

Weinstein, James. 1968. *The Corporate Ideal in the Liberal State: 1900–1918.* Boston: Beacon Press.

Williamson, Oliver E. 1981. "The Modern Corporation: Origins, Evolution, Attributes." *Journal of Economic Literature* 19(4):1537–68.

CHAPTER 8

The economics of governance:
framework and implications

OLIVER E. WILLIAMSON

A leading issue with which the economics of organization is concerned is: Why do we observe so much organizational variety? This question has been relatively neglected on the research agenda, in large measure because neoclassical price theory is poorly suited to address it.[1] Thus orthodoxy holds that the allocation of economic activity between firms and markets is a datum; firms are production functions; markets are signaling devices; contracting is accomplished through an auctioneer; and disputes are disregarded because of the presumed efficacy of court adjudication. The economic purposes served by organizational variety do not arise within – indeed, are effectively beyond the reach of – this framework.

Transaction-cost economics approaches the study of economic organization very differently. It regards firms, markets, and mixed modes as alternative means of organization and views the allocation of economic activity among them as a decision variable. Moreover, it describes firms as governance structures, the internal organization of which has real economic consequences. Its assessment of the contracting process runs the gamut from faceless transactions of the kind that are adequately served by auctioneers to complex bilateral trades in which the identity of the partners matters critically. And transaction-cost economics supplants the legal centralism tradition, under which court adjudication is presumed to be efficacious, with the study of private orderings. As a

---

This research was supported by a grant from the National Science Foundation. Comments by Masahiko Aoki and Mario Rizzo on an earlier draft are gratefully acknowledged.
[1] Leonid Hurwicz (1973, p. 1) plainly concurs: "Traditionally, economic analysis treats the economic system as one of the givens," whereas he proposes that the structure of the economic system be made the object of analysis. Transaction-cost economics adopts this same point of view, but assigns greater importance to the institutional features than does Hurwicz, who emphasizes the incentive mechanisms. For a recent study in the Hurwicz tradition that recognizes, however, that the institutions themselves require special attention, see Masahiko Aoki (1984).

result, organizational variety is not disregarded but located centrally on the research agenda.

Transaction-cost economics joins aspects of law, economics, and organization theory in an effort to deepen organizational insight and develop refutable implications. It approaches the study of firms, markets, and mixed modes as a unified subject in which the economizing of transaction costs is central. Organizational variety is explained by the fact that transactions differ in their attributes, which means that their governance needs vary. Transaction-cost economies are realized by assigning transactions to governance structures in a discriminating way. This approach to the study of economic organization is akin to what Ronald Coase (1972) has characterized as "the direct approach to the problem."

This would concentrate on what activities firms undertake, and would endeavor to discover the characteristics of groupings of activities within firms. . . . In addition to studying what happens within firms, studies should also be made of the contractual arrangements between firms (long-term contracts, leasing, licensing arrangements of various kinds including franchising, and so on), since market arrangements are the alternative to organization within the firm. (Coase 1972, p. 73)

Section 8.1 sets out the rudiments of transaction-cost economics. Section 8.2 elaborates the process features of this approach. And Section 8.3 summarizes its refutable implications. The final section offers some concluding remarks.

8.1   The rudiments

James Buchanan (1975, p. 229) has argued that "economics comes closer to being a 'science of contract' than a 'science of choice' . . . [on which account] the maximizer must be replaced by the arbitrator, the outsider who tries to work out compromises among conflicting claims." The approach taken here adopts the science-of-contract orientation but supplants the arbitrator with an institutional-design specialist. The object is less to resolve conflict in progress than to recognize potential conflict in advance and devise governance structures to forestall or attenuate it. The analysis of transactions requires recognizing the main behavioral attributes of the human agents who are engaged in contracting. It further requires identifying the basic attributes with respect to which transactions differ. The object is to study contracting processes not mainly in ex ante or ex post respects but rather in their entirety.

8.1.1   *Behavioral assumptions*

Economists tend to be rather casual in their statements of behavioral assumptions. This reflects a widespread opinion that the realism of the assumptions is unimportant and that the fruitfulness of a theory turns on its implications (Friedman 1953). Although there is much to be said for this viewpoint, Percy Bridgman (1955, p. 450) reminds social scientists that "the principal problem in understanding the actions of men is to understand how they think – how their minds work." This is especially relevant to the study of alternative means of contracting. As I discuss below, the prevailing view of economic man – a high-powered maximizer given to simple self-interest seeking – effectively removes the study of contract from the research agenda.

The transaction-cost approach makes an effort to come to terms with what Frank Knight (1971, p. 270) referred to as "human nature as we know it." At least three attributes of human nature are important to the study of the economics of process: cognitive competence, motivation, and self- and social-regard. I will treat these under the headings of rationality, motivation, and dignity, respectively. Transaction-cost economics relies expressly and repeatedly on the first two of these. The third has yet to be introduced in a systematic way.

8.1.1.1 *Rationality:* One can distinguish three levels of rationality. The first or strongest form is maximizing. This is the orientation of neoclassical economics, in which firms are reduced to production functions, consumers are characterized as utility functions, institutions are taken as given, and optimizing is ubiquitous. Comprehensive contracting of the Arrow-Debreu kind is an especially ambitious – indeed, mind-boggling – form of maximizing.[2] The need to study alternative means of contracting would vanish if comprehensive intertemporal trading were feasible.

Bounded rationality is the cognitive assumption on which transaction-cost economics relies. This is a semistrong form of rationality in which economic actors are assumed to be *"intendedly* rational, but only *limitedly* so" (Simon 1962, p. xxiv). Regrettably, Simon's simultaneous reference to intended but limited rationality has been resisted by both economists and noneconomists, albeit for different reasons. Economists object to it because they mistakenly interpret limits on rationality in

---

[2] As James Meade (1971, p. 166) puts it, all trading is reduced to a "single gigantic once-for-all forward 'higgle-haggle' in which all contingent goods and services . . . are bought and sold once and for all now for money payments made now."

terms of nonrationality or irrationality. Regarding themselves as the "guardians of rationality" (Arrow 1974, p. 16), economists are understandably chary of such an approach. Other social scientists take exception to Simon's definition because the reference even to intended rationality makes too great a concession to the economists' favored mode of inquiry. The upshot is that bounded rationality invites attack from both sides.

By contrast, transaction-cost economics embraces bounded rationality and maintains that both parts of the definition should be respected. The intended-rationality part of the definition calls for an economizing orientation, and a recognition that competence is limited encourages the study of institutions. Thus intended rationality supports a presumption that parties to a transaction will seek out and attempt to implement opportunities to realize efficiency. Respect for limited rationality elicits deeper study of nonstandard forms of organization. Given limited competence, how do the parties organize so as to utilize their limited competence to best advantage?

Comprehensive contracting is not a realistic organization alternative when rationality is bounded (Radner 1968). If mind is the scarce resource (Simon 1978, p. 12), then economizing on claims against it is plainly warranted. Assessing the efficacy of alternative means of contracting enters the economic calculus largely for this reason. More generally, the concept of bounded rationality recognizes that the problems with which human actors are attempting to cope are very complicated in relation to their cognitive abilities. Heuristic programming, with respect, for example, to Rubic's cube (Heiner 1983, p. 563), is a common consequence.

The weak form of rationality is process or organic rationality. This is the type of rationality with which modern evolutionary approaches (Alchian 1950; Nelson and Winter 1982) and Austrian economics (Menger 1963; Hayek 1967) are associated. But whereas Nelson and Winter deal with evolutionary processes within and between firms, the Austrian approach is concerned with processes of the most general kinds – the institutions of money, markets, aspects of property rights, law, and so on. As Louis Schneider puts it (in his introduction to Menger 1963, p. 16), broad societal institutions of these kinds "are not planned. A general blueprint of the institutions is not aboriginally in anyone's mind. . . . [Indeed,] there are situations in which ignorance . . . works more 'effectively' toward certain ends than would knowledge of and planning toward those same ends."

Although transaction-cost economizing is surely an important factor contributing to the viability of the institutions with which Austrian economics is concerned, the research agendas of organic rationality and transaction-cost economics are rather different. They are nevertheless complementary; each will arguably benefit from the insights of the other (see Chapter 1 in this volume).

8.1.1.2 Motivation: One can also distinguish three levels of self-interest seeking. The strong form is opportunism, by which I mean self-interest seeking with guile. This includes but is scarcely limited to more blatant forms – such as lying, stealing, and cheating. Opportunism more often involves subtle forms of deceit. Both active and passive forms and both ex ante and ex post types are included.

Ex ante and ex post opportunism are recognized in the insurance literature under the heading of adverse selection and moral hazard, respectively. The first of these is a consequence of the inability of insurers to distinguish among risks and of the unwillingness of poor risks candidly to disclose their true risk condition. Failure of the insured to behave in a fully responsible way and to take appropriate risk-mitigating actions is responsible for ex post execution problems. Both of these types of insurance conditions are subsumed under the heading opportunism.

More generally, opportunism refers to the incomplete or distorted disclosure of information, especially to calculated efforts to mislead, disguise, obfuscate, or confuse. It vastly complicates problems of economic organization by compounding the sources of uncertainty. As a consequence, both principals and third parties (arbitrators, courts, and the like) are burdened with much more difficult inference problems. Moreover, it is not necessary that all parties be given to opportunism in identical degree. Indeed, problems of economic organization are compounded if the propensity to behave opportunistically is known to vary among members of the contracting population – since gains can then be realized by expending resources to discriminate among types.

Nicholas Georgescu-Roegen's (1971, pp. 319–20) discussion of behavior that deviates from the rules is consonant with this view of human nature. As he puts it,

observation of what happens in the economic sphere of organizations, or between organizations and individuals, . . . [reveals] phenomena that do not consist of tâtonnement with given means toward ends *according to the rules.* They show beyond any doubt that in all societies the typical individual continually pursues also an end ignored by the standard framework: the increase of what he can claim as his. . . . It is the pursuit of this end that makes the individual a true agent of the economic process. (Emphasis added.)

Plainly, were it not for opportunism, all behavior could be rule-governed. Moreover, this need not imply comprehensive preplanning: Unanticipated events could be dealt with by general rules, whereby the parties agree to be bound by actions of a joint-profit-maximizing kind. Many of the governance structures for which orthodoxy has no adequate explanation have the purpose of deterring opportunism.

As discussed in Section 8.1.2, opportunism is a troublesome source of uncertainty in economic transactions – which uncertainty would vanish if individuals were either fully open and honest in their efforts to realize individual advantage or, alternatively, if full subordination, self-denial, and obedience could be presumed. Open and simple self-interest seeking is the behavioral assumption on which neoclassical economics relies. It is the semistrong form of self-interest seeking. Obedience is the weak (really null) form; it amounts to nonself-interest seeking.

Although neoclassical man confronts self-interested others across markets, this merely presumes that bargains are struck on terms that reflect original positions. But these initial positions will be fully and candidly disclosed upon inquiry; state-of-the world declarations will be accurate; and execution will be governed by the rules. Accordingly, whereas parties realize all advantages to which their wealth, resources, patents, knowhow, and the like lawfully entitle them, these are all evident from the outset. There are *no surprises thereafter*. Issues of economic organization thus turn on technological features (e.g., scale economies), there being no problematic behavior attributable to rule-deviance among human actors.[3]

Obedience is the behavioral assumption that Georgescu-Roegen associates with social engineering. He quotes (1971, p. 348) Adolph Lowe as follows: "One can imagine the limiting case of a monolithic collectivism in which the prescriptions of the central plan are carried out by functionaries who fully identify with the imposed macrogoals. In such a system the economically relevant processes reduce almost completely to technical manipulations."[4] The full identification to which Lowe refers implies stewardship of an extreme kind in which self-interestedness vanishes. Although it is a recurrent theme throughout utopian and related literatures, to project such "mechanistic orderliness . . . [is even] more unwarranted than the basic position of standard economics" (Georgescu-Roegen 1971, p. 348). Problems of economic or-

---

[3] Neoclassical economics operates mainly within this framework. Externalities and public goods are plainly exceptions. Both are inconsistent with the standard neoclassical presumption of simple self-interest seeking with candid disclosure.

[4] The statement by Lowe appeared in Lowe (1965, p. 142).

ganization would be greatly simplified if this condition of obedience were satisfied – or even closely approximated. Robots have the feature that they satisfy obedience requirements at zero social conditioning cost, albeit within a limited range of responsiveness.

8.1.1.3 Dignity: The unrestricted cognitive competence with which economic man is endowed is curiously joined with a naive view of human nature.[5] The evolution from economic to organizational man alters both of these, but one at the expense of the other. Thus the organizational man with which the study of contracting is concerned is cognitively less competent (subject, as he is, to bounded rationality), but motivationally more complex (given, as he is, to opportunism) than his economic-man predecessor. The problem of economic organization that emerges from this statement of the behavioral assumptions can be set forth compactly: Organize transactions so as to economize on bounded rationality while simultaneously safeguarding them against the hazards of opportunism.

Instructive though such a statement is, this conception of the problem of economic organization is arguably too narrow in two related respects. First, transaction-cost economics may be fine as far as it goes, but it does not go far enough; important aspects of economic organization are inadvertently foreclosed. Second, transaction-cost economics can be deepened even within its own terms.

A behavioral feature that, I believe, has a bearing on both of these possibilities is the value, hitherto ignored, that humans place on dignity. This has special relevance for the economics of process, moreover, since the means as well as the ends have a bearing on dignity.

Analyzing the economizing of transaction costs without regard to dignity encourages the view that individuals can be considered strictly as instruments. Such an approach may be excusable in studying the governance process in capital markets and in many intermediate-product markets. But sensitivity to human needs for self- and social-esteem becomes important when the organization of work (labor markets) comes under scrutiny.

Issues of process economics that come up in this last connection include worker participation in decision making and demands for due process. As transaction-cost economics now stands, both are treated in

---

[5] Lief Johansen (1979, p. 499) describes this combination as schizophrenic. Whether organizational man is free of or merely suffers from a different form of schizophrenia is uncertain.

an ad hoc rather than an integrated manner.[6] A more systematic treatment is plainly needed.

Transaction-cost economics has made headway in studying the governance of contractual relations by identifying those transactions for which the demands on cognitive competence and the strains of opportunism are greatest. These are the transactions for which specialized governance is most apt to be needed. The parallel strategy for studying dignity would be to argue that dignity is not uniformly important in all transactions but is especially important for some. The role of transaction-cost economics would thus be to ascertain the transactions for which dignity is most critical and to develop the corresponding ramifications for governance structure.

This would be appropriate if dignity were entirely a private value. The parties in these circumstances would craft governance structures that make due provision for dignity. I submit, however, that dignity has important social consequences. Parties who devise governance structures in view only of their private utilitarian calculus will thus undervalue dignity in relation to its social importance (assuming that positive social valuation applies at the margin). Society is the loser if the political and social competencies of the parties are degraded. Such effects are all the more serious if a private utilitarian approach to dignity in economic transactions impairs not only the political and social competencies of the immediate parties but has adverse spillover on others as well. Such results are avoided only by a recognition that society has a stake in dignity and that otherwise neglected systems-effects many need to be recognized and economic incentives corrected appropriately.

This is a complicated issue to deal with. The approach proposed here is to maintain that dignity is equally valued for all transactions and to ask whether governance structures that are crafted in the light of a utilitarian calculus pose a remediable threat to dignity. Might, for example, certain socially valued forms of participation be denied that, at slight cost, could be restored by a simple change in the character of the governance structure? This approach maintains a sensitivity to trade-offs but avoids the wholesale neglect of social values.[7]

---

[6] For a discussion of concerns for dignity in the context of atmosphere, see Williamson (1975, pp. 37–9). Participation is discussed briefly in Williamson (1980, pp. 34–5; 1982, pp. 15–17).

[7] The virtue of the human-relations literature is that it recognizes, albeit in a language different from that employed here, that dignity is intrinsically important and is systematically undervalued. A problem with much of this literature is that it does not acknowledge tradeoffs. A more productive approach that has better prospects for yielding a predictive theory of organization and for informed social intervention is to adopt the more discriminating orientation described here.

8.1.2   Underlying dimensions

The principal dimensions with respect to which transactions differ are asset specificity, uncertainty, and frequency. The first is the most important dimension, and the one that most distinguishes transaction-cost economics from other treatments of economic organization. But both of the other two dimensions play a significant role.

8.1.2.1 Asset specificity: I have discussed asset specificity and its ramifications at length elsewhere (Williamson 1971, 1975, 1979, 1981, 1983). Suffice it to observe here that (1) asset specificity refers to a situation in which durable investments are undertaken in support of particular transactions and the value of those investments would be much lower in best alternative uses or by alternative users should the original transaction be prematurely terminated; (2) the specific identity of the parties to a transaction plainly matters in these circumstances, which is to say that continuity of the relationship is valued; whence, (3) contractual and organizational safeguards arise in support of transactions of this kind, which safeguards are unneeded (would be the source of avoidable costs) for transactions of the more familiar neoclassical or nonspecific variety. Thus, whereas neoclassical transactions take place within markets where "faceless buyers and sellers . . . meet . . . for an instant to exchange standardized goods at equilibrium prices" (Ben-Porath 1980 p. 4), exchanges that are supported by transaction-specific investments are neither faceless nor instantaneous.

It is common practice to distinguish between fixed and variable costs; but this is merely an accounting distinction. What is more relevant to the study of contracting is whether assets are redeployable or not (Klein and Leffler 1981). Many assets that accountants regard as fixed are in fact redeployable – centrally located general-purpose buildings and equipment are examples. Other costs that accountants treat as variable often have a large nonsalvageable part – firm-specific human capital is one illustration. Figure 8.1 helps to make the distinction.

Thus we can divide costs into fixed *(F)* and variable *(V)* parts. But we can also classify them according to degree of specificity: highly specific *(S)* and nonspecific *(N)*. The shaded region at the bottom of Figure 8.1 is the troublesome one for purposes of contracting. This is where the specific assets are located. Such specificity is responsible for the Fundamental Transformation, a pervasive and important process phenomenon that is described in Section 8.2.1. Some of the leading implications of asset specificity, in its various forms, for the organization of economic activity are developed in Section 8.3.

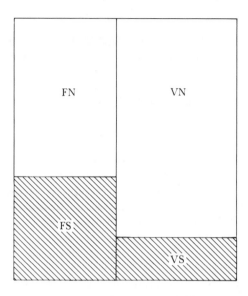

Figure 8.1. Costs (fixed and variable) in relation to assets (specific and nonspecific).

8.1.2.2 Uncertainty: Many of the interesting issues with which transaction-cost economics is involved reduce to an assessment of adaptive, sequential decision making. The basic proposition here is that governance structures differ in their capacities to respond effectively to disturbances. To be sure, these issues would vanish were it not for bounded rationality, since then it would be feasible to develop a detailed strategy for crossing all possible bridges in advance.[8] Similarly, were it not for opportunism, it would be possible to adapt effectively using the general-rule device described above. Confronted, however, by the fact of bounded rationality and opportunism, one must make comparative-institutional assessments of the adaptive attributes of alternative governance structures.

As Friedrich Hayek maintained, interesting problems of economic organization arise only in conjunction with uncertainty (Hayek 1945, pp. 523–4). He (p. 524) thus dismissed equilibrium economics with the

---

[8] Simon has taken the somewhat extreme position that the distinction between deterministic complexity and uncertainty is inessential. What is referred to as "uncertainty" in chess is "uncertainty introduced into a perfectly certain environment by inability – computational inability – to ascertain the structure of the environment. But the result of uncertainty, whatever its source, is the same: approximation must replace exactness in reaching a decision" (Simon 1972, p. 170).

observation that "the economic problem of society is mainly one of adaptation to changes in particular circumstances of time and place." Disturbances are not, however, all of a kind. It is useful to distinguish the origins of the disturbances. In particular, what I refer to as behavioral uncertainty is of special importance to an understanding of the issues in transaction-cost economics.

Although there is a hint in earlier discussions that uncertainty can have behavioral origins (Williamson 1975, pp. 26–37), this idea generally goes unremarked. Thus Tjalling Koopmans (1957, pp. 162–3) describes the core problem of the economic organization of society as that of facing and dealing with uncertainty and distinguishes between primary and secondary uncertainty. Primary uncertainty is uncertainty of a state-contingent kind, while secondary uncertainty arises "from lack of communication, that is from one decision maker having no way of finding out the concurrent decisions and plans made by others"– which he judges to be "quantitatively at least as important as the primary uncertainty arising from random acts of nature and unpredictable changes in consumers' preferences" (Koopmans 1957, p. 163).

The secondary uncertainty to which Koopmans refers appears to be of a rather innocent and nonstrategic kind. There is a lack of communication; but he makes no reference to uncertainty that arises because of strategic nondisclosure, disguise, or distortion of information. (Note that information distortion involves not a lack of information but the conscious supply of false and misleading signals.) Also, the plans to which Koopmans refers are merely unknown. He nowhere suggests the possibility that parties make strategic plans in relation to each other[9] that are the source of ex ante uncertainty and ex post surprises.

Uncertainty of a strategic kind is attributable to opportunism; I will call it *behavioral uncertainty*. It is presumably akin to what Ludwig von Mises (1949, p. 112) refers to as case probability, where "case probability is a particular feature of our dealing with problems of *human action*.

[9] The Holmes-Moriarty dilemma described by Oskar Morgenstern (1935 [1976, pp. 173–4]) is an illustration: "Sherlock Holmes, pursued by his opponent, Moriarty, leaves London for Dover. The train stops at a station on the way, and he alights there rather than travelling on to Dover. He has seen Moriarty at the railway station, recognizes that he is very clever and expects that Moriarty will take a faster special train in order to catch him in Dover. Holmes' anticipation turns out to be correct. But what if Moriarty had been still more clever, had estimated Holmes' mental abilities better and had foreseen his actions accordingly? Then, obviously, he would have travelled to the intermediate station. Holmes, again, would have had to calculate that, and he himself would have decided to go on to Dover. Whereupon, Moriarty would again have 'reacted' differently. Because of so much thinking they might not have been able to act at all or the intellectually weaker of the two would have surrendered to the other in the Victoria Station, since the whole flight would have become unnecessary."

Here any reference to frequency is inappropriate, as our statements always deal with *unique events*" (emphasis added).[10]

Thus even if it were possible to characterize in advance the general propensity of a population to behave opportunistically and perhaps even to screen for trustworthiness, uncertainty would remain. Knowing that one is dealing with a trader who comes from one part of the opportunism distribution rather than another does not fully describe the uncertainties that arise. These added uncertainties can be evaluated only upon projecting the devious responses (and replies) that opportunism introduces. And these can be evaluated only in conjunction with *the particulars of the contract*. Knowledge of particulars, however, does not preclude surprises. The capacity for novelty in the human mind is rich beyond imagination.[11] The issues here are nicely put by Lief Johansen (1979, p. 511), who observes that the study of economic behavior between motivationally complex economic agents is complicated by the fact that the "range of possible messages, offers, threats, etc. which can be given during the process, including the timing of moves, is hard to delimit. Imagination and ability to surprise the opponents may be important points, and very often the 'agenda' will expand during the process." Surprise moves often elicit complex replies. Bounded rationality limits are quickly reached – since the entire decision tree cannot be generated for even "moderately complex problems"[12] (Feldman and Kanter 1965, p. 615).

To be sure, behavioral uncertainties would not pose contractual problems were transactions free from exogenous disturbances – since then there would be no occasion to adapt, and unilateral efforts to alter

---

[10] G. L. S. Shackle (1969, p. 55) likewise remarks that "in a great multitude and diversity of matters the individual has no record of a sufficient number of similar acts, of his own or of other people's, to be able to construct a valid frequency table of the outcomes of acts of this kind. Regarding these acts, probabilities are not available to him." Georgescu-Roegen (1971, p. 83) evidently agrees: "[A] measure for all uncertainty situations . . . has absolutely no meaning, for it can be obtained only in an intentionally mutilated representation of reality. We hear people almost every day speaking of 'calculated risk,' but no one yet can tell us how he calculated it so that we can check his calculations." Events that involve "novelty" cannot be described by probability distributions (Georgescu-Roegen 1971, p. 122).

[11] "By saying that everybody was surprised at the announcement by President Johnson not to seek or accept the 1968 presidential nomination we do not simply mean that the *ex ante* belief in his move had been extremely small: we simply mean that nobody else had thought of it" (Georgescu-Roegen 1971, p. 123).

[12] Inasmuch as a great deal of the relevant information about trustworthiness (or its absence) that is generated during the course of bilateral trading is essentially private information – in that it cannot be fully communicated to others (Williamson 1975, pp. 31–7) – knowledge about behavioral uncertainties is very uneven. The organization of economic activity is even more complicated as a result.

contracts could and presumably would be voided by the courts or other third-party appeal. We would thus observe everywhere an insistence on the original terms of the contract. The ease of enforcing contracts vanishes, however, once the need for adaptation appears. Questions of the following kind then arise: Should maladaptations to changed circumstances be tolerated lest efforts to effect an adaptation give rise to complex behavioral responses by opposite parties who face the prospect of realizing net losses? Can a governance structure that attenuates such behavioral uncertainties be devised? These issues are outside the reach of a neoclassical conception of uncertainty but are nonetheless germane to the study of economic organization.

8.1.2.3 Frequency: Adam Smith's famous theorem that "the division of labor is limited by the extent of the market" is mainly thought to have ramifications for costs of the neoclassical sort. Investments in specialized production techniques will be observed in large markets, since the costs of such techniques are more likely to be recovered in large markets than in small; and general-purpose plant and equipment and procedures will be observed in small markets. Similar reasoning carries over to the study of transaction costs. The basic proposition is this: specialized governance structures are more sensitively attuned to the governance needs of nonstandard transactions than are unspecialized structures,[13] ceteris paribus. But specialized structures come at a great cost, and the question is whether the costs can be justified. The answer varies with the benefits on the one hand and the degree of utilization on the other.

The benefits of specialized governance structures are greatest for transactions that are supported by considerable investment in transaction-specific assets. The reasons here are those described above. The remaining issue is whether the volume of transactions processed through a specialized governance structure utilizes the structure to capacity. The cost of specialized governance structures will be easier to recover for large recurrent transactions. For this reason, the frequency of transactions is a relevant dimension. Where frequency is low but the needs for nuanced governance are great, it may be possible to aggregate the demands of similar but independent transactions. The use of arbitration is an example.

More generally, the object is not to economize on transaction costs

---

[13] This ignores the fact that large firms suffer from bureaucratic disabilities, on account of which it is not the case that a large firm can do everything a small firm can do and more. Unspecialized market governance avoids these bureaucratic disabilities and is sometimes preferred for this reason. See Williamson (1975, pp. 117–31).

but to economize in both transaction-cost and neoclassical production-cost respects. The issue is whether transaction-cost economies are realized at the expense of scale or scope economies. A tradeoff framework is needed to examine simultaneously the production-cost and governance-cost ramifications of alternative modes of organization. A rudimentary apparatus of this kind is developed in Section 8.3.1.

8.2   Process features

The discussion here does not pretend to be an exhaustive treatment of the process features of contract. I merely identify those process features with respect to which transaction-cost economics has an especially close bearing. The first and most important is what I refer to as the Fundamental Transformation, whereby a condition of large-numbers ex ante bidding is transformed into a small-numbers exchange relation during contract execution. The second concerns the limits of legal centralism, on which account private ordering in its various forms emerges. I will then examine the importance of evaluating the contracting process in its entirety, and briefly consider the relation of fairness to contract.

8.2.1   The fundamental transformation

Economists of all persuasions recognize that the terms upon which an initial bargain will be struck depend on whether noncollusive bids can be elicited from more than one qualified supplier. Monopolistic terms will obtain if there is only a single highly qualified supplier, whereas competitive terms will result if there are many. Transaction-cost economics fully accepts this description of ex ante bidding competition but insists that the study of contracting be expanded to include ex post features. Thus, initial bidding merely sets the contracting process in motion. A full assessment requires scrutiny of both contract execution and ex post competition at the contract-renewal interval.

Contrary to earlier practice,[14] transaction-cost economics holds that a condition of large-numbers bidding at the outset does not necessarily imply that a large-numbers bidding condition will obtain thereafter. Whether ex post competition is fully efficacious or not depends on whether the good or service in question is supported by durable investments in transaction-specific human or physical assets. Where no such

[14] See Williamson (1976) for a discussion and critique of the earlier contracting literature in which ex post features were ignored or effectively assumed away. The ex ante – ex post distinctions were originally set out in Williamson (1971).

specialized investments are incurred, the initial winning bidder realizes no advantage over nonwinners. Although it may continue to supply for a long period of time, this is only because, in effect, it is continuously meeting competitive bids from qualified rivals. Rivals cannot be presumed to operate in a condition of parity, however, once substantial investments in transaction-specific assets are put in place. Winners in these circumstances enjoy advantages over nonwinners, which is to say that parity is upset. Accordingly, what was a large-numbers bidding condition at the outset is effectively *transformed* into one of bilateral supply thereafter. The reason why significant reliance investment in durable, transaction-specific assets introduces contractual asymmetry between the winning bidder on the one hand and nonwinners on the other is that economic values would be sacrificed if the ongoing supply relationship were to be terminated.

Faceless contracting is thereby supplanted by contracting in which the identity of the parties matters. Not only would the supplier be unable to realize equivalent value if he redeployed the specialized asset, but the buyer must also induce the other potential suppliers to make the same specialized investments.[15] Thus the parties have clear incentives to work things out rather than terminate the contract. This has massive ramifications for the organization of economic activity.

8.2.2   Legal centralism and private ordering

Most studies of exchange assume that there are efficacious rules of law regarding contract disputes and that these are applied by the courts in an informed, sophisticated, and low-cost way. These assumptions are convenient, in that lawyers and economists are relieved of the need to examine the variety of ways in which individual parties to exchange contract out of or away from the governance structures of the state by devising private orderings. A division of effort thus arises whereby economists are preoccupied with the economic benefits that accrue to specialization and exchange, whereas legal specialists focus on the technicalities of contract law.[16]

The legal-centralism tradition reflects this orientation. It maintains that "disputes require 'access' to a forum external to the original social setting of the dispute . . . [and that] remedies will be provided as prescribed in some body of authoritative learning and dispensed by

---

[15] Alternatively, as described in Section 8.2.3, he could accept supply from an inferior (high-cost) technology in which only general-purpose assets were employed.
[16] The argument here follows Williamson (1983).

experts who operate under the auspices of the state" (Galanter 1981, p. 1). The facts, however, disclose otherwise. Most disputes, including many of those which, under current rules, could be brought to a court, are resolved by avoidance, self-help, and the like (Galanter 1981, p. 2).

The unreality of the assumptions of legal centralism can be defended by pointing to the fruitfulness of the pure exchange model. This is not disputed here. My concern with this tradition is that the law and economics of private ordering has been pushed into the background as a consequence. This is unfortunate, since in "many instances the participants can devise more satisfactory solutions to their disputes than can professionals constrained to apply general rules on the basis of limited knowledge of the dispute" (Galanter 1981, p. 4).

The limitations of general rules and of the application of such rules by disinterested third parties arise from the bounds on rationality to which the courts are subject and from the opportunism to which the parties are given. That the rules are crude rather than refined and fully nuanced is a reflection of the costs of developing refined rules and the difficulty of knowing which rule applies where. The high costs of refining rules are a reflection of bounded rationality. The application of the rules is likewise complicated by bounded rationality (the courts don't know which rule to apply) and by opportunism (each party will represent that the dispute should be governed by the rule most favorable to him or her).

Private orderings will thus presumably arise in support of transactions that predictably experience contractual strain and for which continuity is valued. Inasmuch as the courts are poorly suited to effect continuity, specialized governance appears instead. Specialized third parties – arbitration – is one possibility.[17] Bilateral and unified governance are two others.

The main arguments are those set out above; they are more fully developed elsewhere (Williamson, 1979). The final point to which I want to call attention is that the legal centralism tradition is a comfort to

---

[17] Lon Fuller's (1963, pp. 11–12) remarks concerning procedural differences between arbitration and litigation are instructive: "[T]here are open to the arbitrator . . . quick methods of education not open to the courts. An arbitrator will frequently interrupt the examination of witnesses with a request that the parties educate him to the point where he can understand the testimony being received. The education can proceed informally, with frequent interruptions by the arbitrator, and by informed persons on either side, when a point needs clarification. Sometimes there will be arguments across the table, occasionally even within each of the separate camps. The end result will usually be a clarification that will enable everyone to proceed more intelligently with the case." Many agreements that, were it not for arbitration, would be regarded as excessively hazardous can, in this way, be reached and implemented.

neoclassical analysis in that it avoids the need to engage in the comparative-institutional study of governance. But all institutions, the courts
included, experience cognitive limits and are subject to manipulation.
To characterize contract in terms of legal rules and court adjudication
misses a very substantial part of what the support institutions of contract
are all about (Macneil 1974, 1978).

8.2.3   Contracting in its entirety

Both contract disputes and public policy toward nonstandard contracting commonly focus on contracts at a point in time and without the
benefit of a comparative contractual assessment. This is unfortunate,
since a different and generally deeper understanding of contract
emerges if the main contractual alternatives are expressly identified and
if they are evaluated in an intertemporal, rather than in a point-in-time,
context.

The issues here are akin to those implied in Robert Nozick's (1974, p.
153) remarks on justice: "Whether a distribution is just depends upon
how it came about. In contrast, *current time-slice* principles of justice
hold that the justice of a distribution is determined by how things are
distributed (who has what)" (emphasis in the original). What he refers to
as the current-time-slice approach to justice neglects ex ante bargaining
and evaluates justice in terms of outcomes alone. This has considerable
appeal to those who would use contract enforcement as a means by
which to effect income redistribution or to redress contractual asymmetries that existed between the parties at the outset.

The problem with the ex post approach is that parties who observe
such contract enforcement practices will subsequently strike different
bargains. Some contracts will not go through at all. Other contracts will
be reached on different terms. More generally, the transaction-cost
approach recognizes that administering justice one way rather than
another affects the efficacy of contracting. This means that one can
evaluate the efficiency ramifications of different contract-enforcement
schemes. Unsurprisingly, an examination of the contracting process in
its entirety is especially important for those contracts that are supported
by transaction-specific investments. The issues here are somewhat technical and are developed more fully in Section 8.3.

8.2.4   Process as fairness

Fairness issues of at least three kinds are relevant to an understanding of
contract. The first has to do with participation and has a bearing on the

question of dignity discussed briefly above. The second concerns unanticipated outcomes that are properly described as surprise. The last concerns asymmetric cognitive competence between contracting parties.

8.2.4.1 Participation: Jerry Mashaw (1982) is concerned with participation in his recent examination of due-process ideals for an administrative state. The issues go back to antiquity, however, as the opening quotation in Mashaw's treatise records:

> If you are a man who leads,
> Listen calmly to the speech of one who pleads;
> Don't stop him from purging his body
> Of that which he planned to tell.
> A man in distress wants to pour out his heart
> More than that his case be won.
> About him who stops a plea
> One says: "Why does he reject it."
> Not all one pleads for can be granted
> But a good hearing soothes the heart.
> —The Instruction of Ptahhotep
> (Egyptian, 6th Dynasty,
> 2300–2150 B.C.)

Among other things, failure to provide opportunities to be heard is apt to have demoralization costs of the kind discussed by Frank Michelman (1967). But it could also be argued that such participation is valued for its own sake.

8.2.4.2 Surprise: Karl Llewellyn (1931, pp. 738, 746) notes that "in no legal system are all promises enforceable; people and courts have too much sense," and he subsequently remarks that "when we approach constructive conditions bottomed on the unforeseen, [n]ot agreement, but fairness, is the goal of inquiry. This holds of impossibility, and of frustration; it holds of mistake." I submit that at least some of the unforeseen issues to which Llewellyn refers are those that are properly characterized as surprise within the context of uncertainty discussed in Section 8.1.2. Conditions that give rise to impossibility, frustration, and mistake arguably fall outside of the usual probability calculus. Forcing them in, by insistence that the conditions in question are merely low probability events for which due allowance was made by the parties, is certainly a convenience to those to whom the fiction of comprehensive contracting is appealing. If, however, such insistence flies in the face of reason and common sense, "the people and the courts" will eventually find a way to treat outliers differently. Here as elsewhere, the problem is how to deal with the exceptions in a disciplined manner. Transaction-cost economics, I submit, should help to order the issues.

Taking fairness into consideration is particularly critical when the unforeseen is a consequence of opportunism. In comparing systems that are rigidly governed by legal rules and those that admit legal exceptions, we should recognize that more contracting will take place, and more gains from trade will be realized, in a contracting system in which the more extreme behavioral uncertainties are truncated.

8.2.4.3 Asymmetries: Contracting with minors is an example of asymmetric information in which the courts refuse to enforce contracts. But of course minors are only a specific case where limited competence and contractual naiveté are especially evident. Consumer protection for adults may be warranted for products that are particularly difficult to evaluate and for which reputation effects are weak. The disincentive effects of such protection are nevertheless real, whence its application should presumably be reserved for egregious abuses. Where, however, the "lop-sidedness of bargain result" (Llewellyn 1931, p. 744) is observed to be systematic, the presumption that the lop-sidedness is supported by asymmetric information – which in turn owes its origins to bounded rationality and opportunism (Williamson 1975, pp. 31–7) – is probably warranted.

8.3   Applications

Although "the purpose of science in general is not prediction, but knowledge for its own sake," prediction is nevertheless "the touchstone of scientific knowledge" (Georgescu-Roegen 1971, p. 37). Like other alternatives to orthodoxy, transaction-cost economics must be assessed partly by its capacity to yield new or deeper predictive results.

Some of the implications of the transaction-cost approach to the study of economic organization are presumably evident from the foregoing. In what follows, I will briefly discuss some others – under the headings of vertical integration, nonstandard contracting, the organization of work, regulation, and the modern corporation.

8.3.1   Vertical integration

The main factor to which transaction-cost economics appeals to explain vertical integration is asset specificity.[18] Absent this, autonomous con-

---

[18] The material in this subsection is based on Williamson (1983).

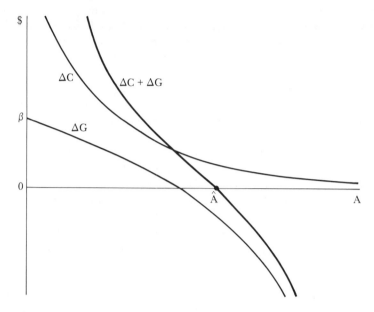

Figure 8.2. Representative differences in net production and governance costs.

tracting between successive stages of production is a mode of organization that economizes effectively on both transaction costs and production costs. As asset specificity increases, however, the balance shifts in favor of internal organization. A heuristic display of what is at stake is shown in Figure 8.2 – where, for convenience, output is assumed to be constant. ΔC refers to production-cost differences between internal and market organization (which is everywhere positive), ΔG refers to governance-cost differences between internal and market organization, $\Delta C + \Delta G$ is the vertical sum (which turns negative at $\hat{A}$), and A refers to the degree of asset specificity.

The production-cost penalty for using internal organization is great for standardized transactions for which market-aggregation economies are great, whence ΔC is large where A is low. This cost disadvantage decreases but remains positive for intermediate degrees of asset specificity. Despite dissimilarities, outside suppliers are nevertheless able to aggregate the diverse demands of many buyers and can thus produce at lower costs than can a firm that produces its own needs. As goods and services become unique (A is high), however, aggregation economies of outside supply can no longer be realized, whence ΔC asymptotically approaches zero. Contracting out affords neither scale nor scope economies in these circumstances.

The governance-cost penalty of internal organization is also positive at low values of asset specificity. The intercept β reflects the bureaucratic-cost disadvantage to which internal procurement is subject (Williamson 1975, pp. 118–30). As asset specificity increases, however, the continuity needs of the parties increase and the cost of market governance becomes great. Furthermore, ΔG declines as the cost of using the market increases in relative terms, eventually becoming negative. The cross-over value at which the sum ($\Delta C + \Delta G$) becomes negative is shown by $\hat{A}$

Several implications obtain immediately:[19]

1. Market procurement has advantages in both scale-economy and governance respects where asset specificity is slight.
2. Internal organization enjoys the advantage where asset specificity is substantial. Not only does the market realize little aggregation-economy benefits but, because of the lock-in problems that arise when asset specificity is high, market governance is actually hazardous.
3. Intermediate degrees of asset specificity give rise to mixed governance in which some firms will be observed to buy, others to make, and all to express dissatisfaction with their current procurement solution. Nonstandard contracts (see Section 8.3.2) may arise in these circumstances.

One can derive further implications from the notion of transaction-cost economizing by recognizing that asset specificity takes a variety of forms and that the organizational ramifications vary among these forms. We can usefully distinguish four types of asset specificity: site specificity (e.g., successive stations that are located cheek by jowl so as to economize on inventory and transportation expenses); physical-asset specificity (e.g., specialized dies that are required to produce a component); human-asset specificity that arises in a learning-by-doing fashion; and dedicated assets that represent a discrete investment in generalized (as contrasted with special-purpose) production capacity – investment that would not be made but for the prospect of selling a significant amount of product to a specific customer. Each type of asset specificity has its distinct organizational ramifications.

---

[19] Further comparative-static implications can be deduced by shifting the cost curves to reflect changing scale-economy and bureaucratic-cost conditions.

1. *Site specificity.* Common ownership is the preponderant response to a condition of asset specificity that arises when successive stages are located close to each other. Such specificity is explained by a condition of asset immobility, which is to say that the setup or relocation costs are great. Once located, the parties are therefore operating in a bilateral-exchange relation for the useful life of the assets.

2. *Physical-asset specificity.* If assets are mobile and the specificity is attributable to physical features, market procurement may still be feasible if the buyer owns all of the specific assets (e.g., the specialized dies) and uses a bidding procedure to select the seller. Lock-in problems are avoided because the buyer can reclaim the dies and reopen the bidding should contractual difficulties develop.[20] Thus ex post competition is efficacious and internal organization is unneeded.

3. *Human-asset specificity.* Any condition that gives rise to substantial human-asset specificity – be it learning by doing or chronic problems of moving human assets in team configurations – favors common ownership, whence an employment relation rather than autonomous contracting characterizes the exchange.

4. *Dedicated assets.* Investment in dedicated assets involves expanding existing plant on behalf of a particular buyer. Common ownership in these circumstances is rarely contemplated. Trading hazards are nevertheless recognized and are often mitigated by expanding the contractual relation to include hostages, thereby to effect equilibration.

Yet another implication of transaction-cost reasoning is that where firms are observed both to make and to buy an identical good or service, the internal technology will be characterized by greater asset specificity than will the external technology, ceteris paribus.[21]

8.3.2   Nonstandard commercial contracting

The transaction-cost approach to nonstandard contracting generates a whole series of predictions about vertical-market restrictions, Robinson-Patman price discrimination, reciprocal sales arrangements (of which the use of identical product for swaps or exchanges is a special

---

[20] See Teece (1982).
[21] This needs to be qualified for certain special cases, but the statement in the text will normally obtain.

case), and two-part pricing. It does not justify such practices in general, but it indicates the extent to which such practices can and often do arise in the service of economic efficiency. Some serve to deter free-riding and curb externalities; others serve to safeguard investments in specific assets. Whether they serve a useful function or not depends, of course, on whether the transactions in question are subject to strain (Do externalities exist? Are specific assets exposed?) and on whether the nonstandard terms afford meaningful relief. Furthermore, inasmuch as some of these same practices can be used to achieve or perfect monopoly, it is appropriate to scrutinize the market-power ramifications of these practices. Such concerns can be disregarded, however, unless the requisite preconditions to support strategic behavior – mainly high concentration together with high barriers to entry – are satisfied. Even where such conditions exist, the causal linkage between the nonstandard contracting practices in question and the enhancement or maintenance of market power needs to be shown. And there are tradeoffs where nonstandard practices simultaneously serve efficiency and promote market power.

The study of many of these practices is facilitated by examining the contracting process in its entirety in the context of what I have referred to elsewhere as the "hostage model" (Williamson 1983). Assume that the product in question can be produced by either of two technologies. One is a general-purpose technology; the second is a special-purpose technology. The special-purpose technology requires greater investment in transaction-specific durable assets and, as described below, is more efficient for serving steady-state demands.

It is common practice to distinguish between fixed and variable costs; but this is not the critical distinction for contracting. The question is whether assets, either fixed or variable, can be productively redeployed (Klein and Leffler 1981). The two technologies in question will thus be described in value-realization terms. The value that can be realized by redeploying variable and fixed costs will be given by v. The nonsalvageable value of advance commitments will be denoted by k. The two technologies can thus be described as

T_1: the general-purpose technology, all advance commitments of which are salvageable, and the redeployable unit operating costs of which are v_1;

T_2: the special-purpose technology, the nonsalvageable value of advance commitments of which are k and the redeployable unit operating costs of which are v_2.

Inasmuch as the second technology poses greater contractual risk, there is an interesting choice between these technologies only if $k + v_2 < v_1$.

Oliver E. Williamson

Assuming that the product is supplied on competitive terms, the supply price under T_1 will be $p_1 = v_1$. The price at which product is supplied under technology T_2 is a bit more complicated and requires that both the stochastic nature of demands and of supplier assurances, if any, be described. Assume in this latter connection that buyers have the option of confirming or canceling orders after demands are registered, and consider the following two contracting scenarios:

1. The producer makes specific-asset investments of k in the first period and receives $\bar{p}$ in the second period if the buyer confirms the order but nothing otherwise, and
2. the producer makes specific-asset investments of k in the first period and receives $\hat{p}$ in the second period if the buyer confirms the order and h if the buyer cancels.

Scenario 2 can be thought of as one in which the buyers post a bond or, more generally, supply a hostage, of h to be delivered upon the cancellation of the order.

If it is assumed that $\bar{p}$ and $\hat{p}$ are break-even prices and that the steady-state costs of T_2 are substantially below those of T_1, it can be shown that $p_1 > \bar{p} > \hat{p}$. It can further be shown that contracting scenario 2 leads to supply on marginal-cost terms if $h = k$. The schematic in Figure 8.3 summarizes the options.

Among the issues to which this model can be applied are the following:

1. Unlawful price discrimination is not necessarily implied by the fact that identical quantities of product are priced differently to two different customer classes if one class offers a hostage but the other does not.
2. Reciprocal sales agreements can promote efficiency if the products in question are supported by investments in transaction-specific assets, especially if the stochastic disturbances to which the products are subject are highly correlated.
3. Product swaps or exchanges (for example, for petroleum and aluminum) are specific illustrations of the general reciprocal-sales argument for which it is especially likely that disturbances will be highly correlated.
4. Nonlinear pricing schemes sometimes serve to safeguard transactions for which specific assets are exposed and promote trading on marginal-cost terms.

An issue related to all of the above, and on which transaction-cost economics also has a bearing, is: Why should parties engage in all of the *indirect* contracting practices if a simple realignment of the incentives

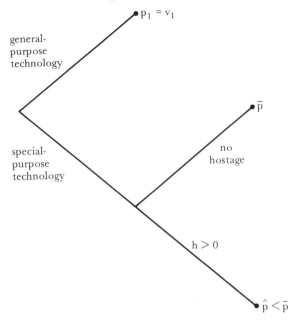

$p_1 = v_1$

general-
purpose
technology

$\bar{p}$

special-
purpose
technology

no
hostage

$h > 0$

$\hat{p} < \bar{p}$

Figure 8.3.

would accomplish the same purposes? Why, for example, should a supplier require a buyer to expose specialized physical assets rather than
have him post a security bond? The answer turns on an examination of
the expropriation hazards that sometimes appear when generalized
purchasing power (money) is used as the bond. To be sure, institutional
(nonpecuniary) safeguards, where specialized assets are mutually exposed, are not without their own disabilities. But the basic point is this:
The simple mathematics of aligning contractual incentives is predisposed to favor pecuniary instruments; as a consequence, the distinctive
benefits that nonstandard contracting institutions afford are typically
ignored. The fact that so many contractual anomalies have long resisted
a rational economic explanation is due in large part to the prevailing
pecuniary or anti-institutional bias.

8.3.3   The organization of work

The transaction-cost approach also generates a whole series of propositions regarding the organization of work.[22] One set of arguments deals

[22] The issues are developed in Williamson (1982).

with the efficiency incentives to surround labor contracts with protective governance structures. The general proposition here is that jobs that involve investments in firm-specific human capital are ones for which the parties – both firm and worker – have a mutual interest in devising a governance structure in which they have confidence.

A second and related set of propositions concerns labor unions (or, more generally, collective organization). Other things equal, unions will appear earlier in firms where workers acquire firm-specific knowledge and skills. Additionally, wherever unions have been organized (for whatever reason), the extent to which a complex governance structure is developed will vary directly with the degree of human-asset specificity.

To be sure, power and other relational considerations also have bearing on work organization. Sociologists and other students of labor organization often emphasize these features to the neglect of efficiency. Although a complete treatment will make provision for all, more attention to refutable implications (and less to rhetoric) is arguably warranted. Transaction-cost economics maintains this orientation.

8.3.4   Regulation

Transaction-cost economics also has ramifications for the study of regulation. Franchise bidding for natural monopolies is one illustration; two-part pricing is another.

8.3.4.1 Franchise bidding: Monopoly supply is efficient where economies of scale are large in relation to the size of the market. But as Milton Friedman (1962, p. 128) observes, "There is unfortunately no good solution for technical monopoly. There is only a choice among three evils: private unregulated monopoly, private monopoly regulated by the state, and government operation."

Friedman characterized private unregulated monopoly as an evil because he assumed that private monopoly ownership implies pricing on monopoly terms. As subsequently argued by Harold Demsetz (1968), George Stigler (1968), and Richard Posner (1972), however, an outcome of monopoly price can be avoided by using ex ante bidding to award the monopoly franchise to the firm that offers to supply the product on the best terms. Demsetz (1968, p. 57) advances the argument for franchise bidding for natural monopoly by stripping away "irrelevant complications" – such as equipment durability and uncertainty. Stigler (1968, p. 19) contends that "customers can auction off the right to sell electricity, using the state as an instrument to conduct the auction. . . . The auction . . . consists of . . . [franchise bids] to sell cheaply." Posner agrees and furthermore holds that franchise bidding is an efficacious way by which to award and operate community antenna television (CATV) franchises.

Transaction-cost economics recognizes merit in the argument but insists that both ex ante and ex post contracting features be examined.[23] Only if competition is efficacious at *both* stages does the franchise bidding argument go through. The attributes of the good or service to be franchised are crucial to the assessment. Specifically, if the good or service is to be supplied under conditions of uncertainty and if nontrivial investments in specific assets are involved, the efficacy of franchise bidding is highly problematic. Indeed, the implementation of a franchise-bidding scheme under these circumstances essentially requires the progressive elaboration of an administrative apparatus that differs mainly in name rather than in kind from that associated with rate-of-return regulation. It is elementary that a *change in name lacks comparative-institutional significance.*

This is not, however, to suggest that franchise bidding for goods or services that are supplied under decreasing-cost conditions is never feasible, nor is it to suggest that extant regulation or public ownership can never by supplanted to good effect by franchise bidding. Examples include local-service airlines and, possibly, postal delivery. The winning bidder for each can be displaced "without posing serious asset valuation problems – since the base plant (terminals, post offices, warehouses, etc.) can be owned by the government and other assets (planes, trucks, etc.) will have an active second-hand market. It is. not, therefore, that franchise bidding is totally lacking in merit, but that those who have favored this mode have been insufficiently discriminating in their endorsement of it" (Williamson 1976, pp. 102 – 3). The selective application of the argument thus has clear ramifications for deregulation – suggesting where such reforms are feasible and where they are not.

8.3.4.2 Two-part pricing: Installation fees paid in conjunction with utility services have some of the attributes of a two-part pricing scheme in which there is both a flat and a variable fee. The variable fee is linked to marginal cost and influences efficient utilization. The flat fee covers fixed costs. The parties to such arrangements have an incentive to create a governance structure in which both have confidence. Victor Goldberg (1976) has argued that regulatory commissions may owe their origins to agency purposes of this kind.

---

[23] The argument was first set out in and is based on Williamson (1976).

8.3.5   Internal organization

Transaction-cost economics has been brought to bear on the study of internal organization in two related ways. One set of issues, which has been of special interest to radical economists, is to explain the evolution of work modes within the factory. This involves an examination of the contracting attributes of the putting-out system, peer groups, inside contracting, and the authority relation. Stephen Marglin (1974) and others contend that hierarchical modes of work organization supplanted earlier modes not because of technology but because they operated in the service of power. But this conceives the issues too narrowly. A microanalytic examination of the *contracting* attributes of alternative modes reveals that hierarchy can and often does yield economies – albeit of a transaction-cost rather than of a neoclassical (technological) kind (Williamson, 1980).

Transaction-cost economics also can be and has been brought to bear on the study of the modern corporation, with special attention to its internal-organization attributes. Both forward integration into distribution (as reported by Chandler 1977) and the invention and diffusion of the multidivisional structure (Chandler 1962) have been interpreted as organizational innovations that economize on transaction costs (Williamson 1975, 1981). An interesting literature is in progress in which these issues are being developed in both conceptual and empirical respects (Armour and Teece 1978; Teece 1980, 1982; Cable and Speer 1978; Fama and Jensen 1983).

8.3.6   Recapitulation

The argument of this section might be summarized this way:

1. Vertical integration is a governance response to the underlying contractual strains that develop between autonomous traders when asset specificity is great.
2. Different types and degrees of asset specificity call for different types of vertical-integration responses.
3. A variety of nonstandard contracting practices owe their origins to the fact that goods and services for which specialized investments are made will be traded on superior terms if the hazards that attend such transactions are equilibrated using hostages or their equivalents.
4. Collective modes of organizing work (including unions) can and often do promote mutual confidence and thereby encourage firms and workers to make investments in firm-specific human capital that would otherwise be refused.

5. The efficacy of franchise bidding for public utilities – and, more generally, of regulation and deregulation – turns fundamentally on whether durable, nonmobile, special-purpose investments in plant and equipment are needed to support the services in question.
6. The hierarchical organization of the corporation and the internal governance thereof is jointly a reflection of bounded rationality, opportunism, and the characteristics of the assets that are employed.

8.4 Concluding remarks

Pretransaction-cost economics takes the organization of economic activity as given and characterizes firms as production functions with a motive of profit maximization (Coase 1972; Smith 1974). Ronald Coase (1972, p. 63) laments this situation, but observes that his classic 1937 article, in which transaction costs were featured, has been "much cited and little used." Vernon Smith (1974, p. 321) nevertheless declares that the orthodox approach is dead and argues that the "new microtheory will, and should, deal with the economic foundations of organization and institution, and this will require us to have an economics of information and a more sophisticated treatment of the technology of transacting."

The transaction-cost approach described in this chapter alerts social scientists to attributes of economic organization different from those to which they are accustomed. The distinctive features of this approach to the study of economic organization are these: (1) a set of behavioral assumptions that describe organizational man as cognitively less competent but motivationally more complex than his economic-man counterpart; (2) a set of underlying dimensions that describe transactions in more microanalytic detail[24] than has previously been employed, with asset specificity as the most distinctive and important of these dimensions; and (3) a comparative-institutional strategy for evaluating alternative modes of organization that assigns transactions to governance structures according to the criterion of transaction-cost economizing.

What has hitherto been regarded as a set of diverse and anomalous contracting practices has been shown to be variations on a common theme: economizing on transaction costs. Although the details differ, the underlying regularities are the same. This is gratifying, since "whenever the capacity to recognize an abstract rule . . . has been acquired in one field, the same master mould will apply when the signs

---

[24] As Llewellyn (1931, p. 751) puts it, "[O]nly in close study of facts salvation lies."

for those abstract attributes are evoked by altogether different elements" (Hayek 1967, p. 50). Transaction-cost economics is nevertheless primitive and in need of refinement. Furthermore, it needs to be joined with other approaches to the study of economic process. I am confident that developments of both kinds will be forthcoming and that the evolving theory of economic organization will be deepened as a consequence.[25]

References

Alchian, Armen. 1950. "Uncertainty, Evolution, and Economic Theory." *Journal of Political Economy* 58(3):211–21.
Aoki, Masahiko. 1984. *The Cooperative Game Theory of the Firm.* New York: Oxford University Press.
Armour, H. O., and David Teece. 1978. "Organizational Structure and Economic Performance." *Bell Journal of Economics* 9:106–22.
Arrow, Kenneth J. 1974. *The Limits of Organization.* New York: Norton.
Ben-Porath, Yoram. 1980. "The F-Connection: Families, Friends, and Firms and the Organization of Exchange." *Population and Development Review* 6(1):1–30.
Bridgman, Percy. 1955. *Reflections of a Physicist.* New York: Philosophical Library.
Buchanan, James M. 1975. "A Contractarian Paradigm for Applying Economic Theory." *American Economic Review* 65:225–30.
Cable, John, and W. Speer. 1978. "Internal Organization and Profit: An Empirical Analysis of Large U.K. Companies." *Journal of Industrial Economics* 27:13–30.
Chandler, Alfred D., Jr. 1962. *Strategy and Structure.* Cambridge: MIT Press.
1977. *The Visible Hand.* Cambridge: Belknap Press.
Coase, Ronald H. 1972. "Industrial Organization: A Proposal for Research." In *Policy Issues and Research Opportunities in Industrial Organization,* ed. Victor R. Fuchs. New York: National Bureau of Economic Research.
Demsetz, Harold. 1968. "Why Regulate Utilities?" *Journal of Law and Economics* 11:55–66.
Fama, Eugene F., and Michael Jensen. 1983. "Separation of Ownership and Control." *Journal of Law and Economics* 26 (June).
Feldman, Julian, and Hershel Kanter. 1965. "Organizational Decision Making," In *Handbook of Organizations,* ed. James March. Chicago: Rand McNally.
Friedman, Milton. 1953. "The Methodology of Positive Economics." In *Essays on Positive Economics.* Chicago: University of Chicago Press. Reprinted in William Breit and Harold Hochman, eds., *Readings in Microeconomics.* 2d ed. Hinsdale, Ill.: Dryden Press, 1977.
1962. *Capitalism and Freedom.* Chicago: University of Chicago Press.
Fuller, Lon L. 1963. "Collective Bargaining and the Arbitrator." *Wisconsin Law Review* (January): 3–46.
Galanter, Marc. 1981. "Justice in Many Rooms: Courts, Private Orderings, and Indigenous Law." *Journal of Legal Pluralism* 19:1–47.
Georgescu-Roegen, Nicholas. 1971. *The Entropy Law and the Economic Process.* Cambridge: Harvard University Press.

---

[25] For similar views see Michael Jensen (1982, p. 10).

Goldberg, Victor. 1976. "Regulation and Administered Contracts." *Bell Journal of Economics* 7(2):426–52.

Hayek, Friedrich A. 1945. "The Use of Knowledge in Society." *American Economic Review* 35:519–30.

1967. *Studies in Philosophy, Politics, and Economics*. Chicago: The University of Chicago Press.

Heiner, Ronald A. 1983. "The Origin of Predictable Behavior." *American Economic Review* 83(4):560–95.

Hurwicz, Leonid. 1973. "The Design of Mechanisms for Resource Allocation." *American Economic Review* 63(2):1–30.

Jensen, Michael. 1982. "Organization Theory and Methodology." Working Paper no. MERC 82-11. University of Rochester.

Johansen, Lief. 1979. "The Bargaining Society and the Inefficiency of Bargaining." *Kyklos* 32:497–521.

Klein, Benjamin, and K. B. Leffler. 1981. "The Role of Market Forces in Assuring Contractual Performance." *Journal of Political Economy* 89:615–41.

Knight, Frank H. 1971. *Risk, Uncertainty, and Profit*. Chicago: University of Chicago Press. (First published in 1921).

Koopmans, Tjalling. 1957. *Three Essays on the State of Economic Science*. New York: McGraw-Hill.

Llewellyn, Karl. 1931. "What Price Contract?–an Essay in Perspective." *Yale Law Journal* 40:704–51.

Lowe, Adolph. 1965. *On Economic Knowledge*. New York: Harper and Row.

Macneil, Ian. 1974. "The Many Faces of Contract." *University of Southern California Law Review* 67:691–816.

1978. "Contracts: Adjustments of Long-Term Economic Relations under Classical, Neoclassical, and Relational Contract Law." *Northwestern University Law Review* 72:854–906.

Marglin, Stephen A. 1974. "What Do Bosses Do? The Origin and Functions of Hierarchy in Capitalist Production." *Review of Radical Political Economics* 6(2):60–112.

Mashaw, Jerry. 1982. "Appropriate, Competent, and Dignified: Due Process Ideals for an Administrative State." Draft.

Meade, James. 1971. *The Controlled Economy*. London: Allen and Unwin.

Menger, Carl. 1963. *Problems of Economics and Sociology*. Trans. F. J. Nock. Urbana: University of Illinois Press. [First published in 1883.]

Michelman, Frank. 1967. "Property, Utility, and Fairness: Comments on the Ethical Foundations of 'Just Compensation' Law." *Harvard Law Review* 80:1165–1257.

Mises, Ludwig von. 1949. *Human Action*. New Haven: Yale University Press.

Morgenstern, Oskar. 1935. "Vollkommene Voraussicht und wirtschaftliches Gleichgewicht." *Zeitschrift fur Nationalokonomie* 6, Part 3. Trans. Frank Knight in Andrew Schotter, ed., *Selected Writings of Oskar Morgenstern*. New York: New York University Press, 1976.

Nelson, Richard R., and Sidney G. Winter. 1982. *An Evolutionary Theory of Economic Change*. Cambridge: Harvard University Press.

Nozick, Robert. 1974. *Anarchy, State, and Utopia*. New York: Basic Books.

Posner, Richard. 1972. "The Appropriate Scope of Regulation in the Cable Television Industry." *Bell Journal of Economics* 3:98–129.

Radner, Roy. 1968. "Competitive Equilibrium under Uncertainty." *Econometrica*. 36:31–58.

Shackle, G. L. S. 1969. *Decision, Order, and Time in Human Affairs*. 2d ed. Cambridge: Cambridge University Press.

Simon, Herbert A. 1962. "The Architecture of Complexity." *Proceedings of the American Philosophical Society* 106:467 – 82. Reprinted in Simon, *The Sciences of the Artificial*. 2d ed. Cambridge: MIT Press, 1981.

1972. "Theories of Bounded Rationality." In *Decision and Organization*, ed. C. McGuire and R. Radner. Amsterdam: North-Holland.

1978. "Rationality as a Process and as a Product of Thought." *American Economic Review* 68:1 – 15.

Smith, Vernon. 1974. "Economic Theory and Its Discontents." *American Economic Review* 64:320 – 2.

Stigler, George. 1968. *The Organization of Industry*. Homewood, Ill.: Richard D. Irwin.

Teece, David. 1980. "Economies of Scope and the Scope of the Enterprise." *Journal of Economic Behavior and Organization* 1(3):223 – 45.

1982. "Towards an Economic Theory of the Multiproduct Firm." *Journal of Economic Behavior and Organization* 3:39 – 64.

Williamson, Oliver E. 1971. "The Vertical Integration of Production: Market Failure Considerations." *American Economic Review* 61:112 – 23.

1975. *Markets and Hierarchies: Analysis and Antitrust Implications*. New York: The Free Press.

1976. "Franchise Bidding for Natural Monopolies – in General and with Respect to CATV." *Bell Journal of Economics* 7:73 – 104.

1979. "Transaction Cost Economics: The Governance of Contractual Relations." *Journal of Law and Economics* 22(2):233 – 61.

1980. "The Organization of Work: A Comparative Institutional Assessment." *Journal of Economic Behavior and Organization* 1(1):5 – 38.

1981. "The Modern Corporation: Origin, Evolution, Attributes." *Journal of Economic Literature* 19:1537.

1982. "Efficient Labor Organization." CSOI Discussion Paper no. 123. University of Pennsylvania.

1983. "Credible Commitments: Using Hostages in Support of Exchange." *American Economic Review* 73:519 – 40.

CHAPTER 9

Capitalism and the factory system

AXEL LEIJONHUFVUD

9.1 Introduction

Economic theorizing utilizes, on the one hand, mathematical techniques and, on the other, thought experiments, parables, or stories. Progress may stagnate for various reasons. Sometimes we are held back for lack of the technique needed to turn our stories into the raw material for effective scientific work. At other times, we are short of good stories to inject meaning into (and perhaps even to draw a moral from) our models. One can strive for intellectual coherence in economics either by attempting to fit all aspects of the subject into one overarching mathematical structure or by trying to weave its best stories into one grand epic.

This chapter attempts to revive an old parable, Adam Smith's theory of manufacturing production, which has been shunted aside and neglected because it has not fitted into the formal structure of either neoclassical or neo-Ricardian theory. The discussion attempts to persuade not by formal demonstrations (at this stage) but by suggesting that the parable can illuminate many and diverse problems and thus become the red thread in a theoretical tapestry of almost epic proportions.

The subject may be approached from either a theoretical or a historical angle. Regarding the theoretical starting point, it is possible to be brief since the familiar litany of complaints about the neoclassical constant-returns production function hardly bears repeating. The one point about it that is germane here is that it does not describe production as a process, that is, as an ordered sequence of operations. It is more like a recipe for bouillabaisse where all the ingredients are dumped in a pot, (K, L), heated up, $f(\cdot)$, and the output, X, is ready. This abstraction from the sequencing of tasks, it will be suggested, is largely responsible for the well-known fact that neoclassical production theory gives us no

I am especially grateful for the comments and constructive help of my UCLA colleague Daniel Friedman. I have also benefited from the comments of Earlene Craver, Christina Marcuzzo, Annalisa Rosselli, David Teece, Oliver Williamson, and the members of Albert Hirschman's seminar at the Institute for Advanced Study.

203

clue to how production is actually organized. Specifically, it does not help us explain (1) why, since the industrial revolution, manufacturing is normally conducted in factories with a sizable work force concentrated to one workplace; (2) why factories relatively seldom house more than one firm; or (3) why manufacturing firms are capitalistic in the sense that capital hires labor rather than vice versa.

9.2   Revolutions: agricultural and industrial

The story of the industrial revolution has often been told around the theme of technical invention and innovation in spinning and weaving, in steel making and power generation, in freight transportation, and so on. Similarly, the agricultural revolution that preceded it sometimes seems just a long catalogue of new crops, new rotations, new ways to drain or fertilize land, new techniques of selective breeding, and the like.

If one looks at the two revolutions from the standpoint, not of technological history, but of a new institutional history, the agricultural revolution becomes primarily the story of enclosures and the industrial one the story of the coming of the factory system and, eventually, of the joint-stock corporation.

It is customary in standard treatments of eighteenth-century English economic history to hail both these organizational developments as obvious examples of progress. Carl Dahlman (1980, pp. 209 – 10) has pointed out that the juxtaposition of the two poses something of a paradox, for one process seems to be almost the reverse of the other. The reorganization of agriculture, known as the enclosure movement, was a move away from the collective "team" working of village land. Each family ended up working their own farm. Correspondingly, it required the unscrambling of joint-ownership rights in land held in common (and of obligations owed to the collective). In the somewhat later reorganization of manufacturing we have the reverse. The coming of the factory was a move toward collectively organized modes of production. It replaced the family-firm craftshop and the putting-out system. The craftshop run by a master craftsman with a couple of journeymen and apprentices and with family helpers had been the dominant type of manufacturing business since the early Middle Ages. Under the putting-out system, an entrepreneur "put out" materials for processing at piece rates by workers who usually worked at home. The factory pulled the work force in under one roof. Later on, the limited liability manufacturing corporation arose to pool individual titles to physical capital in the joint-stock arrangement.

Thus the Dahlman paradox: What is progress in manufacturing is backwardness in agriculture and vice versa! The open field system and enclosures are admirably analyzed in Dahlman's book. The present inquiry concerns the factory system.

9.3   The factory system

Contemporaries tended, of course, to marvel at the new inventions and to be deeply impressed by the (very visible) role of fixed capital in the new factories. The most prominent features of the factories were (a) the size of the work force in one and the same workplace, and (b) the new machinery. The impulse has been to explain (a) by (b), that is, to take for granted that the novel spinning frames, weaving looms, steam engines, and the other new machinery made the explanation for factory organization of the work almost too obvious to require explicit comment.

Some histories of the industrial revolution have taken the line that the new machinery explains the factories. The point has been made, for example, that the early steam engines, with their low thermal efficiency, were very large, stationary ones; consequently, if one wanted to utilize steam power, one had to pull a sizable labor force in under one roof and run the various machines of the factory by belt transmission from a single source. The answer suggested in this sort of illustration is that the new technologies introduced obvious economies of scale (e.g., in power generation) that led quite naturally to large-scale factory production.

Economies of scale were obviously one aspect of the story. But they do not make the whole story. Some 150 years later, small-scale electrical motors removed the basis for the particular type of scale economy just adduced – but did not, of course, thereby undermine the factory system. (At the same time, the economies of scale in generating electricity were even more formidable than they had been in steam power.) We might also check some centuries earlier. The fourteenth-century arsenal of Venice was one of the wonders of the world for the size of the labor force concentrated in it. Yet, the organization of shipbuilding in the arsenal was not that of a single firm; instead, numerous craftsmen, owning their own tools, each with a few journeymen and apprentices, operated within the arsenal and cooperated via exchange transactions in the building and outfitting of ships. In short, the famous arsenal was not a factory and not a firm.[1]

---

[1] See Lane (1973, esp. pp. 162–5). Production by small firms inside a larger facility remained an important organizational form in manufacturing into this century. A famous example is the Winchester Repeating Arms Company, which operated in this manner until the outbreak of World War I. See Buttrick (1952).

There are other examples of large work forces in one location before the industrial revolution. Large woolen manufacturing workshops existed in England since at least the beginning of the sixteenth century. Their size would not have been dictated by machine technology.[2] Although medieval mining was in general organized as independent partnerships of miners, by the sixteenth century, deeper mineshafts with dangerous ventilation and drainage problems raised the capital requirements in mining beyond the means of artisan miners. The mines became capitalist firms. Alum, bricks, brass, and glass were seventeenth-century examples of technology dictating production in sizable establishments.[3] In these instances, the workplaces were factories and were firms.

The putting-out system was also replaced by the factory system. It exemplified capitalist control of production often without capitalist ownership of the means of production.[4] The organization could be large but the workplaces were, of course, small.

It is not all that obvious, therefore, what role should be assigned to indivisible machinery in explaining the emergence of the factory as the dominant form of manufacturing enterprise. Some questions remain. Why, for example, did not the steam engine simply lead many independent masters to locate in the same workplace (and, perhaps, pay rent for the right to attach their new-fangled machines to the overhead steam-powered shaft)?[5]

9.4   The classical theory of the division of labor

There is one contemporary observer whom economists might be particularly inclined to pay attention to, namely, Adam Smith. The *Wealth of*

---

[2] See Mantoux (1962, pp. 33–6). Mantoux was not willing to count the royal manufactories sponsored by Colbert in France as forerunners of the industrial factory system, mainly because they required royal subsidies or patronage for their continued existence.

[3] Nef (1934). Nef also discusses large plants, such as cannon foundries, in various metallurgical branches.

[4] That is, the individual weaver might own his own loom, for instance. The jobber would own the working capital (the materials).

[5] It was tried: "In the Coventry silk weaving industry the experiment of 'cottage factories' was tried. In the centre of a square surrounded by rows of cottages, an engine-house was built and the engine connected by shafts with the looms in the cottages. In all cases the power was hired at so much per loom. The rent was payable weekly, whether the looms worked or not. Each cottage held from 2 to 6 looms; some belonged to the weaver, some were bought on credit, some were hired. The struggle between these cottage factories and the factory proper lasted over 12 years. It ended with the complete ruin of the 300 cottage factories" (Marx 1906, p. 503). Marx mentions other examples "in some of the Birmingham trades."

Nations is, of course, a bit early (1776) for the mechanized, steam-powered, relatively fixed-capital-intensive factory system to have become established as the wave of the future. Even so, it is worth remembering that Smith did *not* dwell much on machinery as one of the "Causes of Wealth." Instead, of course, he made the *"division of Labour"* his grand theme. In fact, Smith (1776 [1937, p. 9]) does treat the role of machinery as important but as secondary and subsidiary to increasing division of labor in his account of economic progress:[6]

[E]very body must be sensible how labour is facilitated and abridged by the application of proper machinery. It is unnecessary to give any example. I shall only observe, therefore, that the invention of all those machines by which labour is so much facilitated and abridged, seems to have been originally owing to the division of labour.

The classical theory of the division of labor was greatly advanced by Karl Marx in *Das Kapital*.[7] In his day, of course, the factory system was the wave of the present. Marx made the use of machinery the criterion of modern industry, which he associated with factories. At the same time, however, he emphatically agreed with Smith that mechanization followed from the division of labor.[8] In Marx's (1906, p. 369) historical schema, capitalism was subdivided into a manufacturing period ("from the middle of the 16th to the last third of the 18th century") and the subsequent modern industrial epoch. Manufacturing, in Marxist terminology, resulted from applying the principles of the division of labor to as yet unmechanized industry.

In Smith's famous pin-making illustration of the benefits of the division of labor, two modes of organizing production were contrasted.

---

[6] See also Smith ([1776] 1937, p. 86): "The greater their number, the more they naturally divide themselves into different classes and subdivisions of employment. More heads are occupied in inventing the most proper machinery for executing the work of each, and it is, therefore, more likely to be invented." And, of course, the opening paragraph itself (p.1): "The greatest improvement in the productive powers of labour, and the greater part of the skill, dexterity, and judgment with which it is any where directed, or applied, seem to have been the effects of the division of labour."

[7] Marx (1906, Pt. IV, Chaps. XIV, XV, pp. 368–556). This is, of course, a far more extensive treatment than we find in Smith. It is far superior to that of J. S. Mill, who had little of any interest to add to Smith. See *Principles*, Book I, Chaps. VIII and IX:1 (Mill 1964, pp. 116–36.) It is worth noting, however, that Mill (pp. 132, 135) too shared the opinion of Smith and Marx that the advantages of division of labor had precedence over "the introduction of processes requiring expensive machinery" among the "causes of large manufactories."

[8] Kenneth Sokoloff's (1983) study of a large 1832 sample of manufacturing firms in the U.S. northeast finds that "the evidence serves to undercut the notion that the early period of industrialization was based on a proliferation of new, machinery-intensive technologies."

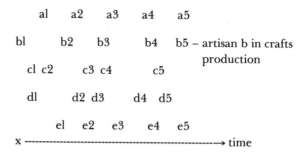

Figure 9.1. Crafts production.

Prejudging matters a little, let us call them crafts production and factory production, respectively.[9]

In *crafts production,* each craftsman sequentially performs all the operations necessary to make a pin. In *factory production,* each worker specializes in one of these operations so that "the important business of making a pin is, in this manner, divided into about eighteen distinct operations which, in some manufactories, are all performed by distinct hands"[10] (Smith 1937, p. 4–5).

Suppose, for illustration, that we have five craftsmen producing a product that requires five successive operations. These must be undertaken in temporal sequence, running from left to right in Figure 9.1. Here each artisan is working at his own pace and the individuals differ in (absolute and comparative) skill across the different operations.

Suppose, next, that we simply rearrange the work in some given workshop as indicated in Figure 9.2. People who previously worked in parallel now work in series. Worker b now performs only operation 2 but does so on all units of output produced by the team. Each individual now has to work at the pace of the team. This, obviously, makes supervision of work effort easier. Note, however, that we do not change the engineering descriptions of the operations performed, we do not change the tools used, and we do not change the people involved. We

---

[9] Marx's distinction between "manufacturing" and "factory production" is a perfectly good and useful one. It is omitted here so as not to burden the discussion with too much terminological baggage.

[10] Everyone recalls his calculation: "Those ten persons, therefore, could make among them upwards of forty-eight thousand pins in a day." Marx checked on pin making in his own day: "[A] single needlemachine makes 145,000 in a working day of 11 hours. One woman or one girl superintends four such machines and so produces near upon 600,000 needles in a day" (Marx 1906, p. 502). The most recent report is Pratten (1980): Today, one operative supervising 24 machines, each of which turns out 500 pins per minute, will make about 6 million pins in a day.

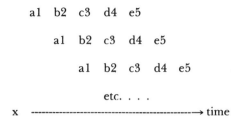

Figure 9.2. Factory production.

might expect output to be unchanged as well, therefore. Yet both Smith and Marx would tell us to expect a large increase in productivity from this reorganization of the work.

The sequencing of operations is not captured by the usual production-function representation of productive activities; nor is the degree to which individual agents specialize. A production function simply relates a vector of inputs to one or more outputs without specifying the method by which the tasks involved are coordinated. Thus Smith's division of labor – the core of his theory of production – slips through modern production theory as a ghostly technological-change coefficient or as an equally ill-understood economies-of-scale property of the function.[11]

The economies achieved by switching from crafts to factory production arise from increased division of labor. In the above example, labor was entirely undivided to begin with, so that the conversion takes us from individual production to *team* production. There are three aspects to this that deserve comment. First, the specialization of labor in team production will require *standardization of product*. Under crafts production, in contrast, the skills and care of individual artisans will be reflected in nonstandard output. Second, serial production requires coordination of activities in the sense of the *time phasing* of the inputs of individual workers. Third, the labor of individual workers become *complementary* inputs. If one work station on an assembly line is unmanned, total product goes to zero.

So far we have supposed that the number of workers and the tools are unchanged and that the only change arises from their improved coordi-

---

[11] Professor Georgescu-Roegen especially stresses the failure of neoclassical production theory to illuminate the fundamental difference between manufacturing processes and agricultural production processes where nature dictates the time phasing of operations. See Georgescu-Roegen (1972), which is reprinted (with several other essays germane to our subject) in Georgescu-Roegen (1976).

nation. But it is obvious that the conversion from crafts to factory production will present opportunities to economize on inputs.[12]

The switch is *capital-saving*. This is an aspect easily missed. The reorganization of production undertaken to increase the division of labor will very often also create opportunities for mechanizing some stage of the process. Hence what we tend to observe is that an increase in fixed capital takes place at the same time. The impression we are left with is that productivity increases are normally due to more capital-intensive technology being adopted.[13] But the pin-making illustration is a counterexample.

In crafts production, each artisan would be equipped with a full complement of pin-making tools. Suppose, for simplicity, that there is a different tool for each of the five stages in the series. Then, four out of five tools are *always idle* when artisans work in parallel under crafts production.[14] In factory production, only one complement of tools is needed, not five.[15]

It is possible that the more decisive capital-saving incentive may be the opportunity to economize on goods-in-process inventories. Suppose that, under crafts production, considerable time (and concentration) is lost in switching from one task to the next. A master craftsman with a thick enough market to allow him to produce in batches would then perform operation 1 x times, before moving on to operation 2, and so on. If his dexterity (as the classical writers used to say) at each task were equal to that of the specialized factory worker, the factory's competitive edge would lie mainly in its lower working-capital requirements. Economizing on goods-in-process is likely to have been particularly important in the evolutionary struggle between the factory and the putting-out system.

[12] Sokoloff has mustered impressive evidence on the efficiency advantages of small, nonmechanized factories over craftshops in the early industrialization of the American northeast. His estimates of total factor productivity show "factories" with more than five employees to be more than 20 percent more productive than artisanal shops. See Sokoloff (1984, secs. III, IV).

[13] Events will sometimes challenge that impression. Swedish economists will recall the Horndal effect (so named by Erik Lundberg). Horndal was a steel mill considered outdated by its controlling corporation, which intended to concentrate production in its more modern plants. Investment in Horndal was therefore stopped altogether. The expectation, of course, was that in a couple of years the mill would not cover variable costs. To the consternation of observers, however, the rate of productivity growth in Horndal kept pace with that of the rest of the industry for many years (Lundberg 1959, pp. 663–4).

[14] It was in fact normal for each craftsman (guild member) to own the tools he was using.

[15] See John Rae (as quoted by Mill 1964, p. 129): "If any man had all the tools which many different occupations require, at least three-fourths of them would constantly be idle and useless."

The switch to factory production will also save on *human capital*. No worker need possess all the skills required to make a pin from beginning to end. Under crafts production, each individual has to spend years of apprenticeship before becoming a master pin maker. In factory production, the skills needed to perform one of the operations can be quickly picked up. The increased productivity resulting from specialization on simple, narrowly defined tasks is the advantage arising from increased division of labor most emphasized by the classical economists. Correspondingly, the decreased investment in human capital is the disadvantage that most concerned them.

9.5 Horizontal and vertical division of labor

There are two dimensions along which the division of labor may be varied. Adam Smith drew examples from both (without, however, making the distinction clear). The manufacture of pins illustrates what we will call *vertical* division of labor. Recall his observation that "in so desert a country as the Highlands of Scotland, every farmer must be butcher, baker and brewer for his own family." When the growth of the market turns slaughtering, baking, and brewing into specialized occupations, we have examples of *horizontal* division of labor.

The distinction is seldom drawn in the literature. This may be in part because those authors, who see the advantages of division of labor as deriving primarily from the concentration of time, experience, and ingenuity on part of individuals on a narrower range of tasks, are looking simply for *all* the differentiations of functions that the expansion of markets will allow. Charles Babbage (1833, pp. 175–6) improved on Smith's statement of the division of labor by making clear how functional differentiation brings comparative advantage into play also inside the individual firm:[16]

That the master manufacturer, by dividing the work to be executed into different processes, each requiring different degrees of skill or force, can purchase exactly that precise quantity of both which is necessary for each process; whereas, if the whole work were executed by one workman, that person must possess sufficient skill to perform the most difficult, and sufficient strength to execute the most laborious, of the operations into which the art is divided.

But there are reasons for making the proposed distinction. An increase in the vertical division of labor requires less skilled labor at the various stages of the manufacturing process. Increased horizontal division of

[16] Babbage found that priority for this statement of the advantages of division of labor belonged to Gioja (1815).

labor does not in general carry this implication and is perhaps more likely to mean an increase in human capital per worker. Furthermore, increased horizontal division is a question simply of *minimum economical scale*, whereas vertical division of labor results from an increasing-returns-to-scale technology.

This implication of pin-making technology may be another reason why the distinction is most often fudged, particularly in the neoclassical literature. Stigler ([1951] 1968, p. 129), in his famous article on the subject, notes the dilemma bequeathed by classical to neoclassical theory:[17]

Either the division of labor is limited by the extent of the market, and, characteristically, industries are monopolized; or industries are characteristically competitive, and the theorem is false or of little significance. Neither alternative is inviting.

Marx saw the significance of the distinction very clearly. The consequences of expansion of the market for a branch of manufacturing, he pointed out, would depend upon the technology. He distinguished two "fundamental forms," namely, "heterogenous manufacture" and "serial manufacture." The latter, of course, was exemplified by Smithian pin making and offered opportunities for vertical division of labor. As an example of the former, Marx used watch manufacturing. All the parts of a watch could be separately manufactured for final assembly. This "makes it . . . a matter of chance whether the detail labourers are brought together in one workshop or not." Heterogeneous manufacture might be carried out under the putting-out system, therefore (Marx 1906, pp. 375ff).

9.6   Social consequences

The competitive impetus to exploit the economies afforded by vertical division of labor would seem to explain, therefore, many of the social consequences of the nineteenth-century factory system that have been the object of so much adverse sociological commentary:[18]

1. When labor is subdivided vertically, less skill is required, less versatility as producer is acquired by the individual worker.

---

[17] Compare Arrow (1979, p. 156): "This dilemma has been thoroughly discussed: it has not been thoroughly resolved." But, surely, there is no genuine dilemma – just our obstinate collective refusal to draw the obvious conclusion and allow the empirical reality of increasing returns to displace the convenient construct of "perfect competition."

[18] See especially Thompson (1967).

The use of child labor at some work stations often becomes
feasible.[19]

2. No normal prospect of promotion or improvement in social
    status is to be expected; the unskilled workman does not be-
    come a master of his guild by sticking to his job for many years.
3. More discipline is required and of a sort that most people will
    find irksome and that most rural emigrants would have to be
    taught; you cannot work at your own pace, you have to be on
    time; random absenteeism must be subject to relatively severe
    sanctions.
4. "Alienation from the product": No worker can take personal
    pride in the output or its quality.

Considerations of this sort do not give one grounds for blundering into
the much controverted subject of the development of standards of
living during the industrial revolution in Britain. The point to be made
is simply that the competitive pursuit of the productivity gains afforded
by the vertical division of labor will explain many of those conditions in
industry that were criticized by contemporary observers.

9.7   The extent of the market

In our simple five-worker example, a doubling of output under crafts
production will require a doubling of all inputs. Under factory production, some economies of scale will *normally* be present. In factory production, "the division of labor depends on the extent of the market" –
and so, therefore, do the scale economies that can be realized. These
will be of two kinds.

9.7.1   Parallel-series scale economies

Suppose, in the example, that one of the workers (worker *d* at work
station 4, let's say) is *idle* half the time after conversion to factory production. Then double the output can be had with nine workers, and the
flow of work would be organized as in Figure 9.3.

This is the source of increasing returns emphasized by Georgescu-
Roegen (1972) as almost universally present in manufacturing – but
not, as all the classical economists agreed, in agriculture. Even on the
sophisticated assembly lines of a large-scale factory some factor ("fund"

[19] Golden and Sokoloff (1984) find that, in the first half of the nineteenth century, even
quite small factories (with five or more employees) were giving a greater share of jobs to
women and children than did artisanal shops.

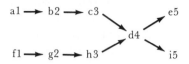

Figure 9.3. Parallel assembly lines.

in Georgescu-Roegen's terminology) is almost bound to have an input stream that is not perfectly continuous. Babbage's "master manufacturer" cannot always divide the work so as to "purchase exactly that precise quantity" of the services of the factor that is technically required to produce his output. A machine that is idle half the time cannot be replaced by half a machine employed all of the time. But it may be possible to double its utilization rate if, say, the machine can be shared between two parallel assembly lines *and* the firm can sell twice the output.

These parallel scale economies are probably never totally exhausted. In our five-stage example, it might be found, for instance, that worker b is busy only 80 percent of the time, in which case a quintupling of output can be had with only a quadrupling of stage 2 workers. And so on. But it is clear that, if we keep the number of serial stages constant, these economies of parallel replication become less and less significant as output is increased. It can in fact be shown that this is a case of assymptotically constant returns (although with a nonmonotonic approach to the assymptote).[20]

9.7.2   Longer-series scale economies

Smith, Marx, and Mill, however, were thinking more of another source of economies of scale, namely, increased vertical division of labor. As the extent of the market grew, opportunities would arise, they thought, for further efficient subdivision of the production process into a greater number of serial tasks. This vertical differentiation would not only be efficient in itself but, as it proceeded, it would open up new possibilities for exploiting scale economies of the Georgescu-Roegen kind.

---

[20] Sokoloff's data suggest that, for nonmechanized factories deriving their competitive advantage solely from the division of labor, economies of scale would tend to be very nearly exhausted already in the size range of six to fifteen employees and totally exhausted at twenty. (For the already mechanized textile industries, the scale economies were much stronger and remained significant up to a far larger scale.) (Sokoloff 1984, sec. III)

9.8 Mechanization and division of labor as a "discovery procedure"

As one proceeds with the analysis of this classical division-of-labor theory, it increasingly escapes the analytical categories of static neoclassical production theory. The classical theory becomes a theory of an *evolutionary process*, rather than a theory of the rational choice between known alternatives.

Recall that Smith and Marx both insisted that the new division of labor *preceded* the mechanization of industry. They also thought that one *led to* the other, and they thought it rather obvious what the causal link was: As one subdivides the process of production vertically into a greater and greater number of simpler and simpler tasks, some of these tasks become so simple that a *machine* could do them. The mental task of analyzing the production process so as to carry through the division of labor leads to the *discovery* of these opportunities for mechanization. Once the principles of the division of labor are mastered, the discovery of how industry can be mechanized follows.

Mechanization, in turn, will renew the sources of economies of scale. Suppose each stage of what was previously a five-stage process is subdivided into two. Suppose further that it is then discovered that stage 4b can be mechanized. But at the old scale of the enterprise, the 4b machine may be idle 90 percent of the time. In that case, the most economical scale of production has multiplied tenfold.

9.8.1 Differentiation of function: capital and labor

The process leads to increasing functional differentiation of both capital equipment and labor. But in one respect the consequences are quite different – and it turns out to be a socially important respect.

Although the tasks that become mechanized tend to be quite simple, completely standardized tasks, the machines very often will be extremely specialized to doing just this one task (or series of tasks) in the production of just one product. This means that they may have no alternative employment. This differentiation of equipment can be observed also in simple handtools:

[S]o soon as the different operations of a labour-process are disconnected the one from the other, and each fractional operation acquires in the hands of the detail labourer a suitable and peculiar form, alterations become necessary in the implements that previously served more than one purpose. . . . In Birmingham alone 500 varieties of hammers are produced, and not only is each adapted to one particular process, but several varieties often serve exclusively for the different operations in one and the same process. (Marx 1906, pp. 374–5)

In the course of this vertical subdivision of the production process, *labor becomes increasingly unskilled.* The sociocultural consequences are disturbing. Adam Smith gradually became so convinced that the division of labor tended to produce an unskilled, illiterate, brutalized proletariat that in the end his *Wealth of Nations* contained two views of the division of labor (West 1964; Rosenberg 1965). In the early chapters, it was The Source of the Wealth of Nations. Toward the end of the book, it became the ruination of the laboring classes. This outlook Marx took over.

From the more narrowly economic standpoint, the vertical subdivision of production makes the machines functionally more specialized or dedicated. A particular machine, as a consequence, may have few alternative uses but is also not easy to replace. With labor, the result is rather different. The individual worker becomes a detail laborer, that is, specialized in the sense that, when at work, he performs only one task. But the task is an unskilled one. The worker, consequently, can be easily replaced and can also easily qualify for alternative tasks. Thus, increasing specialization has quite different implications for the competitive position of capital and of labor, respectively. We will return to this point shortly.

9.9   American and Japanese traditions in production management

The American tradition in production management has made the most of the static advantages of the division of labor: minimal human capital requirements, maximum dexterity in the performance of individual tasks, and minimal time lost in switching between tasks – these are the principles stressed on Henry Ford's assembly lines and in Taylorite time-and-motion studies.

Apparently, Japanese production management violates all of these principles. Each member of a production team is supposed to learn every work station on the assembly line. Human capital input is maximized rather than minimized. But the dynamics of the Smithian evolutionary process are improved. The Japanese teams are better at discovering potential improvements in both products and methods.

9.10   The capitalist firm

Consider next an idyllic thought-experiment of so-called *team production*.[21] A number of individuals come together for the purpose of pro-

[21] Inspired by Alchian and Demsetz (1972).

ducing a particular commodity. In the "Original State," we suppose, there are no marked distinctions of wealth, power, or status among these people. Some of them will contribute their skills and labor, others will commit themselves to bring machines to the joint enterprise.

We may assume that they will decide to take advantage of the Smithian economies of vertical division of labor and so set up production in the form of a single, long assembly line. For simplicity, let there be stages of production, machines, and operatives – one per machine. The product could also be produced by individual artisans using a set of simple handtools or in k shorter assembly lines of n/k workers using less-specialized machines. But we presume, with Smith and Marx, that by setting up on one long assembly line, the collective effort will produce a larger output with the same resources.

The questions are: How many firms will there be? Will the typical firm be a capitalist one? If so, why?

One can imagine the possibility of successive firms, each one buying the output of the stage preceding and selling to the stage succeeding. In half of these firms (one might also imagine), the owner of the machine hires the operative and pays wages, whereas in the other half the worker rents the machine he or she is working with. But these imaginings, of course, fit singularly ill with the ways in which we find modern manufacturing to be organized.

Since the team utilizes the economies of scale due to the division of labor, the enterprise earns a joint rent (or a surplus, if you will). Total sales proceeds exceed the sum of the earnings that the inputs would find in alternative employments. The joint rent is a Sssssnake in this paradise. For how is it to be divided? In our illustration, all the inputs are assumed to be strictly complementary. If one machine is withdrawn from the assembly line, total output falls to zero. If one worker is missing, the consequence is the same. Marginal productivities will not supply the criteria for the distribution of product.

The division of the joint rent becomes a bargaining problem. Let the members of the collective form coalitions among themselves and bargain against the rest. How well might the various coalitions do? How stable would we expect them to be?

Consider first how the bargain might go between the machine owner (capitalist) and the operative (labor) at one of the work stations on the presupposition that the total sum going to this work station has somehow been arrived at. Each can threaten the other to withhold input so that their joint income will go to zero. But the bargaining situation is not symmetrical. There are plenty of unskilled laborers in the market, but few if any substitutes for the specialized machine. This might make us

218   Axel Leijonhufvud

suspect a tendency for the capitalist to walk away with the joint rent, leaving the laborer with a wage equal to alternative earnings. But there is also another asymmetry: The unskilled laborer has many, the specialized machine few, alternative employment opportunities. If, therefore, the laborer could threaten to "fire" the machine, the worker's bargaining position would be very strong indeed. The question becomes who can fire and replace whom? Or: Who owns the work station, the machine owner or the operative?

To get a clue to this question, consider the bargaining situation among the capitalists. Each machine owner can threaten to reduce output and, therefore, everyone else's earnings to zero[22] – until a replacement for the machine can be found. But, again, the market for very specialized machines will be thin, so replacements – and alternative employments – for them are hard to find. Any agreement about the division of earnings among the machine owners would be extremely unstable.[23] So unstable, in fact, that some organization of production that avoids the complementarities between the highly specialized inputs of cooperating owners might be preferred – even at the cost of foregoing the advantages of the division of labor. To sink one's capital into these dedicated machines will not appear to be an attractive investment – unless some stable organizational form can be found.

The solution, of course, is to prevent individual capitalists from owning and controlling specific machines. Instead, a firm is formed and any capitalist who joins has to give up ownership of his machines and accept shares in the firm. Thus the assembly line is vertically integrated into one firm.[24] We might find a market gap between firms along the production chain at some stage where the market in the intermediate product issuing from the stage is thick enough so that firms on both sides of the gap are safe from hold-ups.

The formation of a firm as a solution to the machine owners' bargaining problem has one additional advantage (for them): It creates a cartel

---

[22] In the literature on vertical integration, this is familiar as the postcontractual "opportunistic behavior" of Williamson (1975) or the "hold-up" problem of Klein, Crawford, and Alchian (1978).

[23] Technically speaking, the core is empty since every distribution can be blocked. (It does not seem helpful to insist that the empty core is a transaction-cost problem.) I am especially grateful to Dan Friedman for clarifying the structure of the bargaining situation for me.

[24] That the integration should be vertical does not seem to be necessary in general. In Dahlman's theory of the open field system, avoidance of the hold-up problem explains why the scattering of strips was maintained over the centuries. With arable strips scattered, the individual farmer could not, in some dispute over communal production or distribution issues, threaten to withdraw and thereby to reduce the benefits of scale economies to the village as a whole (Dahlman 1980, pp. 120–30 and 135–8).

of capitalists that bargains as one unit against workers. This cartel will own the work stations. It can fire and replace workers; the workers cannot threaten to fire and replace the dedicated machines. The non-unionized worker is not going to come out of that contest with any part of the joint rent (unless, of course, he or she has some firm-specific capital). As long, at least, as unions can be kept illegal, the factory owners will continue to appropriate all the rent.

Unionization will look like labor's best bet in this situation. Workers cannot pool their labor power, as the capitalists pool their physical capital, in order to hire the machines at a rental that would leave the joint rent going to the workers of the labor-managed firm. Labor will not be owned and specialized machinery is not for hire. The producer cooperative is a possible compromise form but, on the whole, successful enterprises started as worker partnerships are going to end up owning capital and hiring labor – which is to say, end up as capitalist firms. Unions that do succeed in capturing part of the joint rent, on the other hand, might thereby discourage capital accumulation and the further productive subdivision of labor and hence weaken the competitive position of the enterprise over the longer run.

The labor union is a subject on which economics has a less than secure grasp. In neoclassical economic theory, unions are just another pernicious form of monopoly. The alternative "labor relations" tradition tends to reject economic theory and to draw lessons more friendly to unions from labor history. Perhaps the view of the manufacturing firm presented here might provide ground on which theoretical and historical analysis could finally meet?

9.11   Fluctuations and growth

Our representation of the pin-making technology is so simple as to be little more than a metaphor. It is obviously capable of considerable formal elaboration.[25] But at this point the question is whether there are good reasons to prefer it to that other simplistic metaphor, the neoclassical production function. The Smithian production function may well have advantages in areas other than the ones discussed in this essay. It may be worthwhile, in conclusion, to indicate some of these potential applications.

One of the mainstay stylized facts of applied macroeconomics is that employment in manufacturing fluctuates less than proportionally to output over the business cycle. Most macroeconomic models assume a

---

[25] An attempt in this direction is made in Ippolito (1977).

neoclassical constant-returns-to-scale technology and most macroeconomists explain the Okun's law phenomenon as reflecting the hoarding of labor, in particular of workers with firm-specific skills, during recessions. According to this hoarding hypothesis, firms keep workers on during recessions, although they are not needed in production, in order to make sure their skills are available when business picks up again.

The Smithian increasing-returns technology suggests a competing hypothesis. Firms that utilize the scale economies of parallel series (Figure 9.3) will reduce output by shutting down, say, one assembly line of two. But the work station that the two lines have in common cannot be left unmanned. Thus, half the work force cannot be laid off when output is cut in half.[26] By the same token, the laid-off worker cannot by cutting his or her own wage get the line started up again. Individuals are not able by marginal wage-cutting to expand the number of production jobs being offered at the factory in recession.[27]

When the Extent of the Market determines the Division of Labor, economic growth will bring productivity gains. The growing economy will show increasing division of labor not only within firms but among firms. The economy becomes more complex as it expands. When, in our simple illustration, the work of the five artisans was reorganized into a five-man factory, the production process became more complex in the straightforward sense that the number of people cooperating in making any given unit of output increased. It is this increasingly complex coordination (when it can be maintained!) of larger and larger numbers of specialists that shows up as increasing productivity.[28] It is

[26] Marshall's cost curves, which have managed to survive (at least in undergraduate teaching) in uneasy co-existence with neo-Walrasian theory, have a rather natural fit to the Smithian technology. In neoclassical production theory, we cannot be sure that there are any firms to talk about. With the Smithian theory, we at least have no doubts about their existence. Marshall tended to presume long-run decreasing cost for his firms; this property follows directly from the increasing returns of Smithian technology. Marshall's short-run U-shaped average cost schedule gets its downward-sloping segment by the same argument as used above in connection with Okun's Law and its upward-sloping segment, quite conventionally, from the diminishing marginal product of variable factors when fixed factors are kept fixed. Pricing in the markets supplied by these firms, however, should be analyzed in Hicksian, rather than Marshallian terms. We should expect them to be "fix-price" rather than "flex-price" markets.

[27] I very much agree, therefore, with Martin Weitzman that the prevalence of these increasing returns technologies must be taken into account if one is to understand the situation of manufacturing workers in a recession. Unemployment theory, Weitzman argues, must as a first logical requirement explain why unemployed factor units do not set up in production on their own. In the Smithian division of labor case the answer is straightforward: The manufacturing worker simply does not have the skills and knowledge required to make the product as an artisan (see Weitzman 1982).

[28] Another example of an important idea that has not found a home in neoclassical theory but would fit into a Smithian production theory is Erik Dahmen's "development block." In a growing economy, all the component sectors of a Dahmen block have to be completed before any one of them becomes economically viable (see Dahmen 1971).

perhaps overoptimistic to hope that explicit modeling of division-of-labor production would give us an econometric handle on the Solow-Denison growth residuals. But it could give us a better qualitative understanding of how economic development differs from mere economic growth, which would be worth having. An economist used to thinking of production in terms of the Smithian division-of-labor model is likely to be more impressed with the dangers of protectionism, for instance, than colleagues whose thinking runs in neoclassical or neo-Ricardian channels. To the welfare losses arising from impediments to trade in constant (or diminishing) returns models, the Smithian economist[29] would add not only the static loss of scale economies foregone but also the dynamic losses of innovative discoveries foregone when the Smithian evolutionary process is stemmed. Although the loss of competitive improvements never made may be unquantifiable, comparisons between open and closed economies suggest that they are nonetheless the most significant category of welfare losses due to protectionism.

9.12   Conclusion

The theory of the capitalist factory outlined here shares elements with other explanations that have been proposed. It is not to be expected, however, that the proponents of these other theories will be entirely happy with it. The present theory stresses the complementarity of inputs as a central problem as do Alchian and Demsetz (1972), but it does not at all accept their insistence that the bargain between capital and labor is essentially symmetrical. My story has a great many points in common with Williamson's "organization of work" (1980) but differs from his in seeing technological rather than transaction-cost considerations as central. Finally, like Marglin (1974), I recognize an element of power in the capital-labor bargain as essential. Marglin would insist, however, that the capitalists' control of production has no technological or efficiency rationale, whereas I see the capitalists' power as rooted in the efficient, Smithian technology.

References

Alchian, Armen, and Harold Demsetz. 1972. "Production, Information Costs, and Economic Organization." *American Economic Review* 62(5): 777–95.
Arrow, Kenneth. 1979. "The Division of Labor in the Economy, the Polity, and Society." In *Adam Smith and Modern Political Economy*, ed. Gerald P. O'Driscoll, Jr. Ames, Iowa: Iowa State University Press.

[29] This worthy, of course, expects countries with similar factor endowments to export similar products to each other and would not be surprised if trade of this description would reach large volume.

222   Axel Leijonhufvud

Babbage, Charles. 1833. *On the Economy of Machinery and Manufactures.* 3d ed. London: Charles Knight.
Buttrick, John. 1952. "The Inside Contracting System." *Journal of Economic History* 12.
Dahlman, Carl J. 1980. *The Open Field System and Beyond.* New York: Cambridge University Press.
Dahmen, Erik. 1971. *Entrepreneurial Activity and the Development of Swedish Industry, 1919–1939.* Homewood, Ill.: Richard D. Irwin.
Georgescu-Roegen, Nicholas. 1972. "Process Analysis and the Neoclassical Theory of Production." *American Journal of Agricultural Economics* 54(2):279–94.
1976. *Energy and Economic Myths.* New York: Pergamon Press.
Gioja, Melchiorre. 1815. *Nuovo Prospetto delle Scienze Economiche.* Milan: Presso G. Pirotta.
Golden, Claudia, and Kenneth Sokoloff. 1984. "Women, Children and Industrialization in the Early Republic: Evidence from the Manufacturing Censuses." *Journal of Economic History* 44.
Ippolito, Richard S. 1977. "The Division of Labor in the Firm." *Economic Inquiry* 15(4): 469–92.
Klein, Benjamin, Robert G. Crawford, and Armen Alchian. 1978. "Vertical Integration, Appropriable Rents, and the Competitive Contracting Process." *Journal of Law and Economics* 21(2):297–326.
Lane, Frederic C. 1973. *Venice, A Maritime Republic.* Baltimore: Johns Hopkins University Press.
Lundberg, Erik. 1959. "The Profitability of Investment." *Economic Journal* 69:653–77.
Mantoux, Paul. 1962. *The Industrial Revolution in the Eighteenth Century.* Rev. ed. New York: Harper and Row.
Marglin, Stephen A. 1974. "What Do Bosses Do? The Origin and Functions of Hierarchy in Capitalist Production." *Review of Radical Political Economics* 6(2):60–112.
Marx, Karl. 1906. *Capital.* New York: Modern Library.
Mill, John Stuart. 1964. *Principles of Political Economy.* New York: Ashley edition. [First published in 1848.]
Nef, J. U. 1934. "The Progress of Technology and Growth of Large-Scale Industry in Great Britain, 1540–1640." *Economic History Review* 5(1):3–24.
Pratten, Clifford F. 1980. "The Manufacture of Pins." *Journal of Economic Literature* 18(1):93–96.
Rae, John. 1964. *Statement of Some New Principles on the Subject of Political Economy.* New York: Augustus M. Kelley. [First published in 1834.]
Rosenberg, Nathan. 1965. "Adam Smith on the Division of Labour: Two Views or One?" *Economica* 32:127–39.
Smith, Adam. 1937. *An Inquiry into the Nature and Causes of the Wealth of Nations.* New York: Modern Library edition. [First published in 1776.]
Sokoloff, Kenneth L. 1983. "Investment in Fixed and Working Capital during Early Industrialization: Evidence from U.S. Manufacturing Firms." Working Paper no. 311. Los Angeles: University of California.
1984. "Was the Transition from the Artisanal Shop to the Non-Mechanized Factory Associated with Gains in Efficiency?: Evidence from the U.S. Manufacturing Censuses of 1820 and 1850." Los Angeles: University of California. Photocopy.
Stigler, George. 1951. "The Division of Labor is Limited by the Extent of the Market." *Journal of Political Economy* 59(3). Reprinted in Stigler, *The Organization of Industry.* Homewood, Ill.: Richard D. Irwin, 1968.
Thompson, E. P. 1967. "Time, Work-Discipline, and Industrial Revolution." *Past & Present* (December).

Weitzman, Martin L. 1982. "Increasing Returns and the Foundation of Unemployment
    Theory." *Economic Journal* 92:787–804.
West, E. G. 1964. "Adam Smith's Two Views on the Division of Labour." *Economica* 31:
    23–32.
Williamson, Oliver E. 1975. *Markets and Hierarchies.* New York: The Free Press.
    1980. "The Organization of Work: A Comparative Institutional Assessment." *Journal
    of Economic Behavior and Organization* 1(1):5–38.

CHAPTER 10

Rationality, institutions, and explanation

RICHARD N. LANGLOIS

In Chapter 1, I tried to introduce the reader to some of the themes he or she would encounter in this volume. These included: (1) the critique of maximizing rationality; (2) an emphasis on processes and sequences of events; and (3) a concern with the nature and role of social institutions. In this final chapter, I want to explore these themes more deeply. What I say here will, of course, have a good deal of bearing on a program for a New Institutional Economics. Indeed, I will even offer explicitly my own proposal for a research program. But, ultimately, this chapter sets for itself an earlier and more basic task – to sort out some of the methodological issues that surround these three themes.

10.1 The critique of rationality

The trail begins with the crucial but somewhat slippery notion of rationality in economics. One of the best-known and most influential modern discussions of economic rationality is that by Herbert Simon, who put forth the notion of bounded rationality (1955, 1957, 1959) and more recently argued for a distinction between substantive rationality and procedural rationality (1976, 1978a, 1978b). Simon's analysis involves the recognition that individuals often face very complicated decision-problems that they cannot be expected to solve instantly and optimally; such individuals are thus afflicted with bounded rationality, and they must "*satisfice* because they have not the wits to maximize" (Simon 1957, p. xxviii, emphasis in the original). As a consequence, Simon recommends a reduced emphasis on the optimality of particular courses of action (substantive rationality) and greater emphasis on the effectiveness of the procedures used in the choosing (procedural rationality). Simon's critique of maximizing rationality is well taken. None-

I would like to thank Israel Kirzner, Roger Koppl, Brian Loasby, and Richard Nelson for helpful comments.

theless, I will argue that his idea of procedural rationality, if taken literally, is misplaced. The problem with maximizing rationality (if I may put the matter somewhat mysteriously) is not that it is substantive, but precisely the opposite – that it is *too procedural*.

However much economists may wish to distance their ideas of economic rationality from the philosophical doctrines of rationalism, the two must ultimately remain related. Maximizing rationality is closely connected with the rationalist tradition, usually traced from Plato and Descartes, that sees reason as conscious, logical deduction from explicit premises. The criterion for economic rationality is thus the logical consistency of the agent's actions with his or her (explicit) knowledge and preferences. And since, even under conditions of subjective uncertainty, that knowledge and those preferences logically imply a best course of action, the agent is rational only when he or she selects that particular best course.

By this criterion, an economic agent is rational when successful in maximizing some explicit objective (such as utility or profit) within the constraints of well-defined alternatives.[1] Simon's critique of substantive rationality rests on what we might call the argument from complexity. In the real world, this argument goes, problems of economic decision making are frequently extremely complicated: The agent's difficulty in processing masses of information and computing the optimal solution, coupled with natural biases and assorted human frailties, will inevitably prevent him or her from taking the correct rational action.

This understanding of bounded rationality has a good deal of intuitive appeal. But it is important to recognize how little one has to stray from maximizing rationality in order to accept the argument from complexity. The argument in most forms implicitly accepts the Cartesian definition of reason, finding a need for procedural rationality only in the relative difficulty of carrying out the required logical deduction. And this is ultimately quite significant: for if all that's at stake is some constraint on information-processing and computational capacity, then one's satisficing alternative quickly collapses into substantive rationality – satisficing is actually the optimal course of action in view of costly computational resources (Baumol and Quandt 1964). Simon's own conception of bounded rationality is closely tied up with his fascina-

---

[1] In modern economics, this is normally construed as a subjective criterion – the agent is rational when he or she maximizes according to subjectively defined preferences and perceived alternatives. In practice, however, most models assume that the agent is also objectively rational, in the sense that perceived alternatives are in fact the "true" alternatives or (what amounts to the same thing) that all agents perceive the alternatives – and sometimes even the probability distributions over relevant states of the world – identically.

tion with the computer. He often writes as if there really does exist a well-defined optimization problem out there, and the solution to that problem is ultimately the benchmark of rationality; the only difficulty is computational complexity. This is why analogies to chess games or the solution of complex differential equations (e.g., Simon and Stedry 1968) appear so frequently in his discussions. In the end, Simon's theory of knowledge is the Cartesian one, a fact brought out most clearly in his work on so-called artificial intelligence (Dreyfus 1979).

There are, however, a couple of other bounded-rationality arguments in which forms of satisficing behavior and procedural rationality emerge that are *not* logically reducible to substantive rationality. The first, and less interesting, is what Jon Elster (1983, p. 74) calls the special argument for satisficing: We can construct problem situations in which there is simply no substantively rational solution. (For an example, see Frydman, O'Driscoll, and Schotter 1982.) In such cases, the agent is necessarily satisficing, since he or she simply can't be rational according to substantive criteria. The more interesting line of reasoning is what Elster (1983, p. 75) calls the general argument for satisficing.[2] This approach is indeed general in that it effectively extends to *all* choice situations the dilemma of the rational problem without solution. If rationality consists only in the optimal adjustment of means to ends, then rationality must presuppose some framework of means and ends within which the optimization is to take place. But where do these frameworks come from? As a logical matter, they cannot themselves be explained as the result of maximizing choice. For if the choice of frameworks *were* the result of maximizing within some higher framework, the choice of that higher framework would remain unexplained – and so on ad infinitum (Winter 1964, pp. 262–4; Kirzner 1982, pp. 143–5). If we insist that the economic agent is rational only insofar as he or she makes consistent logical choices, then we must consign an important aspect of his or her behavior – the perception of new alternatives and possibilities – to the realm of the nonrational.[3]

---

[2] By "satisficing," I should note, I simply mean any otherwise reasonable behavior that can't be characterized as substantively rational. This is to be distinguished from the narrower sense of satisficing as thermostat-like behavior.

[3] Here we need to make an important distinction between what is nonrational (in that it is not based on fully specified and complete evidence, and thus cannot be placed in the form of a deduction from explicit premises) and what is irrational (in that it is contrary to logical argument). One necessarily misses this distinction if one clings to the neoclassical definition of rationality, since one assumes, in effect, that evidence is always complete. The distinction becomes important when we look at its flip side: It can be not irrational (i.e., not contrary to logical argument) to act on the basis of incomplete evidence – and, therefore, the agent can be rational (in a nonneoclassical sense) even in an open-ended world. (I am indebted to Brian Loasby for suggesting this distinction to me.)

As Littlechild (in this volume) makes clear, this argument does not have to do with the uncertainty faced by an economic agent – at least not with uncertainty as it is construed in conventional modeling. Consider Kenneth Arrow's definition of uncertainty, which I am perhaps unduly fond of quoting. "Uncertainty," he says, "means that we do not have a complete description of the world which we fully believe to be true. Instead, we consider the world to be in one or another of a range of states. Each state of the world is a description which is complete for all relevant purposes. Our uncertainty consists in not knowing which state is the true one" (Arrow 1974, p. 33). The Winter-Kirzner argument is effectively a denial that the economic agent does or could know a collectively exhaustive set of states that are "complete for all relevant purposes."[4] If the argument has to do with uncertainty, it is to the extent that it suggests a broader conception of uncertainty: One can be uncertain not merely about which pregiven state will obtain, but also about which states are possible. This is a view that G. L. S. Shackle has long advocated, and his writings have been perhaps as seminal as those of Simon in the contemporary discussion of economic rationality. Many others – often influenced by Shackle – have also argued for a broader view of uncertainty. Some have talked about "radical" uncertainty or simply ignorance (Loasby 1976); others have suggested the terms "genuine" uncertainty (O'Driscoll and Rizzo 1985) and "extended" uncertainty (Bookstaber and Langsam 1983). My own taxonomic preference is "structural" (as distinguished from "parametric") uncertainty, since that way of putting things highlights the qualitative nature of the distinction between this wider kind of uncertainty and the uncertainty of Arrow's definition[5] (Langlois 1984). This wider conception of uncertainty has lately been creeping into mainstream discussions through a

---

[4] If the accent is on the word "all," then the Simonian argument from complexity is perhaps more appropriate. But if the accent is on the word "relevant," then the Winter-Kirzner argument clearly applies – the agent cannot decide on (neoclassically) rational grounds which states are relevant. The same infinite-regress is at work (see Langlois 1984, n. 14).

[5] The long-familiar way of discussing uncertainty, of course, is to invoke Frank Knight's distinction between risk and uncertainty (Knight [1921] 1971). This has led to much confusion, though, since Knight's uncertainty is subject to several different interpretations. His conception of risk is clear enough: It is what we would now call insurable risk. But his category of uncertainty blurs the distinction between situations of structural uncertainty and situations in which there are well-defined states of the world but simply no objective probabilities to assign those states. Since the so-called Bayesian revolution, we have learned that the absence of objective probabilities is no bar to conceiving of uncertainty along the lines of Arrow's definition. Whether Knight was a radical subjectivist or just an incipient Bayesian is a doctrinal issue into which I have no desire to enter. I would prefer to avoid confusion by banishing the term "Knightian uncertainty" from the discussion.

somewhat different rhetorical channel: the assertion that the agent may be laboring under an optimization problem that is "misspecified" (Cohen and Axelrod 1984).

If one accepts this critique of maximizing rationality in any of its forms, one is left with two choices: either to consign some behavior to the nonrational (and thus to place its consequences beyond the range of economic explanation) or to find a conception of rationality different from that implied by the maximizing criterion.

At the highest level, the latter alternative entails questioning the very idea that reason must involve, and therefore that economic rationality must be defined as, conscious, logical deduction from explicit premises. The implications of this alternative have been most clearly stated by F. A. Hayek (1967, 1973), who identifies a long and well-developed philosophical tradition in which "reason had meant the capacity to recognize truth, especially moral truth, when [one meets] it, rather than a capacity of deductive reasoning from explicit premisses"[6] (Hayek 1967, p. 84). Lawrence Boland makes a somewhat similar distinction. He objects to the maximizing conception of rationality not merely because it limits reason to the process of logical deduction from explicit premises but because of the very fact that it conceives of rationality as a psychological process at all.[7]

The view that rationality is a psychological process is a relic of the late eighteenth century. Even today it is still commonplace to distinguish humans from other animals on the basis that humans can be rational. Thus any criticism of a psychologistic view of rationality might be considered dangerous. Nevertheless, the psychologistic view is based on a simple mistake. It confuses one's *argument* in favor of an individual's decision with the *process* of making the decision. It also confuses being rational with being reasonable – the latter only implies the willingness to provide reasons for one's actions. The reasons may not always be adequate.

The case against psychologistic rationality is rather straightforward. Simply stated, humans cannot be rational – only arguments can be rational. An argument is rational only if it is not logically inconsistent. . . . But, most important, whether an argument is rational can be decided independently of the process of its creation or the psychological state of its creator. (Boland 1982, p. 38)

[6] Hayek (1973, pp. 5, 29) distinguishes the two views of reason as "Cartesian constructivist" versus "evolutionary" rationalism or, in Karl Popper's phrase, as "naive" versus "critical" rationalism. In Hayek's view, it was evolutionary rationalism that characterized the thought of eighteenth-century Scottish moral philosophers such as Adam Smith and David Hume.

[7] Compare Elster's (1983, p. 70) distinction between acting *with* a reason and acting *for* a reason: "Acting with a reason means that the actor has reasons for doing what he does, acting for a reason implies in addition that he did what he did because of those reasons." As Roger Koppl pointed out to me, this is similar to the distinction Alfred Schutz made between "in-order-to motives" and "because motives."

Thus, Boland's alternative is neither substantive *nor* procedural rationality – but rather a situational or institutional conception. (More on this shortly.)

To Hayek, this criterion of rationality consists in nothing so much as the ability to learn from experience. Although this is certainly one aspect of it, I don't think learning fully circumscribes the alternate conception of rationality I'm after. More broadly, I would argue, the criterion of ratonality is the ability to act reasonably, to act appropriately to one's circumstances, to adapt. We will need a name for this, so I will refer to behavior that meets the alternate criterion of rationality as "adaptive" behavior.

10.2   Arbitrariness, problem-situations, and exits

The general argument for satisficing (which ought more properly be called the general argument against maximizing rationality) rests on the arbitrariness of maximization as a criterion of the rational. The power of this criterion is that it supplies a unique outcome as rational: There is only one rational exit. But this apparent uniqueness is in fact illusory. It is bought at the expense of an arbitrary specification of the means-ends framework in which the optimization is to take place. What we are left with is a kind of conservation-of-arbitrariness doctrine. If we want non-arbitrary (rational) behavior, we must specify (arbitrarily) the agent's means-ends framework. If we eliminate this arbitrariness by leaving the framework unspecified – so that the agent is free to choose his or her own framework – then we must impose some (arbitrary) behavioral assumption on the agent in order to arrive at a determinate (unique) result. We can't eliminate arbitrariness without also eliminating determinateness.

The practice of restricting the agent's means-ends framework in order to produce a determinate outcome is what Spiro Latsis (1972, 1976a, 1976b) refers to as single-exit modeling, an approach he finds at the base of the neoclassical research program. As first introduced to economics by Ludwig von Mises, single-exit modeling was an attempt to reconcile a desire for determinate models with a belief in the free will of the economic agent. In a single-exit model, the agent's behavior is not formally preprogrammed. Yet the model has determinate results, because we place the agent in a situation with only one reasonable exit. The agent is free to do as he or she likes; but, by analyzing the logic of the situation, we can determine the unique course of action a reasonable person would take. This is to a large extent an antipsychological method. It doesn't require that we delve too deeply into the motivations of the agent. The constraints imposed by the agent's situation reduce his or her options sufficiently, that a light postulate of reasonable conduct is adequate to secure a determinate outcome.

It was Karl Popper (1957, 1966, 1967) who articulated this idea that theory in the social sciences consists in analyzing the "logic of the situation," although the basic technique goes back at least to Max Weber. What is interesting is that Boland, also citing Popper, offers this situational-logic method as his *alternative* to the "psychologistic" rationalism of neoclassical economics. We thus have situational determinism (a phrase Latsis uses synonymously with single-exit modeling) held up both as the method of neoclassical economics and as the alternative to the method of neoclassical economics. How can this be?

As is normally the case, the paradox turns on the meaning of words. In particular, Latsis and Boland seem to mean different things when they describe a method as antipsychological. Moreover, they have somewhat different notions of what analyzing the logic of the situation entails. Influenced by Simon, Latsis views situational determinism as antipsychological not because it eliminates the psychological conception of rationality, but because it eliminates the psychological *details* of the individual's motivation. Thus, for Latsis, situational determinism uses the problem-situation as a way to avoid considering the agent's internal psychological landscape. "For instance," he says, "in certain situations the *suspension of a vehicle* and *a parachutist's legs* both behave as *shock absorbers*. Yet the internal environments that generate this activity are of very diverse structure and complexity" (Latsis 1976b, p. 18, emphasis in the original). This is nothing other than the ideal-typical method as developed out of the Weberian tradition by Alfred Schutz and Fritz Machlup (Langlois and Koppl 1984). A quick translation of Latsis's physical analogy illustrates the point: We can, in some situations, represent the concrete types "vehicle suspension" and "parachutist's legs" as the ideal type "shock absorber." But this is situational determinism only in a specific and limited sense. The constraints of the situation give one license to replace a diverse and complex set of concrete types with a single ideal type: Because of the nature of the situation, the psychological details just don't matter.

From Boland's point of view, this is psychologism and not analyzing the "logic of the situation" at all. The principle of maximizing behavior programmed into the neoclassical ideal type is not innocent of the psychological conception of rationality merely because the psychology it embodies is an abstract and simplified one. The problem with maximizing rationality is not that it is substantive rationality, but that it is in fact *too procedural*. From Latsis's point of view, by contrast, the act of collapsing the complex psychological process of a concrete agent into the abstract rationality of the ideal type is in fact a transformation to situational logic. The actual decision processes of the agent are replaced by an optimization problem defined solely by the agent's goals and the situation's constraints. Thus, the neoclassical program is psychologism for Boland because it attempts to explain economic phenomena in terms of the psychological states of the agent; and it is antipsychological for Latsis because it makes no reference to the inner environment of the agent.

This is, of course, a little too pat. In fact, the neoclassical program is not as psychologistic as Boland thinks nor as antipsychological as Latsis believes. Psychologism for Boland (1982, p. 30, following Popper) "is the methodological prescription that psychological states are the *only* exogenous variables permitted beyond natural givens (e.g., weather, contents of the Universe, etc.)" (emphasis in the original). Now, it is arguably correct that psychologism of this sort is a long-term goal of the neoclassical program. This is what I described in Chapter 1 as the attempt to construct an institution-free theory. And general-equilibrium theory in the manner of Arrow, Debreu, and Hahn (Debreu, 1959; Arrow and Hahn, 1971) may indeed have accomplished this goal. But as far as the day-to-day positive heuristic of the neoclassical program is concerned, it is clearly wrong to say that psychological states and natural givens are the only exogenous variables: Latsis is quite right that neoclassical modeling takes problem-situations – which are not usually natural givens – as exogenous. This is clearly true of the Marshallian marginalism that Machlup defended in the so-called marginalist controversy (Langlois and Koppl 1984). It is even true of the Stigler-Becker models (Stigler and Becker 1977) that Boland describes as "simple" psychologism. In these models all agents have identical preferences but face different constraints. The constraints are *not* natural givens, however: they are unreduced economic artifacts like budgets and human-capital endowments. Indeed, we can identify a contrapuntal theme within the same neoclassical circles – the attempt to show that economic phenomena can be explained without *any* reference to preferences (Alchian 1950; Becker 1962). I will have more to say about this latter program in a moment.

On the other hand, Latsis is wrong to think that the neoclassical program is antipsychological in any strong sense. If we are considering textbook Marshallian economics, it may be easy to persuade ourselves that not much psychology is at work, that we are studying the reasonable response of agents to a problem at the margin. But if we are looking at models that represent the agent as solving an optimal-control problem with a foot-long objective function, are we really seeing an appeal to the logic of the situation? We might just as well view this kind of maximizing behavior as a form of behavioralism – with a perhaps implausible psychology behind it.

In the end, the neoclassical program is a convolution of psychologism and situational determinism. In most of its manifestations, it takes both psychological states and problem-situations as exogenous. Of course, neither Boland nor Latsis is a fan of this program. Boland wants to eliminate the psychologism; Latsis wants to eliminate the situational determinism in favor of *more* psychology. What is ironic is that the programmatic results of these divergent prescriptions turn out ultimately to be rather similar.

The reason for the similarity has to do with the ambiguity of what it means to add "psychology" to economic theory. Boland is disdainful of psychology. What he wants to add to economics is a more sophisticated philosophy of knowledge. Knowing, he argues, ought to be seen not as a psychological process but as a logical and scientific process. Thus, we should represent actors not as possessing psychologies but as possessing views or philosophies of knowledge; moreover, we should not limit these views of knowledge to inductive philosophies, according to which we build up knowledge by accumulating data, but should consider the Popperian theory of knowledge, according to which we can learn from counterinstances that refute our conjectures[8] (Boland 1982, pp. 178 – 82). The distinction might be encapsulated as learning-from-success versus learning-from-failure.

I think we should follow Boland in this rejection of psychologism. At the same time, however, we should recognize that the distinction be-

---

[8] Ironically – and contrary to what Boland seems to think – Popper himself repudiated his own larger notion of critical rationalism in discussing the rationality principle in economics. "It is necessary," he writes, "to distinguish between rationality as a personal attitude (of which, normally, all individuals with a healthy mind are capable) and the rationality principle. Rationality as a personal attitude consists in the disposition to correct our ideas. Intellectually, in its most developed form, it is a disposition to examine our ideas in a critical spirit and to revise them in the light of critical discussion with others. The 'rationality principle,' on the other hand, has nothing to do with the hypothesis that men are rational in this sense and that they always adopt a rational attitude" (Popper 1967, p. 149, translation mine). This may seem odd, but it connects with what Wade Hands (1984) describes as the division between Popper-sub-n and Popper-sub-s – that is, between Popper's views on the methodology of the natural sciences and his views on the methodology of the social sciences. In discussing the social sciences, Hands argues, Popper abandoned much of his own falsificationist position and came to argue for the rationality principle as a kind of irrefutable "hard core." Whether we should follow Popper in this is another matter. As I've already suggested, Popper's friend Hayek is very willing to associate the conception of rationality in economics with the ability to learn from experience. Hayek, it seems, is more Popperian than Popper (see Caldwell 1984).

tween psychology and the philosophy of knowledge is not at all a sharp one. Boland's recommendation is essentially the man-as-scientist approach that Loasby (in this volume) discusses so well. What is interesting is that Loasby finds this view in the work of a *psychologist,* George Kelly. This begins to suggest, I think, why those who have tried to take up the Simon-Latsis program, who have tried to incorporate more of the agent's internal environment into their models, have often ended up doing precisely what Boland recommends: studying the views of knowledge agents possess and specifying the theories they take with them into their problem-situations (see, for example, Nelson and Winter 1982, chaps. 4, 5). Discussing an agent's psychology and discussing his or her theory of knowledge may be less distinct activities in practice than in principle. In order for the knowledge possessed by the agent to have a role in an economic theory, that knowledge must be *causally adequate.* Boland is right that the agent's knowledge need not be adequate in the sense that it reflects a true and complete theory of his or her situation; but it must be causally adequate in the sense that the knowledge the agent possesses – whatever it may be – provides us with an explanation of his or her behavior (so that we can say it was the "cause" of that behavior). And "explaining behavior" is very often what one means by psychology. Again, this needn't commit us to a simple neoclassical psychology in which preferences are given and unchanging. It may be that Boland would object to some of the theories of decision making that come out of Simonian psychologizing.[9] But that doesn't mean he and the Simonians aren't engaged in activities that are similar for purposes of economic modeling.

From one point of view, this might seem like an untenable claim. It often appears as though there are two conflicting themes in Simon's treatment. On the one hand, his famous notion of satisficing reflects the opinion – consistent with Boland's – that there is in effect too much psychology in economics. "A comparative examination of the models of adaptive behavior employed in psychology (e.g., learning theories), and

---

[9] His main complaint, of course, would be that most theories attributed to the agents are inductivist in his sense: They are theories in which agents acquire knowledge by gathering data. But, even though one may want to reject inductivism as an approach to the philosophy of science, one may still wish to represent an *economic agent* as possessing an inductivist theory. Indeed, there are grounds to argue that inductive learning is precisely the theory held by most people who aren't trained in philosophy (as well as a good many who are). Nor, I think, would Boland deny this. Nonetheless, the idea of modeling economic agents as Popperian falsificationists is an approach worth trying. The picture of man-as-scientist that Loasby paints in his chapter has elements of both inductivism and falsificationism. And, as I will suggest in the next section, one can have a model in which the economic system as a whole is falsificationist – i.e., rejects false conjectures – even when the agents within the system all hold inductive learning theories.

of the models of rational behavior employed in economics, shows," he writes, "that in almost all respects the latter postulate a much greater complexity in the choice mechanisms, and a much larger capacity in the organism for obtaining information and performing computations, than do the former" (Simon [1956, p. 129] 1982, p. 259). In this sense, Simon is calling for economics to *simplify* its treatment of the agent's inner environment. But we can also find Simon seemingly arguing the opposite case – that the psychology of neoclassical models is not complex enough. Consider his famous "molasses" example, which Latsis cites approvingly. Suppose we were pouring molasses into a bowl of irregular shape. How much, he asks, would we have to know about the properties of molasses in order to predict its behavior?

If the bowl were held motionless, and if we wanted only to predict behavior in equilibrium, we would have to know little, indeed, about molasses. The single essential assumption would be that molasses, under the force of gravity, would minimize the height of its center of gravity. With this assumption, which would apply as well to any other liquid, and a complete knowledge of the environment – in this case, the shape of the bowl – the equilibrium is completely determined. Just so, the equilibrium behavior of a perfectly adapting organism depends only on its goal and its environment; it is otherwise completely independent of the internal properties of the organism. (Simon [1959, p. 255] 1982, p. 289)

By contrast, says Simon, we would need more detailed information about the properties of molasses in order to predict its behavior in disequilibrium. "Likewise, to predict the short-run behavior of an adaptive organism, or its behavior in a complex or rapidly changing environment, it is not enough to know its goals. We must know also a great deal about its internal structure and particularly its methods of adaptation" (Simon [1959, p. 255] 1982, p. 289). Clearly, the need to know the agent's methods of adaptation is fully consistent with the Popperian program. But what about the need to know "a great deal about its internal structure"? Again, a certain amount of "procedural rationality" is consistent with the Popper-Boland program: Appropriate behavior may require different decision rules in different situations, and analyzing such behavior may require attention to "the effectiveness, in light of human cognitive powers and limitations, of the procedures used to choose actions" (Simon [1978a, p. 9] 1982, p. 452, emphasis deleted).

10.3   Rationality and system constraints

Having minimized the differences between the Popper-Boland view and the Simon-Latsis view, however, let me now suggest that there is at least one distinction with a difference. Simon's belief that we need to know "a great deal" about the inner workings of the agent is based on a misconception about the nature of social science explanation.

There are several important issues here, and they need to be carefully sorted. The first thing to notice is a certain ambiguity in Simon about the explanandum of economic theory (see Machlup [1967, p. 9] 1978, p. 399). Is economic theory designed, as Simon clearly seems to suggest in the passages above, to predict (or explain) the *behavior of the agent?* Causal adequacy requires that the agent's knowledge explain his or her behavior. But explaining that behavior is not the goal of theory. Rather, as Hayek (1979, pp. 146–7) argues, the social sciences "are concerned with man's actions, *and their aim is to explain the unintended or undesigned results of the actions of many men*" (emphasis added). Similarly, Popper (1965, p. 342) holds that the main task of the theoretical social sciences *"is to trace the unintended social repercussions of intentional human actions"* (emphasis in the original). If this and not individual behavior is the explanandum of theory, then it need not follow that we have to know more about the psychology of the agent – even under disequilibrium conditions – than is implied in the notion of adapting to the logic of one's situation.

Another way to approach the issue is to ask what Simon means by "the environment." It seems that, in both the equilibrium and disequilibrium cases, Simon takes the environment to mean exactly what we have called the agent's situation. Situational determinism, he seems to be saying, is possible in the equilibrium case but not in the disequilibrium one. But if we adopt the view of theory advocated by Hayek and Popper, then the relevant environment must somehow extend beyond the agent's situation to encompass the effects of his or her interactions with other agents. At first glance, this observation would tend to cement Simon's case: the more complicated the environment, the more we need to know about the agent's internal workings. To the contrary, I would argue, a knowledge of the agent's environment serves in some cases – including many of those most relevant to economic theory – as a *substitute* for a knowledge of the details of his or her internal psychology.

First of all, the very idea of taking the agent's situation as exogenous is a way of limiting the demands on his cognitive powers. In general-equilibrium theory, which seeks to reduce economic phenomena to psychological states (utility functions) and natural givens[10] (endowments and

---

[10] These are "natural" givens, of course, only in the sense that the problem-situation they embody encompasses the entire economic universe. This is also presumably what Boland means, though he never puts it this way.

technological possibilities), the cognitive demands on the agent are phenomenal. If instead we permit the agent to respond not to the entire economic universe (or an unreasonably large part of it), but to a manageable subset, then the demands are much attenuated, and what we need to know about his internal landscape is reduced. This may seem an arbitrary procedure: Does the agent not in fact face a problem-situation ultimately identical to the entire economic universe? But this procedure is *not* entirely arbitrary. This is so not merely because, as a subjective matter, agents do not typically conceive of their problem-situations as taking in the whole economic universe. It is so, more interestingly, because the method of situational analysis permits one to take as exogenous the existence of various *social institutions*. As I suggested in Chapter 1, institutions have an informational-support function. They are, in effect, interpersonal stores of coordinative knowledge; as such, they serve to restrict at once the dimensions of the agent's problem-situation and the extent of the cognitive demands placed upon the agent. This is why Joseph Agassi refers to the method of situational analysis as "institutional individualism." The problem-situations that we take as exogenous are not fully arbitrary – they have, as it were, an objective correlative in various "distinct social yet not psychological entities (called institutions, customs, traditions, societies, etc.)" (Agassi 1974, p. 145). These entities – which I will continue to refer to as institutions – are ultimately the result of individual action, but they cannot be reduced to psychological states.

There is also a somewhat different sense in which a knowledge of the agent's environment can act as a substitute for a knowledge of the details of his psychology. If we take seriously the Popper-Hayek program – that the explanandum of theory is the unintended social consequences of individual action – then we can appeal not only to the environment of the agent's problem-situation, but also to the larger environment that his or her actions help form. We can appeal, in effect, to the system constraint (Langlois and Koppl 1984).

As I've already hinted, this is not a new theme in economics. The idea that constraints can substitute – indeed, substitute perfectly – for rational behavior has been put forward by some of the very writers Boland finds most guilty of psychologism. The seminal paper is by Alchian (1950), which I will turn to shortly; but the critical locus of this argument for present purposes is an exchange between Gary Becker (1962, 1963) and Israel Kirzner (1962, 1963) that occurred more than two decades ago in the *Journal of Political Economy*. This exchange has, I feel, been both neglected and misunderstood.

Becker (1962, p. 1) set out to show that "the important theorems of modern economics" can be derived exclusively from considering the "opportunity set" faced by a population of agents – in a manner independent of what one assumes about the behavior of those agents. In particular, he wanted to show that the so-called law of demand – the notion that demand curves slope downward – can be derived even if behavior is capricious or habit-bound rather than rational in the manner of conventional models. Consider, he says, a world of two goods in which agents choose capriciously in the sense that they select their consumption bundles at random. Suppose now that the relative price of the two goods changes, incomes remaining constant. This price-shift changes the opportunity set of the population in that some previously feasible randomly chosen bundles are now ruled out by the constraint of a finite income. Those choosing the infeasible bundles will not be able to pay for them, and will go home disappointed. This means that aggregate consumption of the good whose price rose will necessarily decline. Voilà the law of demand. (The same story applies for habit-bound behavior.)[11]

Kirzner's article set out to show that, despite this incontrovertible argument, Becker still had not demonstrated that all forms of rationality could be eliminated in deriving the important theorems of economics. Becker's story depends crucially on the assumption that price is set on the supply side of the market and that the consumers are just price-takers. The reason that one side of the market can be irrational, Kirzner argues, is that, in effect, the other side of the market is doing all the rational work in adjusting prices to market conditions: "The crux of the matter is that for the market process to work, even within the market for a single commodity, *it cannot be assumed that all market participants are price-takers*" (Kirzner 1962, p. 382, emphasis in the original). For prices to move from one equilibrium level to another requires that

---

[11] Random behavior arguably violates the Popperian criterion of situational appropriateness: A choice of that sort is inappropriate to the situation in the sense that it makes no reference at all to the situation. Incorrigibly habit-bound behavior would probably also violate the criterion, since it is implicit in the situation of this model that a reasonable person would know of the price change and would also realize that he could make himself better off by changing the composition of his bundle. (After the price change, some consumers will find they don't have enough income to continue buying their habitual bundles; but others will find that they have income left over, which is strictly a waste in a two-good world for anyone who prefers more to less.) In a wider context, of course, habitual behavior can certainly be appropriate to the agent's situation. Let me also note in passing that Becker's attempt to derive the law of demand without assuming rationality is really an aggregate version of Paul Samuelson's (1938) frankly behaviorist attempt to construct a demand theory at the individual level that makes no reference to subjective or non-observable theoretical terms (Samuelson 1938). On the failure of revealed-preference theory in this regard, see the excellent discussions by Majumdar (1958) and Wong (1978).

someone somewhere recognize the change in economic conditions and actively adapt to the new conditions.[12]

Becker's reply to this challenge is somewhat confused and ultimately unsatisfactory. He tries to tell a story in which a population of irrational agents (in this case firms) can in fact change the market price. Suppose, he says, that market price is too high in the sense that some sellers could not sell all they wanted at that price. This, he says, would be reflected in the "production opportunity set" that constrains the price and output levels of the firms. This opportunity set "shifts to the left," causing a reduction in the average price offered regardless of the rationality of the firms. As Kirzner quickly pointed out in a rejoinder, this is nonsense. In the short run, the firms can set any prices and quantities they want. And, if the firms are irrational, there is no reason why average price should move toward the equilibrium level. In the short run, then, rationality of some sort is indispensable if markets are to have a tendency toward equilibrium.

In the somewhat longer run, of course, firms cannot go on setting any prices and quantities they like. If there are underlying changes in demand or the scarcity of resources, some previously profitable price and output combinations can no longer be sustained. Some firms – especially those charging higher-than-average prices – may well go bankrupt; and their departure will lower the average price in the direction of equilibrium. But not only do arguments of this sort apply only in the longer run, they are in fact quite complicated and subtle.[13]

What should we learn from this exchange? On the one hand, the assumption of rationality – of some kind – is essential in the short run and difficult (or maybe impossible) to eliminate even in the long run. On the other hand, the system constraint does ultimately remove much of the burden that rationality is often thought – by friend and foe alike – to carry in theory. Rationality, in the limited sense of the method of

---

[12] The best way to understand Kirzner's argument is in the light of his own work (especially Kirzner 1973), which can be understood in part as an attempt to solve precisely this problem: How can we explain the disequilibrium process through which markets move from one equilibrium to another? Although he was certainly defending the necessity of a postulate of rationality, he was not defending the conception of maximizing rationality.

[13] For example, if the behavior of the firms is truly random, there will be no systematic tendency for the pricier firms to go bankrupt first. Moreover, even if the firms are habit-followers – an assumption much more consistent with selection stories – the argument still requires a careful specification of the dynamic selection process supposed to be operating (Winter 1964, p. 240 and passim). Notice, furthermore, that talking about bankruptcy does not by itself eliminate all conscious adjustment even in the long run – it just pushes that rationality back one stage into the process of bankruptcy, which arguably consists in creditors, stockholders, etc., reacting consciously to the actions of the firm.

situational analysis, is necessary for a coherent story; but it is also sufficient for deriving the important theorems of economics.

The role of rationality in basic economic theory (with an emphasis on
the theory of the firm) received an extensive airing in an earlier and
probably more famous exchange: the marginalist controversy between
Richard Lester (1946, 1947) and Fritz Machlup (1946, 1947). It was
largely in reaction to this controversy that Armen Alchian produced his
1950 article "Uncertainty, Evolution, and Economic Theory." "It's
very embarrassing," he said in a recent published discussion (Zerbe
1982, p. 149); "you write an article in response to two misplaced articles, one by a fellow named Lester and one by a guy named Machlup.
Lester was arguing that businessmen do not think in terms of Marshall's
cost calculations and [marginalist theory] therefore cannot be right; and
Machlup says oh, yes they do and therefore it is right. Both of them
irrelevant positions and so you simply apply the well-known evolutionary theory, put it on paper, and it becomes a classic." The article is
indeed a classic, and the issues it raises are crucial to understanding the
relationship of rationality and system constraints in theory.

As his remarks about the Lester-Machlup debate suggest, Alchian set
out in large part to show – as did Becker – that the conclusions of traditional marginalist theory do not depend on the performance of Marshallian cost calculations or other assumptions of rationality. But, in
applying evolutionary theory (or, more correctly, a selection argument)
to economic explanation, Alchian ultimately does something more interesting. (Sometimes even theorizing about the unintended consequences of human action can have its unintended consequences.)

Before considering selection arguments in detail, though, it might be
useful to say a word about the Lester-Machlup debate. For it is a small
irony that Machlup's argument was in fact very much in the spirit of
Alchian's argument, albeit at a slightly different level of discourse. As a
strong proponent of the method of ideal types, Machlup certainly did
affirm the necessity of the rationality postulate – in essentially the situa-
tional-analysis form I have cast it here. But he was also concerned with
the relationship between this rationality postulate and the larger system
constraint. Since the basic results of price theory are derived from
considering the behavior of large numbers of agents, he argued, the
appropriate ideal type is a very general and anonymous one. It is the
system constraint, in effect, that allows us to use an ideal type that is only
"boundedly rational." The tighter the constraint, the less we have to
worry about the informational demands placed on the agent and about
the internal details of his psychology. Thus, like Alchian, Machlup is
saying that the supposed failure of the businessman to perform explicit
Marshallian cost calculations does not invalidate the results of the

theory because (in some sense) the system as a whole obviates such conscious rationality.[14]

The real issue then is whether the relevant system constraint is tight or loose.[15] When the constraints are loose, which often means that social outcomes depend crucially on the behavior of one or a few pivotal individuals (the Schumpeterian entrepreneur, perhaps, or the chairman of the Federal Reserve Board), then we need to know a lot more about the agent's situation and how he perceives it. But very often the interesting explananda involve large-numbers situations with more or less tight constraints. And in those situations we can use a more simplified ideal type. But this does not automatically mean we are limited to Marshallian theories in which we draw conclusions about aggregate outcomes simply by scaling up the behavior of any single representative individual.[16] *This*, I think, is the real message of Alchian's article.[17] It is not so much that we can or should eliminate marginalism in the sense of eliminating any particular motivational assumption: Acting "on the margin," after all, often means nothing more than acting in a boundedly rational way – acting appropriately to the situation one faces on the margin rather than reacting to the total picture. The aspect of marginalism that Alchian calls most seriously into question is its compositional structure – its assumption that aggregate outcomes are just individual outcomes writ large.

10.4 Invisible-hand explanations

The idea that we should pay attention to compositional principles is implicit in the statement of the Popper-Hayek program: We want to explain the unintended consequences of individual action. This is not to say that Marshallian theory does not in fact have this as its goal or that it

[14] Of course, Machlup does at times appear to argue that Lester's businessmen really did perform Marshallian cost calculations. But this is a reflection of the multileveled attack Machlup pursued against Lester. His fundamental methodological position is a form of conventionalism coupled with the ideal-typical method of Weber and Schutz. See Langlois and Koppl (1984).

[15] As we will see, Simon was not far off the mark in distinguishing between situations of equilibrium and situations of disequilibrium – but only because disequilibrium conditions may imply looser system constraints. This is the case, for example, in Becker's failed argument about the opportunity sets of firms in his reply to Kirzner.

[16] More correctly, the representative firm in Marshall is gotten by scaling down aggregate behavior. In any event, I call the resulting compositional principle Marshallian only because the idea of the representative firm comes from Marshall. Perhaps this terminology is unfair to Marshall, for he was always aware of the dangers of using the representative compositional principle for analytic tasks to which it is ill-adapted (see Loasby 1976, chap. 11).

[17] It is this aspect that Nelson and Winter (1982) have seized upon and built into a full-fledged theory.

partakes of a fallacy-of-composition error. Marshallian explanations, based on constructs like the representative firm, do in fact yield the relationships of price and quantity as the unintended consequences of individual action. No competitor consciously intends the particular price or aggregate quantity that obtains in equilibrium; and certainly none intends the condition of zero profit that obtains there. The point is that the Marshallian compositional principle does not exhaust the compositional principles we might reasonably use in explaining aggregate outcomes as the result of individual action.

The best way to understand the issues here is in terms of what the philosophers have taken to calling invisible-hand explanations. The name comes from Adam Smith ([1776, IV. ii. 9] 1976, p. 456), of course, and his description of how the businessman is "led by an *invisible hand* to promote an end which is no part of his intention" (emphasis in the original). It was popularized by Robert Nozick in his discussion of the hypothetical emergence of a minimal state (Nozick 1974, pp. 18–22). And the idea has been developed by Edna Ullmann-Margalit (1978) and by Elster (1979, 1983) in treatments I will draw on here.

At base, to provide an invisible-hand explanation is to do nothing other than to follow the dictates of the Popper-Hayek program:[18] to explain organized social phenomena as the unintended result of individual action. Such explanations are to be distinguished primarily from intentional explanations, which attribute social phenomena to the conscious design of an individual or group.

Ullmann-Margalit distinguishes two "molds" of invisible-hand explanations: aggregate-mold explanations and functional-evolutionary explanations. The first mold speaks primarily to the causal-genetic process by which individual action brings about the aggregate pattern to be explained. The latter addresses the somewhat more complex issue of the pattern's maintenance once established, along with the question of how mechanisms that maintain the pattern relate to those that brought it about in the first place.[19]

These two molds overlap almost completely when, as in the Becker-Kirzner exchange, the phenomena to be explained are the basic con-

[18] I have so far used this term in a way narrower than Boland (1982, p. 178), though I will eventually want to endorse something very like his larger meaning.

[19] Elster (1979, p. 30) appears to make this distinction in a somewhat different way. Unfortunately, his terminology is idiosyncratic and rather confusing, in that he refers to causal-genetic explanations that do not speak to the issue of maintenance as invisible-hand explanations. I prefer to follow Ullmann-Margalit (and Nozick) in using this term as the catch-all category. Any explanation that casts its explananda as the undesigned results of individual action is, for my purposes, an invisible-hand explanation. This would include explanations in which some (or even all) the agents know, suspect, or guess at the overall outcome their decentralized actions would lead to, so long as the pursuit of that outcome is not the principal motivation for their actions.

cerns of price theory. The focus here is not on the formation and maintenance of organized social structures but on the response of observed prices and quantities to changes in such things as tastes, resource availability, expectations, government policies, and so on. As a consequence, the accent is on the causal-genetic aspects of the process and not on functions or mechanisms of maintenance.

As I've already suggested, Becker was not the first to argue that these questions might be tackled without assuming maximizing behavior by a representative agent. Alchian's 1950 article is an attempt to show that there is "an alternative method which treats the decisions and criteria dictated by the economic *system* as more important than those made by the individuals in it" (Alchian [1950] 1977, p. 19, emphasis in the original). He begins by arguing, very much in the spirit of our earlier discussion, that, in a world of uncertainty, profit maximization is not a well-defined notion and thus not a guide to action.[20] Profit, he says, is not something that one maximizes ex ante. Positive – not maximum – profit is something that is awarded ex post by the economic system; it is often as much a result of good luck as of good planning. What's more, he says, it's possible to get results in the absence of foresight by the agents that look very much as if such foresight had been present:

Assume that thousands of travelers set out from Chicago, selecting their roads completely at random and without foresight. Only our "economist" knows that on but one road are there any gasoline stations. He can state categorically that travelers will *continue* to travel only on that road; those on other roads will soon run out of gas. Even though each one selected his route at random, we might have called those travelers who were so fortunate as to have picked the right road wise, efficient, foresighted, etc. . . . If gasoline supplies were now moved to a new road, some formerly luckless travelers again would be able to move; and a new pattern of travel would be observed, although none of the travelers had changed his particular path. The really possible paths have changed with the changing environment. (Alchian [1950] 1977, p. 22, emphasis in the original.)

This is clearly an invisible-hand explanation.[21] Translated into the eco-

[20] Unfortunately, his argument here is not a very good one and is based on what most present-day students of decision making under uncertainty would regard as a misunderstanding. But substituting the special or general arguments against maximizing rationality (discussed earlier) saves his conclusions entirely.

[21] Alchian (1977, p. 22) asserts immediately that his approach "embodies the principles of biological evolution and natural selection." Despite the resonance of this association and its continued presence in the literature, I will try to refrain from dragging in biological evolution unless absolutely necessary. My reason for this reluctance is less the confusion and misunderstandings that invariably attend the comparison with biology than it is a desire to stress the notion of an invisible-hand explanation. Such explanations are not limited to mechanisms fully (or even partly) indebted to the biological notion of evolution, but rather comprise a wide range of selection and filtering principles.

nomic realm, it says that changes in the economic environment (in tastes, factor scarcity, etc.) can affect economic variables not only through the adaptation of the existing population (as portrayed in conventional theory), but also through the selection of a whole new population.[22]

It is not my intention to discuss in detail the mechanism that Alchian proposes or to survey the many other relevant ideas in this highly suggestive article. What is more interesting for present purposes is the seemingly paradoxical subsequent history of the selection-mechanism argument – in which arguments of the sort Alchian advanced served in some hands as a way of *justifying* the more conventional sort of marginalist theory, and in other hands formed the basis for an *alternative* to that program.

The locus classicus of the argument that natural selection considerations serve to reinforce and justify the conventional approach is, of course, Milton Friedman's much-cited 1953 article, "The Methodology of Positive Economics."

Let the apparent immediate determinant of business behavior be anything at all – habitual reaction, random chance, or whatnot. Whenever this determinant happens to lead to behavior consistent with rational and informed maximization of returns, the business will prosper and acquire resources with which to expand; whenever it does not, the business will tend to lose resources and can be kept in existence only by the addition of resources from outside. The process of "natural selection" thus helps to validate the hypothesis – or, rather, given natural selection, acceptance of the hypothesis can be based on the judgment that it summarizes appropriately the conditions for survival. (Friedman [1953] 1977, p. 35)

This is an interesting, if in many ways odd, sort of argument.[23] Notice

[22] This is not to say that Alchian wishes to eliminate rationality. Rather, he recommends, in effect, that we start with a model in which there is no conscious adapting and then add conscious adapting to it – in contrast to the (still) conventional approach of starting with complete rationality and perfect information and then attempting to add uncertainty. Indeed, he describes his view as seeing the economic system "as an adaptive mechanism which chooses among exploratory actions generated by the adaptive pursuit of 'success' or 'profits'" (Alchian [1950] 1977, p. 1). This accords well with the conclusions we drew in the Section 10.3 from the Becker-Kirzner exchange: that we need both the system constraint and an assumption of bounded – adaptive – rationality.

[23] It is no less odd for being, as it were, tacked on to a line of argument in the rest of the paper that is unrelated – if not contradictory. The main thrust of the article is, of course, the well-known assumptions-don't-matter thesis. This has lately been interpreted – with Friedman's concurrence – as a defense of the methodological position called instrumentalism, which holds, roughly speaking, that theories are neither true nor false but merely useful or not; and successful prediction is the only test of usefulness (Boland 1982, esp. pp. 143, 171). Thus, to appeal to some other – arguably deeper or more satisfying – theory for added support is at best irrelevant and may even introduce the suspicion that there is more to theory-choice than predictive success.

how strong the claim is. Friedman is not merely asserting that, for purposes of basic price and allocation theory, the conclusions one arrives at with selection arguments are often the same as those reached using marginalist reasoning.[24] Rather, he is arguing that the two approaches are fully isomorphic in their conclusions – marginalism is in effect a sufficient statistic for the selection approach under all circumstances. (And, therefore, parsimony dictates that marginalism be the approach of choice, with selection relegated to the role of backup defense and heuristic device.)

The key to understanding what's going on in this strong form of the identity argument – and why it's wrong – is to notice that Friedman has effected a subtle shift in the explanandum of the selection explanation.

I have been careful so far to limit my discussion of invisible-hand explanations to cases in which the phenomena to be explained are concerns of basic price theory such as changes in prices and quantities. But there is another class of explananda in the social sciences with which we might be concerned (and with which the explananda of price theory are often confused). That is, we could see our invisible-hand explanation as seeking to explain *behavior patterns* and the organized social structures – institutions, in the broadest sense – that they form. This is an altogether different matter; and it moves us into a world in which the two molds of invisible-hand explanations do not overlap completely and in which we have to concern ourselves with the issues of functionalism.

We can see this clearly in Elster (1983, p. 57; see also 1979, p. 31), who suggests that the only successful functional model in the social sciences[25] is "the attempt by the Chicago school of economists to explain profit-maximizing behavior as the result of the 'natural selection' of firms by the market." It's not explicit whom he has in mind here, but he presumably means the discussions by Alchian or Friedman that we've just examined. But is it obvious that *profit-maximizing behavior* is the phenomenon to be explained? Or is it – once again – the basic phenomena and concerns of price theory that are the explananda? If the latter, it is confusing for Elster to cast these questions in the functionalist mode at all. The sort of Marshallian partial-equilibrium comparative-static questions that (under this view) Friedman and Alchian are interested in are questions of change from one stable position (equilibrium) to another. There is thus no question of a *change* being maintained by a feedback mechanism of some kind. What are maintained, of course, are the equilibrium positions before and after the change. There is certainly a

[24] A conclusion, by the way, that I think is quite supportable as a first approximation and that, in my reading, is borne out in the models of Nelson and Winter (1982, p. 175).
[25] By which he presumably means that it meets all the criteria for a cogent functional explanation, not necessarily that it is unassailable.

question of what maintains these equilibria, but the mechanism involved enters only indirectly into the explanation of the changes in
prices and quantities. Indeed, as Machlup (1963) points out, the equilibria are only conceptual devices used to make sure that all *cetera* are kept
paria during the transition.[26] (Of course, whether economists really
treat equilibrium this way is another matter.)

   But the point is that, in arguing so strongly for the isomorphism
between selection and marginalism, Friedman is necessarily moving
into the realm in which functionalist considerations are important. That
is, he is implicitly doing just what Elster suggests – using selection as a
way of explaining the pattern called profit-maximizing behavior. He
then associates this behavior pattern with the profit-maximizing behavior that is an intermediate term in the marginalist explanation of price
and quantity changes. The selection explanation, he says in effect,
thereby adds credence to our use of profit maximization as a basis for
marginalist theory and reinforces withal a commitment to marginalism.

   The problem with this argument is that the selection model does not
in fact provide an assurance that the profit-maximizing behavior pattern will always maintain itself in the economy or, relatedly, that the
behavior that does result from the selection process can be meaningfully
identified with the profit-maximizing behavior in marginalist theory.
The counterarguments are mostly due to Winter (1964), although
some are already adumbrated in Alchian. Even if we can assert that we
can define some behavior as profit maximizing in a way that's meaningfully related to the concept of the same name in marginalist theory, we
are by no means assured that such behavior will always result from the
selection process. A change in the environment implies a disequilibrium
situation; and, in disequilibrium, we cannot speak unambiguously about
a firm's relative deviation from profit maximization, since to do so
"presumes a particular state of the environment, but the environment is
changed by the dynamic process itself" (Winter 1964, p. 240). To put it
another way, what is profit maximizing in disequilibrium may not be
profit maximizing in equilibrium. This raises the issue of definition:
What is profit maximizing? If we assert that we mean profit maximization to be whatever behavior is best adapted in equilibrium, this immediately raises a second issue: If those firms who would be profit maximizing in the eventual equilibrium are badly adapted to disequilibrium,
they may be selected out before the equilibrium is reached, leaving in
equilibrium only firms that by definition *aren't* profit maximizers.[27]

---

[26] For a discussion see Langlois and Koppl (1984).
[27] These two arguments are what I have elsewhere christened the disequilibrium problem and the path-dependency problem (Langlois 1984). At a broader level, of course,
one might well question on methodological grounds whether it is meaningful in any

If the two approaches – selection and maximizing marginalism – are not thus isomorphic in the manner Friedman suggests, the two must go their own way as separate programs. Selection arguments are not justifications of marginalism but hints at an alternative. It is this view that has animated the work of Nelson and Winter (1982), who cite Alchian's article as inspiration. Their approach clearly reflects invisible-hand explanation, and a careful analysis of it would illustrate many of the issues with which I'm concerned. Nonetheless, I will pass up the temptation to treat this work in detail. Instead, I will look to a different (though related) area: the explanation of social institutions.

10.5   Explaining institutions

In Chapter 1, I described the dual role that social institutions play in economic theory. In their first role, institutions form part of the situation in which the actor finds himself or herself; they serve as behavioral guides that reduce the knowledge and cognitive skills necessary for successful action. In this sense, then, institutions enter theory as exogenous residues of the past.[28] But these institutions are themselves the result of past human actions, of previous situations in which actors found themselves. Such institutions are thus fair game for theoretical explanation; and this – the Menger program – is the second role of social institutions: to play the explananda of invisible-hand explanations.

In attempting explanation of this sort, however, we must confront a number of issues that we had previously been able to skirt. Institutions, as we have seen, are orderly and more or less persistent behavior patterns. At a more abstract level, they are the rules or sets of rules that constrain or govern organized patterns of behavior. In either case, institutions are structures. And explaining them requires attention both to their origins and to their maintenance.[29]

---

sense to identify the theoretical term "survivorship" from the selection approach with the term "profit-maximizing behavior" from the marginalist theory; but this I won't pursue here. I should note that the attempt to identify survival with maximization also raises a question of tautology, which I will address below.

[28] Whether models that incorporate institutions in this way exhibit "hysteresis" in the sense of Georgescu-Roegen (1971, p. 123ff.) is an issue into which I don't want to enter. My suspicion, for what it's worth, is that the answer would be "no," since situational analysis may be understood as a way of "substitut[ing] for past causes the traces left in the present by the operation of those causes" (Elster 1983, p. 33; cf. Elster 1976).

[29] To put it another way, we have to switch from what Roger Koppl (in an unpublished manuscript) calls level-one invisible-hand explanations to what he calls level-two explanations.

As we have seen, explanations that focus on the origin of an institution are what Ullmann-Margalit calls aggregate-mold explanations. These are causal-genetic stories about how individual actions unintentionally led (or might have led) to the development of some social or economic structure. The paradigm of this has long been Carl Menger's theory of the origin of money (Menger 1963, pp. 152ff.; 1981, p. 257), in which the self-interested actions of traders lead from a barter economy to one in which a single commodity has become the universal medium of exchange. The other approach, which Ullmann-Margalit calls the functional-evolutionary mold, focuses not on the process through which the structure emerged but on the processes that maintain the structure once established.

It is important to distinguish this functional mold from the more naive doctrines called functionalism, which assert, more or less baldly, that we can explain a structure simply by finding out what function it serves. Consider Elster's schema for a valid invisible-hand explanation in the functional mold.[30] An institution or behavior pattern X, he says (1979, p. 28; 1983, p. 57), is explained by its function Y for group Z if and only if

1. Y is an effect of X;
2. Y is beneficial for Z;
3. Y is unintended by the actors producing X;
4. Y (or at least the causal relationship between X and Y) is unrecognized[31] by the actors in Z; and
5. Y maintains X by a causal feedback loop passing through Z.

As both Elster and Ullmann-Margalit point out, the problem with much that passes under the name functionalism is that it operates as if criterion 5 – the existence of a feedback mechanism – is either unnecessary to successful explanation or can be inferred from some combination of criteria 1–4.

This is certainly correct. But what exactly have we explained by

[30] Again, this is not his terminology.
[31] A word about criterion 4 is in order. Elster holds it to be necessary to a successful functionalist explanation. An explanation that meets criteria 1–3 and 5 but not 4 is what he calls a filter explanation. These are explanations in which (A) the agents eventually become aware of the nature of the institution that is evolving and of the function it serves for them, and (B) this awareness then leads the agents consciously to maintain the institution. In other words, the institution is created organically but maintained pragmatically (to use Menger's terms). Although a filter explanation of this sort may not be a successful functionalist explanation in Elster's sense, it should still certainly count as an invisible-hand explanation in the wide sense in which I'm using that term.

showing that some institution has fulfilled all five criteria? Ullmann-Margalit (1978, p. 284) puts the matter well: "The basic question of the functionalist-evolutionary mold is this: given that a certain social pattern or institution exists, *why is it in existence?*" (emphasis in the original). Thus the functionalist mode differs from the aggregate mold in that the latter provides "a chronicle of (a particular mode) of emergence," whereas the former is concerned with "establishing *raisons d'être*" (emphasis altered).

The concern with functions is, of course, a legacy of the biological analogy that inspired much of functionalism. The biologist can be more or less safely concerned with function alone, since he or she can rely on a generally agreed-upon process – natural selection – that both provides the feedback mechanism of criterion 5 and deflects attention away from causes: for in evolutionary biology, the source of a structure is random variation or mutation; and what is random is inexplicable. This attitude carries over to functionalist explanations in the social sciences.

It should be noted and emphasized that an explanation of this type involves no commitment as to how the scrutinized pattern actually originated. For all that it tells us the pattern in question could have come into being as a result of intentional design and careful execution,[32] or, for that matter, it may have originated (somehow) through people's "stumbling upon establishments, which are indeed the result of human action, but not the execution of any human design." (Ullmann-Margalit 1978, p. 284. The internal quotation is from Adam Ferguson 1767.)

This also helps us to see, I think, the connection between functionalism and the optimization-and-equilibrium approach in economics. To say that a structure has a function is to say that it solves some kind of problem for the group in question – a problem usually cast in terms of the selection mechanism thought to be operating. The structure is functional because it solves a problem linked to the group's relative success or survival; the structure is efficient in some sense. There are a number of intricate problems here that I won't delve into. My point is merely that this functionalist problem is easily recast in the form of an operations-research problem.[33] That is to say, we can easily transform

[32] That the structure originated through intentional design is, of course, ruled out in Elster's formulation of a functionalist explanation – but not in most formulations.
[33] The alert reader will notice a connection here to my earlier discussion of situational analysis. This replacement of the functional problem by a mathematical optimization problem sounds a bit like situational analysis. But there is an important difference. The idea of situational analysis in the manner of Popper is to analyze the actual situation faced by an individual agent as that agent perceives the situation. This may or may not imply optimization – merely rationality in a broad sense. The substitution of an optimization problem for the functionalist problem, on the other hand, is an "as if"

the functionalist explanation into an intentional explanation: It is as if the agents possessed certain information and consciously brought about certain outcomes in view of that information. This procedure is closely related to the Friedman arguments discussed above, and it is at the root of most of the discussions – and confusions – about perfect information and its absence.

It is, of course, a quick jump from saying that something is functional to saying that it is optimal, especially when we get to choose (within limits) the superimposed operations-research problem that we think. best captures the functional problem. This is not an incidental matter, since there is often enough leeway that we can find, for any given structure, a corresponding operations-research problem to which the structure is an optimal solution. This is a problem even in biology, where functionalism is governed by a natural selection argument that is relatively strict and clear (by social science standards, at any rate). Biologists Stephen Jay Gould and R. C. Lewontin (1979) have identified what they call the "Panglossian paradigm"–after Voltaire's Dr. Pangloss – according to which every observed biological structure is presumed to reflect an optimal adaptation to its environment. They have their arguments for why this "best of all possible worlds" view should be banished from biology – reasons that involve attacking the presumption that selection is the exclusive mechanism for evolution and that it always operates tightly when it *is* the mechanism. The arguments against Panglossianism in the social sciences are similar and necessarily stronger. Here there is no presumption that natural selection or something similar is the *sole* mechanism operating. Social institutions may be susceptible to invisible-hand explanations employing any number of selection or filtering processes, and may also involve elements of intention. This makes it a much trickier business to specify the problem that the structure solves and, not incidentally, makes it easier to find a problem to which the structure is an optimal solution.[34] Moreover, even when we can specify a well-defined process that operates somewhat like natural selection, the conclusions of our operations-research model are

---

exercise: it is as if the agents were attempting to solve a certain (global) problem (whose optimal solution becomes a normative standard). The agents may in turn be represented as if they were solving their own little pieces of the global problem (with any inability to solve this superimposed global problem labeled a "market failure"), but, as I argued earlier, this has no more claim to being situational analysis than it does to being behavioralism with an implausible behavioral assumption. Moreover, my suspicion is that it is this superimposition of the operations-research problem – and not situational analysis properly understood – that really lies behind the complaints of Latsis.

[34] Alchian provides a humorous example of this in Zerbe (1982, p. 178).

still subject to the disequilibrium and path-dependency problems outlined in the Section 10.4 (see also Langlois 1984).

My point here is not that we ought to do away with functionalist explanations or analyses of the "problem" a structure solves. For one thing, the notion of a function or problem-solution is actually necessary, within the evolutionary mold, to save the selection mechanism from tautology; the problem provides an independent criterion of survival value, so that survival does not become its own explanation (Gould 1977, p. 42). But even from the somewhat different perspective of the aggregate mold, the notion of a function serves a purpose: It draws our attention to the mechanisms that maintain a structure. And, since the mechanisms that maintain the structure can often be quite different from those that brought it into existence in the first place, an explanation that excludes the maintenance function is incomplete.[35]

At the risk of leaving out the punch line, I will not try to apply these considerations to the explanations of social institutions discussed in this volume (or elsewhere). In the case of the game-theoretical models offered by Schotter, one would want to ponder the extent to which these models are part of a causal-genetic explanation or of a functionalist one. Do the game-situations represent a true intentional explanation or are they "as if" explanations of what in fact arose through unintentional processes? To what extent do these models (qua functionalist explanations) satisfy Elster's five criteria? Schotter (in this volume) is clearly sensitive to many of these issues; but there remains room for a thorough methodological study. We can ask similar questions about Williamson's transaction-cost paradigm, as I have in fact attempted in part elsewhere.[36]

---

[35] In Menger's theory of money, the mechanisms that bring about the universal money-commodity are the same that maintain it as the monetary unit – the individual efforts to increase liquidity and reduce transaction costs. But consider Edelman's theory of government regulatory commissions (Edelman 1964). Voters, he asserts, are plagued with vague fears about and a sense of powerlessness over certain phenomena they can't control. The fear of monopoly, he says, is one of these. In order to gain votes, politicians make symbolic gestures to placate these fears – in this case, the formation of regulatory commissions. Voilà the *origin* of such commissions. But, once in place, the commissions, usually facing no real monopoly problem they have not themselves created, are quickly captured in the familiar way by those they were supposed to regulate. Thus a quite different mechanism *maintains* them once created; they serve the functon of cartelizing the industry and are kept in business by the political action of that industry. The full invisible-hand explanation – and the full impact of what Kenneth Boulding (1978, p. 195) calls "the law of political irony"—requires both types of explanation.

[36] My (1984) paper is in some measure an attempt to appraise in methodological terms similar to these the transaction-cost paradigm as applied to explaining the internal organization of firms.

252   Richard N. Langlois

10.6   The New Institutional Economics: A program

We are now in a position to tie together – as promised – the themes that (I have argued) run through the essays in this volume and characterize the movement in economic theory those essays reflect. What follows is a "program" for what I have been calling the New Institutional Economics.[37] I will not pretend that this program represents anyone's ideas but my own. Nonetheless, I think that Chapter 1 offered some evidence that it is at least consistent with, and perhaps even captures the spirit of, much of what my fellow authors have to say. Here goes:

1. Situational analysis: Use the method of situational analysis. That is, assume that the agent is rational in the sense that he acts appropriately to or reasonably in his or her situation. This should be seen as a kind of bounded rationality assumption, in the sense that it does not grant the agent unreasonable cognitive powers or an inappropriate level of information. This approach would certainly include the classic economic principle that the agent prefers more to less all things considered; but it would not include maximizing rationality in any strong sense. It would also admit of other kinds of reasonable action in certain situations, including satisficing (in the narrow sense), rule-following behavior, entrepreneurship (in the sense of Kirzner or of Schumpeter), and so on.

2. Institutions I: Pay attention to the existence of social institutions of various kinds as bounds to and definitions of the agent's situation. This is the dual role of institutions in its first guise.

3. Invisible-hand explanations: Practice careful invisible-hand explanations. In its widest compass, this is what I described above as the Popper-Hayek program: explaining economic phenomena as the unintended result of human action. As we saw, such explanations can take many forms; but those forms probably do not include naive functionalism or unreflected "as if" explanations. A careful explanation would also include careful specification of the relevant explananda.

3A. Compositional principles: In formulating invisible-hand explanations, be attentive to alternate compositional principles, including various kinds of filters and selection processes.

[37] I will leave it to the reader to translate this program into Lakatosian or Kuhnian terms if he or she finds it necessary. I should note that I consider this "program" broadly consistent with that offered by Boland (1982, p. 178) as well as with my own earlier (and more Lakatosian) suggestion in a different context (Langlois 1982).

4. Institutions II: Use this program to explain not only the basic
phenomena of price theory but also the nature and origin of social
institutions. This is the dual role in its second guise.

References

Agassi, Joseph. 1975. "Institutional Individualism." *British Journal of Sociology* 26:144–
55.
Alchian, Armen. 1950. "Uncertainty, Evolution, and Economic Theory." *Journal of
Political Economy* 58(3):211–21.
Arrow, Kenneth J. 1974. *The Limits of Organization.* New York: Norton.
Arrow, Kenneth J., and Frank Hahn. 1971. *General Competitive Analysis.* San Francisco:
Holden-Day.
Baumol, William J., and R. E. Quandt. 1964. "Rules of Thumb and Optimally Imperfect
Decisions." *American Economic Review* 54:23–46.
Becker, Gary S. 1962. "Irrational Behavior and Economic Theory." *Journal of Political
Economy* 70:1–13.
1963. "A Reply to I. Kirzner." *Journal of Political Economy* 71:82–3.
Boland, Lawrence A. 1982. *The Foundations of Economic Method.* London: Allen and
Unwin.
Bookstaber, Richard, and Joseph Langsam. 1983. "Coarse Behavior and Extended Un-
certainty." Provo, Utah: Brigham Young University. Photocopy.
Boulding, Kenneth E. 1978. *Ecodynamics: A New Theory of Societal Evolution.* Beverly Hills,
Calif.: Sage.
Caldwell, Bruce J. 1984. "Disentangling Hayek, Hutchison, and Popper on the Method-
ology of Economics." Greensboro: University of North Carolina. Photocopy.
Cohen, Michael D., and Robert Axelrod. 1984. "Coping with Complexity." *American
Economic Review* 74(1):30–42.
Debreu, Gerard. 1959. *Theory of Value.* New York: John Wiley.
Dreyfus, Hubert L. 1979. *What Computers Can't Do: The Limits of Artificial Intelligence.* Rev.
ed. New York: Harper Colophon.
Edelman, Jacob Murray. 1964. *The Symbolic Uses of Politics.* Urbana: University of Illinois
Press.
Elster, Jon. 1976. "A Note on Hysteresis in the Social Sciences." *Synthese* 33:371–91.
1979. *Ulysses and the Sirens: Studies in Rationality and Irrationality.* Cambridge: Cam-
bridge University Press.
1983. *Explaining Technical Change.* Cambridge: Cambridge University Press.
Ferguson, Adam. 1980. *An Essay on the History of Civil Society.* New Brunswick, N.J.:
Transaction Books. [First published in 1767.]
Friedman, Milton. 1953. "The Methodology of Positive Economics." In *Essays on Positive
Economics.* Chicago: University of Chicago Press. Reprinted in William Breit and
Harold Hochman, eds. *Readings in Microeconomics.* 2d ed. Hinsdale, Ill.: Dryden
Press, 1977.
Frydman, Roman, Gerald P. O'Driscoll, Jr., and Andrew Schotter. 1982. "Rational
Expectations and Government Policy: An Application of Newcomb's Problem."
Southern Economic Journal 49(2):311–19.
Georgescu-Roegen, Nicholas. 1971. *The Entropy Law and the Economic Process.* Cam-
bridge: Harvard University Press.
Gould, Stephen J. 1977. *Ever Since Darwin.* New York: Norton.

254   Richard N. Langlois

Gould, Stephen J., and R. D. Lewontin. 1979. "The Spandrels of San Marco and the Panglossian Paradigm: A Critique of the Adaptationist Programme." *Proceedings of the Royal Society of London.* B205:581–98.

Hands, Douglas W. 1984. "Karl Popper and Economic Methodology: A New Look." Paper presented at the History of Economics Society Meeting, May 22, 1984, Pittsburgh.

Hayek, F. A. 1967. *Studies in Philosophy, Politics, and Economics.* Chicago: University of Chicago Press.

   1973. *Law, Legislation, and Liberty.* Vol. 1, *Rules and Order.* Chicago: University of Chicago Press.

   1979. *The Counter-Revolution of Science.* 2d ed. Indianapolis: Liberty Press.

Kirzner, Israel M. 1962. "Rational Action and Economic Theory." *Journal of Political Economy* 70:380–5.

   1963. "Rejoinder." *Journal of Political Economy* 71:84–5.

   1973. *Competition and Entrepreneurship.* Chicago: University of Chicago Press.

   1982. "Uncertainty, Discovery, and Human Action." In *Method, Process, and Austrian Economics: Essays in Honor of Ludwig von Mises,* ed. Kirzner. Lexington, Mass.: D. C. Heath.

Knight, Frank H. 1971. *Risk, Uncertainty, and Profit.* Chicago: University of Chicago Press. [First published in 1921.]

Langlois, Richard N. 1982. "Austrian Economics as Affirmative Science." In *Method, Process, and Austrian Economics: Essays in Honor of Ludwig von Mises,* ed. Israel M. Kirzner. Lexington, Mass.: D. C. Heath.

   1984. "Internal Organization in a Dynamic Context: Some Theoretical Considerations." In *Information and Communications Economics; New Perspectives,* ed. M. Jussawalla and H. Ebenfield. Amsterdam: North-Holland.

Langlois, Richard N., and Roger Koppl. 1984. "Fritz Machlup and Marginalism: A Reevaluation." Working Paper no. 14, Fairfax, Va.: Center for the Study of Market Processes, George Mason University.

Latsis, Spiro J. 1972. "Situational Determinism in Economics." *The British Journal for the Philosophy of Science* 23:207–45.

   1976a. "The Limitations of Single-Exit Models: Reply to Machlup." *British Journal for the Philosophy of Science* 27:51–60.

   1976b. "A Research Program in Economics." In *Method and Appraisal in Economics,* ed. S. J. Latsis. Cambridge: Cambridge University Press.

Lester, Richard A. 1946. "Shortcomings of Marginal Analysis for Wage-Employment Problems." *American Economic Review* 36:63–82.

   1947. "Marginalism, Minimum Wages, and Labor Markets." *American Economic Review* 37:135–48.

Loasby, Brian J. 1976. *Choice, Complexity, and Ignorance.* Cambridge: Cambridge University Press.

Machlup, Fritz. 1946. "Marginal Analysis and Empirical Research." *American Economic Review* 36:519–54.

   1947. "Rejoinder to an Antimarginalist." *American Economic Review* 37:148–54.

   1963. *Essays on Economic Semantics.* Englewood Cliffs, N.J.: Prentice-Hall.

   1967. "Theories of the Firm: Marginalist, Behavioral, Managerial." *American Economic Review* 57:1–33.

   1978. *The Methodology of Economics and Other Social Sciences.* New York: Academic Press.

Majumdar, Tapas. 1958. *The Measurement of Utility.* London: Macmillan.

Menger, Carl. 1963. *Problems of Economics and Sociology.* Trans. F. J. Nock. Urbana: University of Illinois Press. [First published in 1883.]

1981. *Principles of Economics*. Trans. Robert Dingwall and Bert F. Hozelitz. New York: New York University Press. [First published in 1871.]

Nelson, Richard R., and Sidney G. Winter. 1982. *An Evolutionary Theory of Economic Change*. Cambridge: Harvard University Press.

Nozick, Robert. 1974. *Anarchy, State, and Utopia*. New York: Basic Books.

O'Driscoll, Gerald P., and Mario J. Rizzo. 1985. *The Economics of Time and Ignorance*. Oxford: Basil Blackwell.

Popper, Karl R. 1957. *The Poverty of Historicism*. London: Routledge and Kegan Paul; Harper Torchbooks, 1964.

  1965. *Conjectures and Refutations: The Growth of Scientific Knowledge*. New York: Harper Colophon.

  1966. *The Open Society and Its Enemies*. 5th ed., rev. Vol. 2. Princeton: Princeton University Press.

  1967. "La rationalité et le statut du principe de rationalité." In *Les Fondements Philosophiques des systèmes économiques*, ed. Emil M. Claassen. Paris: Payot.

Samuelson, Paul A. 1938. "A Note on the Pure Theory of Consumer's Behavior." *Economica* 5:61–71.

Simon, Herbert A. 1955. "A Behavioral Model of Rational Choice." *Quarterly Journal of Economics* 69:99–118.

  1956. "Rational Choice and the Structure of the Environment." *Psychological Review* 63(2):129–38.

  1957. *Administrative Behavior*. New York: The Free Press.

  1959. "Theories of Decision-Making in Economics and Behavioral Science." *American Economic Review* 49:253–83.

  1976. "From Substantive to Procedural Rationality." In *Method and Appraisal in Economics*, ed. Spiro J. Latsis. Cambridge: Cambridge University Press.

  1978a. "Rationality as Process and as Product of Thought." *American Economic Review* 68(2):4.

  1978b. "On How to Decide What To Do." *The Bell Journal of Economics* 9(2):494–507.

  1982. *Models of Bounded Rationality*. Vol. 2, *Behavioral Economics and Business Organization*. Cambridge: MIT Press.

Simon, Herbert A., and Andrew Stedry. 1968. "Psychology and Economics." *Handbook of Social Psychology*. Reading, Mass.: Addison-Wesley.

Smith, Adam. 1776. *An Inquiry into the Nature and Causes of the Wealth of Nations*. London: W. Strahan and T. Cadell; Glasgow edition, Oxford: Oxford University Press, 1976.

Stigler, George, and Gary Becker. 1977. "De gustibus non est disputandum." *American Economic Review* 67:76–90.

Ullmann-Margalit, Edna. 1978. "Invisible Hand Explanations." *Synthese* 39:282–6.

Winter, Sidney. 1964. "Economic 'Natural Selection' and the Theory of the Firm." *Yale Economic Essays* 4:225–72.

Wong, Stanley. 1978. *The Foundations of Paul Samuelson's Revealed Preference Theory: A Study by the Method of Rational Reconstruction*. London: Routledge and Kegan Paul.

Zerbe, Richard O., ed. 1982. *Research in Law and Economics*. Vol. 4, *Evolutionary Models in Economics and Law*. Greenwich, Conn.: JAI Press.

Index

Abel, A., 94n, 106
Abernathy, William, 13, 22
Adams, J. A., 61n, 103n, 106, 112
advertising, 33–4, 38, 119n, 121, 127, 158
Afghanistan, 127
Agassi, Joseph, 237, 253
agricultural revolution, 204–5
Alchian, Armen, 13n, 16–17, 22, 30, 38, 82n, 83n, 91n, 106, 174, 200, 216n, 218n, 221, 232, 237, 240–1, 243–7, 250n, 253
Alcock, John, 97n, 106
Alexander, Richard, 86n, 106
Allais, Maurice, 82n, 106
Allen, William, 82n, 83n, 106
Alluisi, E. A., 103n, 106
Allyon, T., 82, 107
American Institutionalist School, 2, 4, 5, 155n
American Medical Association, 127
Anderson, J. R., 95n, 106–7
Aoki, Masahiko, 171n, 200
appreciative (versus formal) theory, 9–10, 136–8, 139, 141, 143, 151
Armour, H. O., 198, 200
Arrow, Kenneth J., 11, 13n, 22, 29, 38, 46, 51, 55, 56, 59, 68, 85n, 107, 173–4, 212n, 221, 228, 232, 253
arsenal of Venice, 205
artificial intelligence, 227
"as if" approach, 17, 60, 68, 106, 135, 173, 249n, 250–2
asset specificity, 179–80, 184–5, 187, 189–95, 197–9, 215–16
Atkinson, R. C., 61n, 114
Aumann, R., 123, 132
Austrian School, 1, 4, 28–9, 174
authority relation, 198 (see also employer-employee relation)
Averch-Johnson hypothesis, 35
Axelrod, Robert, 18n, 22, 80n, 107, 229, 253
Ayres, Clarence, 2
Azrin, N. H., 82, 107

Babbage, Charles, 211, 214, 222
Bacon, R., 140, 151
Baddeley, A. D., 103n, 107
Baily, Martin, 139, 148, 151
Baker, R. A., 103n, 115
Baldwin, R. D., 61n, 107
Balestri, A., 54, 56
Barnes, P., 103n, 115
barriers to entry, 14–15, 35, 55, 165, 193
Barro, Robert J., 94n, 107
Battalio, Raymond C., 82, 107, 110
Baumol, William J., 127, 132, 226, 253
Beasley, C. M., 95n, 107
Becker, Gary, 232, 237–40, 241n, 242–3, 244n, 253, 255
behavioralism, 2, 4n, 233, 250n
behavioral view (of social institutions), 118
behaviorism, 4, 238n
Ben-Porath, Yoram, 179, 200
Berndt, E., 139, 151
Binford, J. R., 103n, 111
Blackwell, David, 100n, 101n, 107
Blaug, Mark, 2, 22
Blue Cross/Blue Shield, 163
Boehm, Stephan, 1n
Boland, Lawrence A., 229–35, 236n, 237, 244n, 252n, 253
Bookstaber, Richard, 228, 253
Borgin, G., 86n, 106
Boulding, Kenneth E., 32, 251, 253
bounded rationality, 20, 32, 45, 173–4, 177, 180, 182, 186, 189, 199, 225–7, 240, 244n, 252
brand-name capital, 165–6
Bransford, J. D., 95n, 107
Brennan, Geoffrey, 117, 132
Bridgman, Percy, 173, 200
Broadbent, D. E., 103n, 107
Brown, Roger, 97n, 107
Brunner, Karl, 94n, 107
Buchanan, James M., 1n, 97n, 107, 117, 132, 172, 200
business cycles, 92–4, 219–20
Buttrick, John, 205n, 222

256